Everything

DENIS COUGHLAN

WITH TADHG COAKLEY

www.**HERO**BOOKS.digital

Contents

« CHAPTER 1 »

Madden's Buildings

BLACKPOOL MADE ME. Madden's Buildings made me. I know this now.

Of course, I was a product of my parents and my family and the time I grew up in too. But I can't overstate the influence that my surroundings – my place – had on me, as a child.

And the older I get the more strongly I feel it. I had a very happy childhood. I grew up with my mother and my father and my Nan and my two sisters, Anne and Catherine – Anne two years older than me and Catherine two years younger. I was in between.

We lived in number 14 Madden's Buildings, in Blackpool, Cork.

I WAS BORN on the 7th of June, 1945. One month previously the German Forces had unconditionally surrendered, signalling an end to World War II in Europe but the conflict was still going on in the Far East. On June 7th the Allied Forces won the battle of West Hunan against the Japanese.

A three-piece suit cost £5, 17 shillings and six pence in Roches Stores in Cork. *Gone with the Wind* was showing in the Pavillion.

Cork United (the League of Ireland champions) had just beaten Linfield 5-1 in the Inter-City Cup. Later that summer, Cork would beat Cavan to win their third All-Ireland football championship – their first win since 1911. On that day Jack Lynch would win his fifth All-Ireland medal in five years. Earlier in

September, Tipperary beat Kilkenny in the hurling. Fermoy would be the senior football champions of Cork in 1945 and a club by the name of Glen Rovers would retain their hurling title, beating Carrigdhoun in the final.

The *Cork Examiner* reported that there would be no relaxation of rationing and that special supplies of sugar to make the season's jam would not be available. The Cork Gas Consumers' Co. announced a 1d (penny) reduction per therm in the price of gas; for Quarterly Consumers the standard price was now 21.2 pence for the first 20 therms. Overseas and cross-channel travel was very restricted and exit permits were only allowed by the government when such travel was proven to be in the national interest.

Ireland's Taoiseach was Éamon de Valera and our president was Douglas Hyde – soon to be replaced by Sean T. O'Kelly.

I WAS ACTUALLY born in 43 Upper John Street, at the back of Murphy's Brewery, closer to the city centre. But I was only in John Street for a few months and then we moved to Madden's Buildings, which is all I remember of my childhood. And I lived there until the day I got married on the 3rd of April, 1970, when I was nearly 25 years-old.

There were four terraces of houses – 76 homes in all – split by two narrow streets. The 38 houses on our street, we called 'Our Buildings' and the 38 on the other street we called 'The Other Buildings'. Our Buildings were closer to the city centre and number 14 was near enough to the end of the terrace.

There were a lot of children around Madden's Buildings, you always had a friend to play with, and of course I had my two sisters. Anne had dark hair and she was very outgoing. She went to the same school as me, St Vincent's, until Holy Communion. Catherine went there, too, later. She wasn't as extrovert as Anne, she was quieter.

The people were very neighbourly in the Buildings, all the doors were left open; the windows were left open, they were never locked. We could all go in and out of our friends' houses without any bother, all day long, and we did.

All the men in the Buildings worked outside the home and the women worked in the home. That's the way it was, then. My father, John Coughlan worked in Murphy's Brewery. He was born in 1908 and he was originally from Johnson's Lane. That's called Burke's Avenue now, off Gerald Griffin Street, at the back of

Neptune Stadium. He had three sisters, Mary, Nancy and Kitty – he was an only boy like me. Both my father's parents died young, as did my mother's father. I was born when my father was 37, but people got married later in life those days.

My father had a very difficult job in the brewery. The most physical job there, anyway. At the time the furnaces had to be kept going 24 hours a day, to boil the water, hops and barley for the stout. For his eight-hour shift my father shovelled the coal into those furnaces, with two other men. They did three shifts, one every third week. He was a fit man, he had very strong hands.

My favourite shift for my Dad to do was six in the morning until two in the afternoon. During the summer holidays that gave me a chance to go down as far as O'Connell Street where there was an old stone water trough on the Watercourse Road. The horses drawing wagons on their way down to the quays used to stop for a drink of water and I waited there for my father to finish his shift. I walked home with him then, which was a big thrill. That trough is still there to this day, but when was the last time a horse drank out of it, I don't know.

Other times I might have to bring his lunch down to the brewery. Again, that was thrilling. All the workers busy coming and going; the noise and the sense of purpose about the place. The huge buildings and the yard, with the high stack towering above it all – magical to a small child.

My father was a lovely man. He was a very gentle man. He was quiet for the most part, but was a lovely singer too.

MY MOTHER, MARGARET was an O'Flaherty. She and her brothers and sisters were born across from Madden's Buildings in a little row of six cottages, which was called Foley's Row. And that's where my grandmother was born and reared too, but then they all moved to number 3 Madden's Buildings.

There were eight children in my mother's family; five girls (Nora, Kitty, Lily, Maura, and my mother, Margaret) and three boys (Denis, Willie and Joe) and their mother, Kitty was widowed young. Her husband, Denis – whom I'm called after – died of tuberculosis in his forties in the 1920s. He was in the British Army during World War I, like so many other Blackpool men.

When all the O'Flahertys – my aunts and uncles – got married, they moved out of number 3, but none of them lived far from Madden's Buildings. They all finished school at a very early age – including my mother – and went into some kind of work. There was one, Aunt Nora – I think she might have been the eldest – who went into service in St Patrick's Hill, working as a maid for a well-off family. And then, at 17 or 18, she went to England where she remained all her life. Another aunt, Kitty also went to London.

Their brother, Denis also went to England, to Newcastle, and they had no contact with him for over 20 years. That was talked about on a regular basis because nobody knew whether he was alive or dead. When they eventually found him through the Legion of Mary, he came home and lived with my Nan for a bit. That was a very joyous occasion; it was a big moment for the family, Nan especially – I remember it well. They were a very united family, the O'Flahertys.

When my mother was 15 or so, she left school to work in a place called Cohen's. They were a Jewish family and they used to make garments on St Augustine Street, near the Grand Parade. I often heard her telling us afterwards that Ben Dunne, the father, who started Dunnes Stores, used to work in Cohen's before he left to open up his own shop in Patrick Street. My mother's sister, Lily also worked in Cohen's. I think my mother worked there until she got married to my father in 1942 when she was 25 – she was nine years younger than my father.

When all my mother's brothers and sisters married and moved out, I was sent down to stay with my grandmother at number 3. Her name was Kitty but of course we called her Nan. I lived with her from about the age of seven on. She would have been about 65 by then.

◄◄◆►►

MADDEN'S BUILDINGS ARE still the striking low-sized terraces they always were, with their distinctive sandstone and reddish brick exteriors. The numbers in golden writing on the red tiles in the lintel above the doors. A matching plain tile over the lintel on the window.

They were built in 1886 on the site of an old cattle market. Paul Joseph Madden was Lord Mayor of Cork in 1885/6, hence the name. The initiative was part of a movement to eradicate slum dwellings from the northside of Cork city and was the first such initiative under *The Artisans' and Labourers' Dwellings Improvement Act* of 1875 which gave local councils special powers. The Buildings were built at a cost of £5,846 and they still, to this day, retain much of their original fabric and now represent a part of Cork's social architectural heritage.

The Buildings were known as 'corporation houses', let out by Cork Corporation (now Cork City Council). They were 'affordable' or social housing made available to those lucky enough to get them, and our family was one of those lucky families, among 75 others. Rent was paid every week and when the last family member died, the house went back to the Corporation and a new family could live in it.

The four rows of 76 houses are 'sandwiched' between Great William O'Brien Street at the 'upper end' or west, and Watercourse Road at the 'lower end' or east.

Farranferris (Farna, as we knew it) was only five minutes' walk away at the top of Seminary Road – more popularly known as Water Lane. It was a secondary school for boys – a seminary – run by the Diocese of Cork, with the hope that some boys would have a vocation and go onto become priests after their Leaving Cert. Many did become priests and even bishops, while others distinguished themselves in commerce, sports (hurling in particular) and many other facets of life. Everybody from Farranferris came through Madden's Buildings to get into town because the bus was at the bottom of The Buildings on Watercourse Road. The boarders, the priests, everybody. It was a huge flow-through when they were allowed out and they all came back the same way, later in the day.

The Bishop's Palace was down the road from the college while a couple of hundred yards further on, the North Monastery Christian Boys School (CBS) stood proudly.

At the top right-hand corner of Madden's Buildings was a harness maker, while at the bottom right-hand corner was a blacksmith. So, horses were always coming and going at one time or another. We spent hours, as children, after school, watching the horses being shod.

The garda station was next to the blacksmith's; we had always had a fear going by there, for some strange reason. Kilroy's Mineral Water factory was next door to that, but thoughts of stealing a free bottle of orange were quickly dismissed as the guards might be watching.

Denny's slaughterhouse was beside that – they were well known for sausages and black pudding. We could hear the screeching of the pigs from our house and if the wind was blowing from a particular direction, the smell of the pigs enveloped practically all of Blackpool.

Many smells drifted in the Blackpool air during the days of my youth. The fermenting grain from the distillery, the horse manure from the blacksmith, the pigs in Denny's, the hops and barley from Murphy's Brewery, the smoke from its high chimney stack which could be seen from many parts of Cork. My childhood boast was that my father made the smoke come out of that chimney.

In 'outer' Blackpool, Goulding's Fertilizer factory and Sunbeam Wolsey were big industrial complexes which gave great employment. Gouldings operated in an actual glen, hence the name Glen Rovers, and many of the men who played for Glen Rovers or St Nicholas worked there. Through his friendship with Jack Lynch, Sir Basil Goulding made a gift of a field in Spring Lane which is now part of the Glen/St Nicks complex.

Straight across the road from the Buildings was 'The Distillery' (now internationally known as Irish Distillers). Paddy Whiskey and Cork Dry Gin were made there. Now they are distilled in Midleton along with Jameson and other international products.

On the other side of the Buildings (the 'top end', close to number 14), along Great William O'Brien Street, many small shops were spread about, over which their owners lived. Each of these would have its own unique household items; for instance, you might go to one shop for milk and another for eggs and so on. My mother was great friends with many of the men and women who ran those shops, and we would often be sent down there for 'the messages' – groceries.

I KNOW I'M biased but so many brilliant and successful people lived in Blackpool and were born and raised within a *poc fada* of Madden's Buildings.

James Barry (1741-1806) lived on Water Lane. His house is still there and still occupied. Barry is best remembered for his six-part series of paintings entitled, *The Progress of Human Culture* in the great room of the Royal Society of Arts in London.

In my time, Neil Toibín, the actor and comedian, lived on Redemption Road, beside the Bishop's Palace. He was well known for his many parts on stage, in films and on TV. I remember his father always wore a bowler hat and spoke to you in Irish whenever you met him.

Joe Lynch, the actor, lived in Water Lane around the same time, a few hundred yards away from Neil Toibín. Joe became best known for his part in *Glenroe* and *Bracken* as 'Dinny Byrne'.

Willie Cotter lived on Seminary Road. He was sports editor of the *Cork Examiner* but was better known for his career on the League of Ireland soccer team, Cork Athletic. Willie won league and FAI cup medals in the 40s and 50s including the league/cup double in 1951.

A hundred yards from Willie Cotter, right at the end of Water Lane, Donie O'Sullivan lived. He won senior county championship medals with Glen Rovers and St Nicholas and an All-Ireland senior hurling medal with Cork in 1954.

Tom Buckley (whose family had a pub) also grew up nearby. Tom played with Aston Villa in the 50s whilst Roy Keane's mother lived almost next door. Her maiden name was Lynch.

The sculptor, Seamus Murphy R.H.A. lived and worked at the top right corner of Madden's Buildings. He was internationally famous, although we didn't know that as children. We were fascinated watching him carving out statues and headstones, marvelling at the form taking shape out of the stone.

◄◄◆►►

EVERY SINGLE HOUSE in Madden's Buildings was exactly the same. I've already described the exteriors, with the distinctive bricks, lintels and tiles. Each house had a door and a window facing onto the street. Inside, the hall was narrow and there was lino on the floor and a gas meter on the wall. We had to put a shilling into the meter to keep the gas going.

We had the front room on the left and the kitchen straight ahead. It was a small kitchen. There was a fireplace in the kitchen and two side chairs, a table with four or five small chairs around it. There was the gas cooker that my mother cooked on and then the back door out to the small yard where we had a shed for the coal and our toilet.

The fire would be going in the kitchen a lot in winter and my father was an expert at lighting the fires because of his work. It was our job (my sisters and myself) to clean it out first. But when Dad was working nights and we'd come home from Mass at eight o'clock in the morning, the fire would be blazing for us – a great welcome on a cold morning. But my parents had to spare the fire too, because coal was expensive and money was scarce.

There was a picture of the Sacred Heart in the kitchen, of course, and a radio on the counter top and that was it for decoration.

The front room was the 'good room' and that had a fireplace too, but it was almost never lit. Two armchairs and a sideboard, maybe. There would be net curtains at the window – our only window that faced out on to the street – giving a small bit of privacy, at least.

The door of the front room was *never* opened because the room was almost never used except for special occasions, like Christmas Day or if a very important visitor came – which almost never happened. And that was the same in almost all the houses in the Buildings except for the homes with large families. In those, the front room was converted into a third bedroom.

There were two bedrooms upstairs and nobody had any privacy. I shared a room with my two sisters, and my parents had the other one. Later I slept in my mother and father's room, especially on the weeks of night-shifts, until I moved to my Nan's house at number 3.

There were no fireplaces or heating upstairs and it could be freezing in winter. A skylight let in the cold along with the light. The skylight remained closed all winter long and we weren't allowed to use the iron bar to lift it, in case the window would crash down and we'd hurt ourselves.

When I went back to visit my mother in the house years later – this was after my father died and she was living there on her own – I used to look at it and wonder... *How did we live here at all? How did the five of us all fit... in such a small house?* But the fact is that there were much bigger families than ours living in Madden's Buildings and they managed it too. You did what you had to do, those days.

For example, there were people living not far from us, and they used to keep pigs. This is right in the middle of the city. They used to collect the food waste at lunchtime and feed the pigs with it. They came down the street with wheelbarrows for the waste food or if they had a donkey and cart, they would use that to collect the waste. It was as primitive as that.

In reality, Madden's Buildings was a lovely place to live. Everything we needed was nearby. My father had steady work just a stroll down the road, but a lot of the people who lived around us didn't have far to walk to work. With Gouldings and Sunbeam and the distillery and the brewery, Blackpool was a great source of employment.

My father's three work-shifts were: 6am to 2pm, 2pm to 10pm and 10pm to 6am. In the morning when he arrived home from the night-shift he used to come up the stairs to bring my mother a cup of tea, and he sat on the bed and talked to her.

And she'd say to him every morning, 'Anything strange, John?'

Every morning that's what she used to say. I suppose it was her way of finding out if anything happened at work, or just to get any news out of him, but it always struck me as odd to say that every day to a man just home from work.

After my father finished work at six in the morning, he went straight to Mass at Saint Mary's Church on Pope's Quay, run by the Dominicans, and he'd be home by seven. He did that every morning. Then he brought the cup of tea up to my mother and then my mother and I and my two sisters got up and we went to half-past seven Mass in the North Presentation Convent. I did that every day of my life until the day I got married and moved out of Blackpool.

That wasn't unusual those days. You wouldn't see streams of children going to Mass at half past seven but that's what our family did, anyway. Of course, during Lent, everybody would go to Mass, every single day. All the parents and children, that was a given.

My mother and father had a strong faith; that was the way we were brought up and the Rosary was said every night. Our upbringing was very Catholic, but, again, that wasn't uncommon in Cork in the 40s and 50s.

I never heard my father say a swear word once, not once in my whole life. But he'd be very strict at the same time too. And we were certainly reared in a strict environment, with both my mother and father – there is no doubt about that. But, while my father was strict, he was fair too, and honest. Very good living, that's how I'd describe the way he lived his life.

My mother was a loving mother but she could be a serious woman too. That wasn't unusual. Her own sisters – who we got to know very well growing up – and the other ladies all around, they all had this sense of propriety, of doing right, living a good life. Rearing their children strictly and well. Some of us might break the rules now and again but if we did, we knew we'd pay for it in some shape or form.

MY FATHER WAS strict, definitely. You would get a belt, even around the head. But it was the same in all households, probably worse in some. My father was never cruel and he didn't lose his temper. If you got a belt, it was because he felt it was needed for your own good. And we had to be toughened up too, it wouldn't do to be soft at all.

For example, one day I had a fight with a neighbourhood boy in the Buildings and he beat me up. I came in home and I was crying. I might have been 10 or 11. My father came in from work later and saw me.

'What's wrong with you?' he said.

I didn't want to tell him.

'Go on, tell him,' said my mother. 'Tell him.'

So, I had to tell my father what happened and he pulled me up by the shoulder and brought me out and he said, 'Go on and sort it out with him, now. Finish it off'.

My heart sank. The young fellow wasn't even out but they got him out and of course he gave me a good beating for the second time. My Dad wanted me to fight my corner, but in the heel of the hunt I ended up with two hidings instead of one.

But you couldn't be going in home whinging, either. Times were tough those days and you had to stand up for yourself. It was the same at school. School could be hard; you'd want to watch it with the other boys – the older ones especially. Some of that would be classified as bullying now, but that wasn't really a word we used at all then. I'm not saying it was right and I wouldn't like to go back to that aspect of those days, it's just the way it was.

MY MOTHER AND father never went out to socialise. We never had a childminder once in our lives, or at least that's how I recall it. I guess most of my father's socialising was done at work, or when he went to matches.

My mother had a friend, Mrs Ahern who lived on the southside, and they would visit each other maybe once a month. But that was the only outing she had, apart from shopping for groceries.

Most of the socialising my mother did was with the other women in the Buildings. On summer evenings the mothers would sit out on the footpath to get some sun. They used to sit on stools on the northern side of the street and the sun would come around in the afternoon and shine on them. Our house was on the opposite side – it was in the shade – so my mother brought her stool over and sat with the other women, and they would be chatting away, some of them knitting.

You'd have five or six women at one end of the Buildings and another five or six at the other, talking away the whole time.

On summer Sundays we used to listen to matches on the radio in the kitchen – the wireless we called it – Munster Championship or All-Ireland games, with our great heroes Jack Lynch and Christy Ring playing, if Cork were involved. Some of the neighbours would come in and I'd be put under the table – the room was so small. My sisters might be sent out to play. There would be great excitement in the kitchen, I remember that well, listening to the legendary Michael O'Hehir commentate.

I never dreamed as a child I would ever meet those three great men, let alone get to know them as well as I did.

MY FATHER HAD a gadget – well we called it the gadget but it was a piano accordion. He used to take that out and play it for us, particularly on winter nights. This would really only be at the behest of my mother – if we were getting a bit boisterous or whatever.

She might say, 'John, bring down the gadget, there, and we'll have a few songs.'

So, my father used to go upstairs and he had it on top of a wardrobe, because he didn't want us getting at it. He brought it down and strapped it onto his shoulders and he'd start playing away.

And we'd all start singing. There were always sing-songs in our house, especially at Christmas. That singing stood to me later, when I was in sixth class in the North Monastery Primary School. We had a teacher, Denis Murphy who played football with Cork in the 50s. Denis was from St Finbarr's. Every Friday afternoon he'd have us singing, he'd ask some lads in the class to sing. It got to be very popular because it was nearly like getting a half-day and we loved it.

One Friday in school a boy sang, *Meet me in St Louis* – I'll never forget that. That is over 60 years ago, but I remember it like it was yesterday. And every time I hear it on the radio or whatever – Bing Crosby used to sing it – I think of that lad singing in that classroom all those years ago, when I was a boy.

Brother Cordial was another teacher in primary school. He had a choir and I was in it, and we used to sing in competitions in the City Hall and places like that. So, we got a great grounding in music and some of it was operatic that you'd still hear on the radio. And we all knew a few songs to sing.

I remember learning the *Croppy Boy*.

It was early, early in the spring
The birds did whistle and sweetly sing,
Changing their notes from tree to tree
And the song they sang was Old Ireland free

I remember learning *The Stone Outside Dan Murphy's Door* too. And my father taught me those while he was playing the gadget. He had a song-book with all the words and he'd teach me the words and the airs, and I was able to sing them later in sixth class.

I never played the gadget, we weren't allowed to play it, really. I tried it once or twice in my father's absence, but I was hopeless. My father taught himself to play it – there were no music lessons that time – but I hadn't a hope, I couldn't manage it at all. He never played with other musicians, but if there was a wedding or some event – which would be seldom enough – they'd ask him to bring the gadget and play a few tunes, and he would.

Years later, when I was playing with St Nicholas and Glen Rovers there was always a sing-song when you got back. Or if we were playing at a tournament, after the game everyone would go to the pub and have a sing-song.

There were very famous sing-songs in Blackpool on the night of winning a county championship. Win or lose, there would be singing and lots of it. And it would be all about the singing not the drinking. I myself was a Pioneer when I played hurling and football, and drink never interested me when I was young. I used always sing *The Wild Rover* at those events, a great old come-all-ye.

No matter who you were, you would be asked to sing. I always had a great love of the sing-song.

MY SISTERS AND I walked to school and then we came home for our lunch in the middle of the day, but of course we called it our dinner.

The food those days was basic. Plenty of potatoes and cabbage. You might get dessert once a week. And we might have a fry once a week – sausages and rashers. But an egg was a treat, not like the staple it is today. So, the fry would not include an egg; we'd have the egg boiled and that would be a separate tea, which we had at 6pm.

We'd have tripe, drisheen, all the traditional Cork foods too, and we ate anything we got. You couldn't be picky, that wasn't on at all. Fish on a Friday, of course, whether you liked it or not. I never minded fish.

Sunday dinners were the same as any other day but my mother baked on Sundays, so there would be cake when you'd come home. That was something to look forward to. There were no bought cakes those days, that just didn't happen. Like most people, we couldn't afford it.

One thing we did dread was Saturday mornings. My mother used to line the three of us up in the kitchen, to give us senna. This was made from senna pods and she used to make it herself in a jug. It was a laxative and it was dark green in colour. You'd look into the jug and groan inside if she had made a lot of it. She'd give me a big spoon of it and then to Anne and Catherine, and back to me again until the jar was empty.

Every Saturday morning, God we hated that part of the week. I can still taste it all these years later and then the rumbling in your stomach – you'd hear it and you knew what was coming next.

WE WORE BOOTS quite a lot, to school and so on; Wellington boots too, in winter. We would have to save our good shoes.

My father used to mend our shoes. He had a last, which is what shoemakers use. It was made of solid iron. My mother would go into town, into Matthews I think, and bring home a square of leather and he'd cut the shape of the shoe out of the leather and finely trim it at the edges and tap it all into place. My mother and father had to do things like that because a strip of leather was a lot cheaper than a new pair of shoes. So, they repaired things that we'd throw out today without a second thought.

My father was very good with his hands, but I didn't take after him in that regard at all.

I HAD SO many friends growing up that there are too many to mention. I was always outdoors playing and there were so many boys living in the Buildings and nearby, we were never stuck for company or something to do. We had a wealth of activities to keep us occupied, which led to a very happy childhood.

Most of the 38 houses in Our Buildings contained children of one age or another and it was the same for the Other Buildings. We had enough to play hurling matches with full teams, us against them. I also had a lot of first cousins growing up nearby and I was very friendly with one of them especially, Denis Goggin from Thomas Davis Street, who was the best man at my wedding.

Sometimes we'd go across to the Other Buildings and the boys there would chase us back to our own. And sometimes they'd come over to us and we'd chase them back.

While the street of Our Buildings was very narrow, it was also very quiet, so we could play away on it. There were no cars – you might get a car going past us only once a week, it would be a real novelty. So, we had great freedom and great movement; we were always on the go, outside.

They were simpler times and we lived simply. For example, there was no fuss at birthdays. Mine was on June 7th but if you got a present, it was something you needed, certainly nothing fanciful and there weren't parties or anything like that. It just didn't happen and that wasn't only us, it was the same for everybody.

And while I wouldn't describe myself as a 'happy go lucky' child, I was very happy – always. I was blessed, really. We never wanted for anything, we felt we had everything we could ever want for.

◄◄◆►►

WHEN I WAS seven or eight, I started going down to my Nan's at number 3. She was living on her own and her house was close to the Watercourse Road end or bottom of the Buildings. I used to go down, initially, after my tea in the evening, bring my pyjamas with me, sleep in the house with her and come back to my own house the following morning. As I got a bit older, I used to go down earlier and I'd eat with Nan too. And I kept my clothes there.

I'd say in her day my grandmother might have been a tough lady because she basically had to rear eight children on her own, and they were tough times. Her husband died in his early forties leaving her with the eight. Nora might have been 17 by then, but some of the others were quite young.

I had to be polite to my Nan, as nearly all children were those days. But she was a loving woman and she was always very kind to me. I enjoyed living with my grandmother, Kitty O'Flaherty immensely.

I was very naive. When I used to say my prayers – which I did every night – I would pray to the Blessed Virgin, whose picture was on Nan's wall. Well, I *thought* it was the Blessed Virgin. I only found out many years later – when I saw the picture somewhere else – that it was the Mona Lisa who I had been praying to, all that time. I'm sure Nan thought it was the Blessed Virgin too; they were more innocent times for us all, in so many ways.

But I had a certain amount of freedom at number 3 too, that I didn't have at home. For example, after the FA Cup final of 1955 I became very interested in soccer, it seemed quite glamorous to me. Professional soccer in England, especially. And in Nan's house every Saturday at five o'clock I used to turn on the wireless. I'd ask, of course, but there was never a problem and I'd sit down beside it and listen to Eamonn Andrews call out the results of the day on *Sports Stadium* on the BBC. And I'd listen to every single result, from start to finish. Afterwards, I would be able to tell somebody how Stranraer got on, let alone Manchester City – my team.

There was a cinema in Blackpool with the very exotic name of The Lido and Nan liked to go there every Saturday evening at seven o'clock, and she would bring me with her. Now, this was a great treat at the time. And she only brought me, never Anne or Catherine or any other grandchildren. Of course, I was delighted with this.

Nan used to wear a black shawl; she never ever wore a coat of any description. It was always only the shawl. We'd go out to The Lido and it was literally only a few hundred yards from where we lived – number 3 was near the Watercourse Road. Nan would sit in the back row, on the hard seats and all the other elderly ladies would be sitting there as well, all wearing black shawls. I'd sit on the row just in front of them.

At The Lido, you had films with all the stars of the time, whom I idolised. Roy Rodgers, Gene Autrey, Randolph Scott. Humphrey Bogart, of course. I don't remember the women actors as well, I must admit. As a child I didn't have as much interest in them.

Every so often during the film I'd get a tap on the shoulder, and that meant I'd get a sweet. One or more of the ladies would have sweets and they used to give me some. Happy days, I was spoiled rotten by them.

I loved living with Nan, sweets or films aside. She was a very interesting woman. She used to tell me about the First World War and all the young men from Madden's Buildings and Blackpool who went away and fought in it. Her husband, Denis was one of them and he survived the war, but I don't remember any specific stories about him.

If dance music ever came on the radio – céilí music or anything like that – she'd get up and dance around the floor for me. She'd hoist up her skirts and everything. She used to try to get me up to dance with her but I couldn't dance at all, not for love nor money.

She used to shout 'Up the Munsters!' when she'd be dancing – I guess it referred to the Royal Munster Fusiliers, which was the regiment that many Blackpool men were part of, but I never asked her what it meant.

As I got older, I also had a bit more freedom to stay out later and I had my own room at number 3, unlike at number 14.

Looking back, it was a lovely time in my life. Not only did I grow up in one loving home with my sisters and my mother and father in Madden's Buildings; I was blessed to have grown up in two, with my lovely grandmother, Kitty O'Flaherty who meant everything to me.

◄ ◄ ◆ ► ►

THE RACES AGAINST the Other Buildings was a big event. We had teams and one from each team raced off from the same place around the Buildings with all his teammates cheering him on. The first runner back won and then your team was 'one up' or 'one down'.

The races were held in opposite directions. If I started the race running towards the brewery, my opponent would run away from it. So, when I came to Watercourse Road I went left and left again back down to the other Buildings. And then I could see him coming against me. And I immediately had a very good idea if I was winning or he was winning; I was able to judge because where we passed each other told me whether I was ahead or behind.

And I think that's where we developed our athleticism and speed. We learned how to run and how to pace ourselves; how to really sprint and how to compete. They have to coach young people how to run now, but we knew how to run because we were running all the time. Which we used to good effect when we began to play hurling and football. We never played hurling or football on the street because it was so narrow and windows could be broken.

We had marbles, of course, and we had a particular game of handball – well, we called it handball. We used paper balls and my father made the best paper balls. He used to roll up a newspaper and tie it tightly with twine and you'd still have the ball a week later, no matter how much we played.

We had two goals, with pullovers or jackets for posts, maybe 20 yards apart and one boy played against another. You threw the ball up and hit it hard with your hand (like in handball) and tried to score goals against the other fellow who was guarding his goal. Both players couldn't leave their line. Your opponent tried to catch the ball and hit it back as quickly as possible before you got yourself set up again. The first to six won the game and we had great competitions in that.

One of the strongest parts of my game as an adult was my ability to catch the ball – I could manage it in any environment, really – and I'm sure playing that handball game helped me develop that skill.

WHEN WE WERE very young, we were interested in games and sport, but only the games we played ourselves and from our immediate area. In our innocence we weren't very conscious of sport in the wider world – at least I wasn't.

But I was playing with my friend, Sean O'Callaghan in the Buildings one day – I can remember the exact date, even though I was only nine – it was on a Saturday, the 7th of May, 1955. We were playing on a tricycle (we all played with whatever was to hand) and we were the only children on the street. Out of the blue he said, 'Who's going to win the match today?' He told me that Manchester were playing Newcastle in something called the FA Cup, a big game in England. I'd never heard of it. I'd never heard of those places, either, but I didn't let on to Sean.

For some reason, I said I was going for Manchester and I learned afterwards it was Manchester City. I found out years later that Newcastle United won. It took me a long time to figure out how Sean knew so much about soccer; it turned out his father was a League of Ireland referee.

From that day in May 1955 I have remained a Manchester City supporter. I must be one of the oldest City supporters in Ireland at this stage. We had many lean years until lately, so I was delighted in 2012 when we won the Premier League, our first championship since 1968.

BY ALL ACCOUNTS my father was a very good hurler.

Where he lived, growing up off Gerald Griffin Street, there were two teams. They were great rivals and they were called after the nearby cathedral of St Mary's and St Anne's. St Mary's had their club-rooms on Coburg Street, next to Jerh O'Connor's Funeral Home.

My father captained St Mary's when they won the Cork county junior championship in 1933.

As a consequence of that he was picked on the Cork junior team the following year and they made it as far as an All-Ireland semi-final. But my mother often told me afterwards that you could play with anybody that time, you could move clubs much more easily than you can now.

Glen Rovers were keen for my Dad to go out and play senior hurling with them but he had a lot of friends in Dillon's Cross through my mother's family. There were five girls in her family and they all had boyfriends, a good few of whom were from over there and played with Brian Dillons. So, my father ended up playing with that club too.

The only county championship Brian Dillons ever won was in 1938 and my father played centrefield on that team.

MY FATHER WORKED six days a week, but sometimes on a Saturday he might get a half-day and if he did, my sisters and myself and himself would go for a walk. He'd take us for a long walk and there was no backing out of it, we had to go whether we wanted to or not.

During the week, after school, my mother brought us for walks out the Commons Road – 'to keep us off the streets' as she used to say. My father brought us too, if he was on the night or morning shift. We walked all the way up to Kilbarry, which was about three miles away – in the country, basically. So that's a good six-mile walk, which is a serious walk for a child.

There was a soccer pitch up around Kilbarry – that was also the location of the old Glen Rovers ground – and my father used to bring me to a lot of junior soccer matches there. Some Saturdays in the winter we also walked over to Musgrave Park; he liked to watch rugby matches too. I think I got my love of all sports from my father. There was a rugby player working in Murphy's Brewery and he played for Sunday's Well and my father liked to go and support him.

Going to a match was the highlight of my father's weekend and the highlight of mine. In the summer, on Sundays, we went to the Cork Athletic Grounds to hurling and football games. We walked all the way even though from Blackpool it's a good walk for a child. On the way home he'd stop into a pub in MacCurtain Street and have a pint, and I would have a bottle of lemonade.

Of course, that was the height of Christy Ring's tenure and Glen Rovers were very successful at the time, winning five county championships in the 50s. And whenever they won, the team and all the supporters carried the cup back to the club in a mighty and noisy procession. That began at Murphy's Brewery and it used to pass the bottom of our Buildings. The team, bearing the cup, were led by a pipe band and throngs of fans walking alongside their heroes, cheering. And hundreds more proud Blackpool people used to flow out of Slattery's Lane, Foster's Lane, Green Lane and Madden's Buildings to share the joy and celebrate the win along the Watercourse Road and Thomas Davis Street.

A particular memory of mine, at matches in the old Cork Athletic Grounds (now Páirc Uí Chaoimh) was the scoreboard. When I began playing organised sport, when I was nine or 10, it was with a team called Cuchulainns – an offshoot of Glen Rovers. The players were mainly from Gurranabraher. The man in charge of the team was called Jimmy O'Rourke and he also looked after the old wooden scoreboard in the Athletic Grounds. My father and I used to always go behind the goal at the City End of the ground where the scoreboard was.

Jimmy knew me, of course, and he used to bring me up into the scoreboard. I loved that. I vividly remember being high up in the scoreboard looking down at the crowds of people for big games – there were huge attendances at matches those days – and the likes of John Lyons, Joe Hartnett, Vincie Twomey, Donie O'Donovan and Christy Ring on the pitch for Cork, St Nicks or the Glen, and the old stand below on my left – it used to be on the river side of the pitch those days. I'll never forget those Sundays as a child.

Looking down, the river on my left and the houses of Montenotte above it. Blackrock Castle out in the distance and the harbour beyond, as far as the eye could see… I thought I was looking down over the whole world, seeing everything.

BESIDES HURLING, FOOTBALL and soccer, there were a lot of other organised sports in Blackpool. Virtually everybody – the men especially – were involved in some activity and took it very seriously.

There was pigeon racing (every second house seemed to have a pigeon loft out the back and there were many of them in Madden's Buildings). The fathers of a lot of my friends had lofts and we used to spend time in them watching the birds – they were fascinating.

Going with the harriers (hounds) was very popular. The Blackpool Harrier Club (also known as the Northern Harriers Blackpool) was up above in Gouldings Glen near the railway line. And many extended families kept that tradition going and bred marvellous dogs for it.

Another great pastime was bowling – that's road bowling – and there would be big scores of bowls out the roads featuring famous Blackpool bowlers, up Dublin Hill towards Carrignavar or over near Blarney, with huge crowds and lots of betting.

Boxing was the preference of some lads (including my friend, Owen Wills and the great John 'Kid' Cronin, who was masseur to Cork, Glen Rovers and St Nicholas teams for years). The Glen Boxing Club was very successful, winning many championships, under the guidance of famous men like Ned Regan, Mickey Lucey and Kid Cronin. They had their clubroom and training facilities on Spring Lane.

These sports were deeply embedded in the culture of Blackpool when I was a boy, and they were very popular, very well organised and passed on from one generation to the next.

◄ ◄ ◆ ► ►

I WENT TO two primary schools. First, St Vincent's, on St Mary's Road, which was for children aged four to eight or nine. After that I went to the North Monastery Primary School.

St Vincent's was for both boys and girls, but we were separated in the classroom. It was run by nuns from the Religious Sisters of Charity. There were no male teachers in the school, it was an all-female staff.

There was a lovely teacher there, a Miss Coffee. I remember falling one time in the school yard splitting myself above the eye. She brought me down to the North Infirmary to be looked after and she gave me a Crunchie, which was a real treat.

Some of the nuns were very strict and harsh. If they caught you talking in the line (*an líne*) – the lines just outside the classroom – they would stand you up on the desk and leather the legs off you. The boys all wore short pants that time and the girls wore skirts. Then you'd go home and you couldn't hide it because you were wearing short pants or a skirt and your mother would say, 'What happened your leg?' She'd see the marks on your legs – and it would be the two legs. And you'd have to tell the truth, and then next thing is your mother would be off up to the nuns, there'd be war.

We used to get up to devilment too. We were children after all. For example, there was a big yard close to Blackpool Church with a tall gate in front of it. Out of that yard every morning came a team of horses pulling a float. The float was huge – or it seemed huge to us as children – about 15 feet long, and it was flat and you had the driver at the front and he had a whip for the horses. The float was on its way to the Cork docks for a day's work, but it passed Madden's Buildings every morning around 8.45am.

When we got to a certain age, we used to hang around the corner of the Buildings before school. When all the mothers were gone in off the street, we'd jump on the back of the float from behind. It was highly dangerous because the wheels were very big. Three children could hang on to it but you had to tuck your knees in and pull up your legs underneath at the same time. And you had to mind your school bag – you didn't want to drop that, under a wheel especially. All the time the driver used to be trying to get us off. He'd be lashing down with his whip at us. We thought this was great fun.

We used to hang onto the float as far as O'Connell Street, and we jumped off there and headed on to school. That was a big thrill, to get a lift almost all the way to school, first thing in the morning.

CHILDREN WERE TREATED differently those days and one thing you would never expect was praise. I can hardly ever remember being praised, either at home or at school, it just didn't happen. It's gone the other way now, completely, but praise wasn't done in my time.

I made my First Holy Communion in St Vincent's and then I went on to the North Monastery, which was literally across the road on St Mary's Road.

The Mon – as it was and still is called – was an all-boys school those days, and all the teachers were male too, either Christian Brothers or lay teachers. That was a big culture shock for me. It was a much bigger school and I was there for four or five years until I did my Primary Certificate exam.

Denis Murphy – Mr Murphy as we called him – was probably the teacher I remember most. He was a lovely man. I was sad to learn of his death recently. As I said earlier, he used to have us singing on Friday afternoons. He lived in digs in Gerald Griffin Street over a shop, Mrs Forde's where my mother got her messages.

There was a Christian Brother in The Mon called Brother McCormack, who was from Moate in County Westmeath. He had a great influence on us, he was a lovely man. I know the Christian Brothers got a hard time, after, and some of them deserved it, but of all the ones who taught me in primary or secondary school there was only one I could complain about and he was dealt with by the Brothers themselves for his misbehaviour, years later. All the rest of them were good teachers and we got a great education from them.

In fairness, primary school in The Mon was very good for all activities and most boys would take part in something, so it was a great basis for education and it really stood to me. The brothers let us play matches between classes. And we picked the teams ourselves in the classroom and then everybody would troop up the hill to St Vincent's where the old Mon Field was. No bother. Nowadays so many children opt out, but in my time everybody did something.

I HAD MANY great friends in The Mon and I still have some of them to this day. Because there was so much sport – from athletics to hurling – we formed strong bonds.

I had one great pal, Anthony Kennedy who lived in Ballyvolane and at that time living in Ballyvolane would be like living in Mallow today. We thought it was miles and miles away. He used to walk in to school from Ballyvolane every morning, and he'd call for me on the way and we'd go to school together. He used to go his aunt in Blackpool for his dinner at 1pm.

On the days when we had to go to the Mon Field – which was two miles away up at the top of Fair Hill – he used to bring his bike. Coming home he gave me a spin down, on his crossbar, and we had the two hurleys and two school bags, and me on the crossbar. Without exaggeration, we hopped on the bike at the

Mon Field and he wouldn't have to pedal again until we got to my house; it was downhill all the way and there wasn't much braking, either.

We had no fear those days, but when I drive down Fair Hill and Peacock Lane now and I see their steepness, I shiver. The speed myself and Anthony went down those hills was crazy. If my mother ever knew, she'd have gone through us.

Walking home from The Mon on normal days only took me 10 minutes. I walked down Peacock Lane or Johnson's Lane, where two of my father's sisters still lived at the time. We had an hour and half for our dinner in the middle of the day, but I used to go in home, gulp down my dinner, and be back up in the school yard playing a few minutes later.

Like all children we especially loved the summers. We never went on holidays or anything like that, but we never felt deprived; it was the same for everyone else we knew. We never looked for holidays, either – never. Depending on my father's shift work we might get one or two half-days in Youghal in the summer. This was a big treat and we'd be looking forward to it for days. We walked in to Kent Station in the city – quite the walk – and got the train at 2pm. There was fierce excitement and huge crowds of Cork people heading to the seaside. We got the 6pm train back, then.

When we were a bit older and we were allowed to go further afield, a gang of us would go out as far as Murphy's Rock and have picnics there. In those days that was well out in the country. The grotto in Blackpool was really the end of the city and the start of the country in the 1950s.

We also went to Goulding's Glen – straight across from the Glen Rovers Complex now. Spring Lane was all part of Gouldings, where they used to make the fertilisers. Those days there was a river running though it – it still does, as a matter of fact, but then it was very clean and we used to swim there in summer. All the children in Blackpool used to troop out and gather there, and spend the day. In those days, children were safe on their own, there was no danger at all.

A few parents might be there to supervise with the water, and we swam away all day long. Chatting, eating, picking blackberries or just playing – whatever children do.

◄◄◆▷▶

I MENTIONED MANY of the famous and talented people who lived close to where I grew up but there are four who really stood out and had a huge influence on me as a child.

Willie Cotter was one. He was an absolute gentleman. He lived up the hill from the Buildings. He was one of the greatest Irish soccer players of all time but he never went abroad because of his job as sports editor in the *Cork Examiner*. He had an amazing career with Cork Athletic and also represented Ireland, playing for the Irish League in Glasgow.

As a youngster, my father took me to the Mardyke to see Willie Cotter playing. The old stand is still in the same place and the dressing-rooms are still across the pitch – a red brick building.

Willie used to cycle down through Madden's Buildings on the way to the Dyke and sometimes he stopped and gave me a crossbar to the match with him – having asked my mother or father first, of course. You couldn't do that today; under any circumstances you couldn't possibly do it. I thought I was the whole man arriving to the Mardyke with Willie and everyone looking at us, walking past the inevitable queue to the gate. As a bonus, with Willie, I'd get in free to the match.

Donie O'Sullivan was another great influence and role model. He won county medals with the Glen and St Nicks and an All-Ireland with Cork in 1954, and he lived right at the bottom of the hill by Madden's Buildings. He ended up as Managing Director of Musgrave's in Dublin. He also used to take me to matches – to the Athletic Grounds – when he was playing for Cork. This would be on the crossbar of his bike too, and if he broke his hurley, he'd give it to me after the match and my father would fix it for me. I was so small at the time that I would be able to use the broken bit for myself.

Donie Leahy was another great man. He won a full soccer international cap with Ireland and his father played with the Glen along with all the Leahys. Some Sundays I used to go to matches in Turner's Cross if Evergreen United or Cork Celtic were playing. This was when I was around 12 and I was allowed to go alone (if my father was working the day-shift he couldn't bring me). The odd time I used to take the bus and it cost 3d (three old pence) and we got 6d pocket money a week those days, so 3d was a lot. And it was three pence to get into Turner's Cross as well so then I'd have to walk home – all my pocket money would be gone.

Anyway, the first day I did that, I was standing there at the bus stop and Donie walks by and says to me (and I don't know how he would have known me) ... 'Are you going to the match?'

'I am.'

'Come on and walk with me, so,' he said.

That was his warm-up: walking from Blackpool to Turner's Cross to play Shamrock Rovers or whoever. And I'd get in to the match for free as well, when I was with Donie, so I'd still have my sixpence in my pocket at the match and I could treat myself to something nice on the way home.

Only 10 yards away from Donie O'Sullivan's house there was a pub, Buckley's (it isn't a pub anymore). They were a lovely family; one of them, Derry, became a priest, a Kiltegan Father. His older brother, Tom Buckley was a great soccer player. Under-age, he played with a Cork city club called North End and was signed by Aston Villa. From there, he used to send me the newspapers from Birmingham every week. Every week, imagine. They were claret and blue newspapers, sent in the post to me and I only 10 or 11. And I have a soft spot for Aston Villa to this day as a result.

It is amazing now to think that I was surrounded by such greatness, even in humble circumstances in Madden's Buildings. Famous men bringing me to watch them play in big matches, or Tom – a soccer superstar – sending me newspapers all the way from Birmingham.

I'm sure, too, that those exceptional men had a formative influence on me, when I could see such greatness, close-up as it were, along with such kindness. I often wonder if I drew inspiration from them and I hope I was as kind to children whom I came across when I was playing for Cork and Munster later on. I hope if children looked up to me the way that I looked up to Willie Cotter, Donie O'Sullivan, Donie Leahy and Tom Buckley, that I gave something back to them and that I merited, in some small way, their admiration.

WHENEVER I GOT inside any of the grounds I went to – the Athletic Grounds, The Mardyke, Turner's Cross or Musgrave Park, or even up to the old Glen Field – I was always drawn to the dressing-room. I'd always want to be as close as possible to it. 'What are you going over there for?' my father used to say to me. And I'd say, 'I love to see the players, Dad'. I loved being early to the game too, soaking everything in. I watched the players arrive and I watched them go out on to the pitch and I'd be riveted by them – entranced.

And, for some reason, I gained an uncanny knack of knowing before the match started which team would win. Time and time again I'd have a sense of who would win on the day and I was almost always right. Whether it was hurling, football, soccer or rugby. Now, looking back, I think it had something to do with how the players carried themselves, their body language. Players used to straggle out that time and I'd be right there beside the dressing-room watching each one, player by player. And I'd go back to my Dad, or if I was on my own, I'd make up my mind which team would win and – invariably – I'd be right.

This stayed with me even after I stopped playing, myself, years later. Sitting in the stand, from looking at the players, individually and collectively – whether it was Cork, St Nicks or the Glen, or whoever was playing – I'd have a very good idea which team would win.

I've lost all that, now. They come out 30 or 40 minutes before games these days and they do intensive warm-ups and I have no sense, no idea at all, of who will win. But I really could do it, one time.

◄◄◆►►

MY FIRST HURLEY came from a man who worked with my father in Murphy's Brewery. He used to play for St Vincent's and his name was Rory O'Connor. He broke his hurley and my father must have said something to him because he gave the broken bit to my father who brought it home and cut it down for me – that was my first hurley. I'd say I was eight at the time. Your first hurley is a big moment – it only happens once.

My first pair of boots were given to me by my father's sister, Nancy. She bought them for me just when I entered The Mon primary school – I was probably around eight. And a year later, she also gave me my first pair of sports socks, they were blue and white, The Mon's colours.

My first club was Cuchulainns – an underage branch of Glen Rovers. Jimmy O'Rourke, the man in the scoreboard, was running some of their teams. How I got playing with them was this: every Saturday and Sunday I'd go up to the old Glen Field with my father. We were always taken for walks, my sisters too. It's a wonder I still love going for a walk on the northside, but I do. Above in the field we watched the Glen training or St Nicks, and there was a junior soccer pitch nearby. Depending on which club was playing, we might watch those matches, as well. And I brought my hurley with me no matter where I went.

And because of the fact that I had a hurley, they asked me would I play underage for the Glen; they didn't know where I was from or anything. And I said I would. And the team they had was Cuchulainns, which I wasn't aware of at the time. A lot of them came from Gurranabraher but others came from Blackpool.

I think my very first team, this would be under-12, was called Father Barrett's – he was a former curate or parish priest in Blackpool.

Now, those days there was no communication about matches and you'd never know if you had a match or not. So, I used to stand at the bottom end – the Watercourse Road end – of the Buildings on a Saturday. And if I saw the lads coming along with Jimmy O'Rourke, I knew there would be a match out in the Glen Field and I'd run in and get my boots and hurley – that was all I needed. And I'd walk away up with them. I didn't know any of the boys at the beginning, but I went along anyway and got to know them over time and I became great friends with some of them.

In fairness, they were after walking from the top end of Gurranabraher all the way down to Blackpool and then they had to walk up as far as Kilbarry where the pitch was. That's three or four miles, including a serious hill for the last bit of the walk, with a match in between. But we all walked everywhere those days and we were all incredibly fit and hardy – naturally so.

But then, if they were playing a match anywhere else, I wouldn't know about it. I'd be waiting in my usual place and if there was no sign of the lads, I'd know there might be a game somewhere else, or maybe there'd be no game – I just wouldn't know. And that would be a disappointment and I'd trudge off home. I loved to play so much as a boy, it was all I wanted to do.

Sciath na Scol was the big competition at the time and I played in that in 1957. This was and still is the primary schools' championship in Cork. The big player in Cork that time was Corny Mulcahy, and he played for the North Mon. His club was Na Piarsaigh. His father had a fish shop in the English Market.

Another player was Roger Tuohy. He was Na Piarsaigh as well and didn't we both end up playing centrefield for Cork in the All-Ireland final of 1969 against

Kilkenny 12 years later. We beat Greenmount in the final in Douglas that day in 1957 – even at that age there was southside-northside rivalry, and for me it went on a long time. So that was my first hurling medal.

Greenmount had two very good players. One was Gerald McCarthy, whom I didn't know at the time (but would get to know very well, later) and another lad who was very big. We called him 'Bánie'; we didn't have a proper name for him. We called him that because he had very bright blond hair. He turned out to be Phil O'Callaghan, who would go on to win his first cap for the Irish rugby team 10 years later.

There was a huge crowd at the final, all along the grassy bank surrounding the pitch. My father was among them, which gave me great pride – we had both gotten the bus out there together.

Underage in clubs that time had three main categories, under-12, under-15 and minor (under-18). I played for the Glen at all levels in hurling and for St Nicks in football. I suppose, even at 12 or 13 I was considered a prospect. Now, I can't honestly say that I thought I was any good. But somebody must have seen something in me that I didn't see myself. The North Mon won the Cork under-14 schools championship in 1958 and I was on that team when I was nearly 13.

I was on the Glen minor panel when I was 13 too, which, when you look back on it was crazy. And we won the county in 1958 and '59 but I was only a sub and never got medals (much to my mother's irritation). In the team photo I'm tiny alongside some of the other lads, but I caught up with them eventually.

Funnily enough, St Nicks won the county minor championship in 1958 too, probably with exactly the same players as the Glen had. We all played both hurling and football in those pre-specialised days. But I was only 13 for that too, so I was too young to get my game.

As I said earlier, women were resilient those days, they had very hard upbringings. The wives had to fight their corners and support their children, not least my mother and my grandmother who were both widowed quite young. When the Glen won the minor championship in 1959, she must have heard it at Mass or something, that they had presented the medals the previous night. When she came home she said, 'Did you get a medal from the Glen for winning the minor county?' I was only 14 and I never got a medal, there weren't enough to go around.

'No,' says I, 'I didn't.'

'Well I'm telling you now. You go down to such a fellow and you tell him that if he doesn't give you a medal you're never again playing for the Glen.' (I'm still very friendly with the same man, he's 80 now, but he was secretary of the underage at the time.)

Oh my God. I was absolutely terrified all the way down to the man's house, near the church, having to say this. Anyway, I plucked up my courage and I knocked at the door. 'My mother says that if you don't give me a medal, I can't play for the Glen anymore,' I told him.

The innocence of it. You'd do anything your parents told you that time. Nowadays, it is so different. I didn't even have the cop on to not go near his house and then go home, and tell my mother that I said it to him and he'll see what he can do. But we were pure gormless those days.

I never got the medal. But I'm in the photograph, and, as Christy Ring once famously said to a player who was taken off during an All-Ireland final and was very angry about it, 'Don't worry about it, boy, you're in the photograph'.

Not that there was any question of me never playing again for the Glen, and the same man – and he's a lovely man – knew that too.

MY FATHER WAS at the *Sciath na Scol* final which was, as I said, a big thing for me. Luckily the work shift he was on suited him, otherwise he might not have been able to go.

I went through three stages in relation to my father watching me play. I think it's very strange; I've never heard of it in any other player.

Up to the age of 12 I loved my father being at my matches, including the *Sciath na Scol* games. Then, between the ages of 13 and 17 I didn't want him to go to the St Nicholas/Glen Rovers/Cuchulainns games I was playing in, at all.

To this day, I'm not quite sure why, but I just didn't want him watching me play.

Sometimes I'd know he was there – and he knew I didn't want him there, but he'd go, anyway. Those games could be in Churchfield or Fair Hill, or in our own pitch. I'd be looking out for him before the game, to see if he was there, and sometimes I spotted him, half-hiding behind a tree or a pillar. He knew it upset me but I suppose he couldn't bring himself not to go, either. I was his son, in fairness.

Now, this was a stage too, where I wasn't playing well and I knew I wasn't playing well. I probably wasn't doing as badly as I thought, but I couldn't bear for my father to see me playing badly. I honestly don't know what was behind it. When I got home after a game, and he might be at home before me, he pretended he wasn't at the match and he asked me how I got on, knowing full well that I hadn't played well.

This went on for some years and there was nothing sinister about it – it was something that just got into my head. One night in Madden's Buildings I was lying awake, and the way my bed was aligned meant I could actually see down the stairs from my pillow. There were no doors, no TV, it was very quiet in the house. And my parents must have thought I was asleep because I heard my mother saying to my father, 'John, why are you always at him?'

And my father said, 'But he has it, Margaret… he has it'.

I didn't know what he meant at the time. As an adult and a father myself, of course, now I fully understand. And my father was hard on me, at times, to get the best out of me. I suppose he felt there was more in me, that I could do better. Of course, in hindsight too, I realise that I wanted my father to be proud of me – it meant everything to me. I think a lot of this was down to the lack of confidence I had in myself, especially growing up.

No matter what my father said to my mother that night, I still didn't want him at my games. But you wouldn't talk back to your parents those days, either, the way children would today. I could hear him at times during those matches, and there might be a bit of criticism there. Or perhaps I only perceived it as such, I don't know. At games these days, you'd hear much worse altogether, but that was then and this is now.

That period lasted until I was about 17. And for some strange reason – maybe I had a bit more confidence or I felt I was playing a bit better – suddenly I didn't want him missing any of my matches. I went from one extreme to the other.

And this was particularly true when I began to play for Cork, when I was 18. Then I took great pleasure in being able to give him stand tickets and in going to matches with him – those days he could come with me to the game. If I was playing in the National League in the Cork Athletic Grounds I got the bus down and my father came with me. Or if I was playing with the Glen in the championship, I'd be looking after him, and introducing him to people, and that gave me great pleasure and great joy.

In 1968, just as I was settling into a regular place on the Cork hurling and football senior teams – when I was 23 years-old – my father died suddenly. And I missed him terribly then, because I was beginning to make a name for myself; I was really coming into my own as a dual-player and he would have enjoyed that immensely. I know he would, but it wasn't to be.

Now, he did see me play in one senior All-Ireland final – that was in 1967. And he did see me win senior county championships with St Nicks and the Glen. The sad thing is that he could have had such great enjoyment for many more years, had he lived.

At least I gave him five years of pleasure and joy watching me play for my clubs and my county. And thankfully, after I was 18 I took pleasure and joy in that too. At least I have that, and it is a great consolation, even after all these years. In fact, it means everything to me.

◄◄◆►►

1963 WAS AN exciting time. I was 18 and I was on the Cork minor football team. I was also playing senior football with St Nicks and had been for two years. Moving from minor to senior was a massive step up, needless to say. We got to the county senior final in 1963 when I was 18, so we had a good team, and I came on as a sub that year in the final. We were beaten by a point by UCC – not for the last time, unfortunately. But I never won anything playing underage with the Glen or St Nicks.

I wasn't on the panel for the Cork minors in 1963 for any of the early Munster championship games. And I never got near a minor hurling team for Cork, at any stage at all.

How I ended up on the Cork minor football team – straight into the team, not having been on the panel – was this: I was due to play a match for St Nicks against Mayfield and I was told before the match that if I played well, I might be on the Cork team against Kerry for the upcoming Munster final.

The man that told me this was David O'Brien and he was a selector for Cork at the time. He was very well known in The Glen and St Nicks as a mentor and for being involved in underage teams for years and years. Now, it wasn't because

I was playing for St Nicks that I'd get any special treatment – David was very tough, he'd tell you what was what if you weren't playing well and you wouldn't be getting a swelled head with him, that's for sure. But I must have been playing fairly well that year, and I must have played reasonably well against Mayfield because I ended up on the Cork minor football team at corner-back.

So, my first game for Cork was in the 1963 Munster minor football final against Kerry and it was on in Killarney on July 14th. Not only was it the first time I ever put on a Cork jersey, it was also the first time I ever set foot in County Kerry. I'd never been beyond Macroom – I had played a few games there for St Nicks.

We were picked up in cars from the old GAA headquarters in Cook Street and we headed west. Would you believe I got a fright at my first sight of the Kerry mountains – I'd never seen mountains before, and I can still remember the fear I felt when we were going down the hill by Glenflesk. I don't know what I was afraid of – I was probably nervous about the match too; remember, I'd never before been on a Cork panel, let alone on the team.

I was in awe of Killarney that day and the crowd – the seniors were playing after us and Fitzgerald Stadium was packed with over 30,000 people. I'd never played before such a crowd and it was all so different for me.

The match was a draw and I remember the score, it was eight points each. It was remarkable for one thing in particular: Tony Barrett, who was playing on the '40' for Kerry scored all their eight points. I became very friendly with him when I used to go to the Gaeltacht in West Kerry years later – he was from down there and we used to meet up.

That was my first match for Cork – the first of many, but of course I didn't know that. It was a big moment for my family too. My father was at the game and he made his way over when we came off the pitch and he gave me a big hug afterwards outside the dressing-rooms. And that hug was unusual, it wasn't really done at the time at all. It was my first every hug from my father and it is still very special to me now, over half a century later.

I USED TO look forward to those hugs afterwards, if we won a county final or something. He'd make his way onto the pitch and give me a big hug. Considering how young he was when he died (59) and how young I was when he died (23), I am now very grateful I did have those moments, especially because I lost so much time with him, upon his untimely death.

My mother couldn't bring herself to go to matches when I was playing. She was too nervous – afraid I'd be hurt or whatever. Only once did she see me play and she lived to a good age, thank God. That was the 1967 All-Ireland final with my father and my father's sister and her husband. It was the only time, ever – she just couldn't bring herself to go.

Instead, on the day of a big game – and I only heard this from other people, my mother wouldn't have told me this at all – she used to go down to the church in Blackpool from 3pm until 5pm, until the game was over. She'd be down there, or when my own children were born, she'd look after them and she would take them out the road or something to pass the hours away from a radio or a television.

Kerry cleaned us out in the minor final replay, it was 1-11 to 0-4. And my father couldn't go to that game, he was working – you couldn't swap around shifts those days. Just as well, maybe.

Despite the disappointment, it was great to play for Cork. And that year I was also – amazingly – on the Cork under-21 football team. While I had only one year as a Cork minor footballer, I played four years for the Cork under-21s. What's even stranger is this: even though I was corner-back for the minors, I played centre-back on the under-21 team. This despite the fact that I was marking fellows three years older than me.

We beat Kerry in the 1963 under-21 Munster final in Clonakilty by a score of 2-3 to 1-4. Kerry were hot favourites; they had a star-studded team. Now, we had a very good team too because Cork had won the minor All-Ireland in 1961 and players like Ray Cawley, Brendan Larkin and Gussie Harrington had come through. We also had Mick Coughlan from St Nicks – he was a great footballer. That was a proud day for the Hayes family because brothers, Flor and Tim F. were both on the team. Tim F. was only 17 and didn't Flor score 2-1 of our total of 2-3 the same day. The match was played in March, 1964 – I'm not sure why it was deferred.

That was my first Munster medal, which I was very proud of, especially because I was so young.

Unfortunately, the All-Ireland under-21 championship was not to begin until the following year, in 1964, which meant that Cork could go no further after beating Kerry. But to be playing under-21 at county level when I was only 18, especially against teams like Kerry, was a huge step-up and brought on my football game in leaps and bounds.

I didn't get on the Cork under-21 hurling team until my final year, in 1966, when I was 21. To be honest, I didn't come near the Cork minor hurling panel for the simple reason that I wasn't playing well enough. But training with the Glen Rovers senior team and eventually breaking into that team in 1964 would be a huge development for me. And the 1966 tour of the US with the Glen would be a further massive advance in my hurling.

PEOPLE TO THIS day tell me I was a better footballer than a hurler or vice versa but it didn't matter to me at all what team I was on or which game I played. You played on whatever team you were picked for and that was it. And I wasn't concentrating on one or the other. To be honest, at club level everybody was a dual player then.

Not only that, I can honestly say that I had no preference for hurling or football at this stage in my career. As long as I was getting a game, as long as I was playing, I was happy. I enjoyed it immensely and there were no complications, for this simple reason: they were all knock-out competitions. Every match was a final and you went from one to the other seamlessly. From hurling to football and from club to county. Back and forth, it didn't matter and the knock-out system facilitated that. If I was playing an All-Ireland final next Sunday and the Glen were playing today, I'd play for the Glen and then move on to the next game and vice versa.

In 1964 I was picked on the Cork junior football team. And this came completely out of the blue – I didn't know then and I still don't know where it came from. I wasn't training with them, I wasn't playing with them and nothing – not a word – was said to me in advance. I had played with the under-21 team the previous year and I was on the 1964 under-21 team too, but still, being picked for the junior team was a big surprise.

I only found out when the team was published in the *Cork Examiner*. All the Cork teams, at whatever grade or whatever age group, would be listed in the paper on the Wednesday morning before the match. That's because it would be announced in advance at the county board meeting on the Tuesday night.

That Wednesday morning somebody said to me – this must have been at work or somewhere – that I was playing with the Cork junior team the following Sunday.

'How do you know?' I said.

'It's in the paper,' he said.

When I got home, I went back out to buy the paper. And when I looked at the team, there were four Coughlans on it. Four. One of the Coughlans was Denis. Well, I thought... *there surely isn't another Denis Coughlan playing football in Cork.*

Then I got notification, but that was the first I'd heard of it.

We played Kerry in the Munster Championship in Macroom and we beat them. And we played Clare in the Munster final and we beat them, above in Kilrush, with a scoreline of 2-5 to 1-4, our defence holding strong.

Then we played Roscommon above in Roscommon and we got into what was called the 'Home final' against Meath and that match was a draw. We beat them in a replay thanks to some great defending again, with a scoreline of 2-9 to 0-10. We played London in the final and it was set for the Cork Athletic Grounds. We were in big trouble in the first-half, losing 2-3 to 0-3 at half-time. It wasn't looking good at all. But – not for the last time in my career – the Cork defence were the difference between losing and winning. We held them to just a single point in the second-half and sneaked home by a point, 1-8 to 2-4.

And so, on the 18th of October, 1964, at the age of 19, I won my first All-Ireland medal.

GLEN ROVERS HAD a great year in 1964, winning our 20th senior county championship, beating St Finbarr's in the final. I came on as a substitute and had the honour of playing alongside Christy Ring for the first time. Christy was 44 years of age and I was 19, quite a difference. But he inspired the Glen with a great goal before half-time. We went from 0-6 to 0-4 down just before half-time to 3-6 to 0-6 ahead after 10 minutes of the second-half, with our captain, Ring driving us on. He won his 13th county medal that day, an extraordinary achievement – and he went on to play for three more years. My friend, Finbarr O'Neill was in goal and had a great game. Some famous Glen names were on that team, including Joe Salmon, Jerry O'Sullivan, Patsy Harte, Andrew Flynn and Jackie Daly. A lot of those players would also be playing for Cork.

Officially, 24,000 people attended the game, but in fact it was much more because the crowd broke down a gate and thousands more poured in. That was a huge day for me as a hurler. I never actually thought I'd play senior hurling for the Glen. It never crossed my mind, it wasn't even a dream. You'd hear of fellows dreaming of playing football or hurling for Cork but I never did.

THE SAD FACT of the matter was that in sport I didn't have any confidence at all – I never felt that I would be good enough – ever. Unfortunately, that affliction never ended for me. I might know that some days I played a good match but I never thought I could *ever* play with the likes of Charlie McCarthy, Gerald McCarthy, Con Roche, Justin McCarthy or Tony Maher. God, I used to watch all those hurlers and I looked up to them all so much, even though they were only my own age.

It might be very hard for someone to think that I had such a lack of confidence, given the county teams I was on and the games I played, but that's just the way it was.

I genuinely thought that every player I played against – every single one – was better than me. And this plagued me more at club level. If I was marking somebody, say while playing for the Glen, I used to think that he was twice the hurler I was. And I wouldn't be trying to convince myself of that – I sincerely believed it. And this was when I was established as a Cork senior, winning All-Irelands.

I went through that for my entire career, from start to finish. In every single game. In both football and hurling.

I've never really talked about this before but that's just the way it was. Later, people might say something complimentary to me about a game I played in or that I seemed in control of the ball or had plenty of time on the ball – and I always thought… *If they only knew what was going through my head during those games.*

I was very nervous before games too, and this was especially true of St Nicholas and Glen Rovers matches. And when I began playing football and hurling for Cork this got worse because I always felt that I had to play twice as well to justify myself.

Playing for your club and your county are completely different because at county level everybody is equal, but at club level they aren't – there is a ranking. At county level, you are there on merit and you only have to look after yourself. The other fellow would take care of himself – you knew that – so all you had to think about was your own game. But in the club, the extra responsibility was huge. Or at least I felt it to be huge, anyway.

And the most amazing thing in my career looking back is that I can truly say I almost never missed a match. Almost never, in 30 years. Through injury or suspension or for any other reason. I was very lucky, really.

◄◄◆►►

I WAS VERY friendly with many of my contemporaries in Glen Rovers. Some of those friendships have lasted nearly 60 years, I'm happy to say, and they mean far more to me than any medals or memories of winning matches or glory or anything like that.

When I broke onto the senior team, I was very pally with Finbarr O'Neill and Denis O'Neill (no relation) and Paudie McCarthy from Commons Road. The four of us were the best of pals. We were all Pioneers too – I don't know if that had anything to do with it.

Finbarr had a car, and that was a huge thing at the time. He was the eldest of us (I was maybe 18) and he used to drive us to matches. Particularly in the summer months, when there were many festivals going on around Cork, West Cork especially. And St Nicks were often invited to play at these; there'd be football tournaments built around them.

And the four of us would head off in Finbarr's car, which was a Mini Minor. I can still remember the registration number… LPI 206. After the match then, we might go to a dance and there would be no drink involved at all. And I loved spinning around in the car, meeting new people, seeing new places, having fun with the lads. Driving around West Cork on those long summer nights was like being on holiday.

In my teenage years I did almost no travelling, and I had no holidays apart from the half-day trips to Youghal on the train, or my trips to Cobh in a delivery van.

Then, in 1963, I went on my first holiday. I was 18 years-old.

I went with my friend, Owen Wills, who played football with St Nicks and a bit of hurling with the Glen but Owen was mainly a boxer. He was a brilliant boxer and he boxed for several years in the National Stadium in Irish championships.

So, myself and Owen went on holidays to Butlins, in Mosney, County Meath. That was a famous holiday resort at the time. It was my first holiday ever and I think it was Owen's too. And it was a big deal for us both. I think we booked it through an office they had in Cork at the time and we paid in full, in advance.

Now, this was the week after the Munster minor football final in July (which I had never expected to be part of) and the holiday was complicated by the fact that the match was a draw. Much to my horror the replay was set for the following Friday night, when I was supposed to be in Mosney with Owen. I had a decision to make. Would I cancel the holiday altogether and lose all the money paid in advance? Or would I go on my holidays as planned for the week and miss the replay?

Little did I know that this was to be the pattern of my life. Anyway, I compromised – I decided to go on the holiday as planned but to come home early on the Friday in time for the replay which was being played in Cork.

When you went to Butlins that time you were allocated a table and chairs for the week. A place at the dining table in the main restaurant in the resort. And each place had a number and you had to return to the same number and place for every meal. You got all your meals as part of the deal – it was a full-board holiday. When Owen and I sat down to our first meal in Butlins there were two Dublin girls sitting opposite us. And we realised straight away that we'd be sitting opposite them all week. I'm sure they realised it too. We were stuck with them and they were stuck with us for the week.

I had to leave early on the Friday morning to play the replay in Cork. But one of the girls must have been taking photographs because she said she'd send them on to me. So, I gave her my address thinking no more of it; thinking I'd never hear from her again, let alone meet her. I was wrong about that.

Her name was Margaret Hallinan but now it's Margaret Coughlan, and it has been since April 3, 1970. On April 3, 2020 we celebrated our 50th wedding anniversary. Because of COVID-19, it was a strange celebration – we were cocooning at home in Cork. Not the celebration we had planned in the Rosscarbery Hotel with our children and grandchildren. But it was a celebration, nonetheless.

After Mosney in 1963, Margaret – good to her word, I'd learn that about her – sent on the photos and we exchanged letters for a while. But we were both very young and living our own lives, she in Dublin and me in Cork. Over the next few years, we didn't meet much and there were no phones so all we had was the odd letter. But I did meet her the next time I went to Dublin to a rugby international – our first date, I guess. I went to two games in Dublin in February and March, 1964 (Ban or no Ban), but to be honest, I was more interested in meeting Margaret than in the matches.

Then Margaret went to Edinburgh to qualify as a nurse. But she came back without completing her training and I guess I might have had something to do with that.

IN A FEW years I was playing with the Cork senior team and the only time we'd see each other was when I'd be playing a match in Dublin. Maybe a National League game or an All-Ireland semi-final or final. Which was rare enough. Margaret never came to Cork during that period but by 1968 we had a decision to make, really. Margaret was working in a Dublin solicitor's office, O'Connor and Bergin on the quay by O'Connell Bridge.

So, in Christmas of 1968 she did come down for a visit to meet my family, and this was her first time in Cork. That must have gone well, because she came in 1969 again. And there was a job going in Cork in a solicitor's office, a man called John O'Meara – he had been a rugby international in the 1950s – and he was based on the South Mall. So, when Margaret came down in '69 she went for an interview for the job and, lo and behold, didn't she get it. She took it and came to Cork permanently then. And the rest, as they say is history.

And when I think of all the decisions in my life, the decision for me to go on that holiday was the most important one I ever made. Ever. For over 50 years, I have known this. And of all the gifts I have been given in my life, Margaret is the greatest and I give thanks for her every single day. Because I know that as long as I have her, I have everything I need, everything I could possibly have dreamed of.

Everything.

Madden's Buildings.

Front: My Dad, Catherine and Anne, my aunt Lily; Back (from left): my aunt Maura, my Nan (in the striped dress), my Nan's sister, Bridget, my aunt Kitty and my Mam.

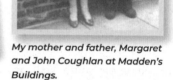

My mother and father, Margaret and John Coughlan at Madden's Buildings.

Me, aged five.

My father (sitting behind the cup), captain of the St Mary's team of 1933, winners of the City Division junior championship.

who had been living in Ballintemple since 1962 – used to drive by every day. He worked in Shell just down the road and he used to stop to have a chat with Liam by the main gate.

This was 1963 and I had just been picked on the Cork minor football team. And Liam never introduced me to Christy Ring or anything like that, but he might have told him at some stage, 'I've a fellow from the Glen working with me, now'. I never knew.

I USED TO just watch them talking when I was eating my sandwich. What I was thinking, I have no idea; maybe I was trying to imagine what two such great men would be talking about. I found it amazing that Liam Dowling and Christy Ring were just there, chatting right there on the road before me every single day.

In Sherrard's there would always be something to do and I really liked that. They had the agency for lawnmowers, for the English company Hayters, and they had one specific model, a petrol machine called the Hayterette. In my spare time I was expected to take a lawnmower out of a box and assemble it. And in the early summer a lot of those machines were delivered and sold.

◄ ◁ ◆ ▷ ►

O'CONNOR'S OF NORTH Gate Bridge were the undertakers who made all the arrangements for my father's funeral in November of 1968. And after the funeral, we paid them immediately. My mother and all the women of her generation would be very fastidious about paying their bills. It was a huge ethical stance that you paid what you owed and you did it immediately – people those days couldn't bear to owe money.

So, we asked O'Connor's for the bill and my mother gave me the money and I duly paid for the funeral. When we got a message from O'Connor's two weeks later for me to go down and see Mr O'Connor, my mother was alarmed. Her big concern was that we hadn't paid him enough, that there had been some problem or mistake with the bill, so she sent me straight down to find out.

When I went down, there was no issue with the bill. On the contrary, he was very pleasant and he said that he was impressed with the way that I had handled the funeral – how I had interacted with all the mourners. He told me that they were looking for a manager and asked would I consider taking the job. The business had grown over the years and they needed somebody to manage the running of the company; all the timings, bookings, the staff and the complex specific arrangements – tailored for every individual funeral.

At the time I had been working for a company called Trux Limited – I had moved from Sherrard's the previous year. In Trux I was managing the stores and I was happy to work there, they were a good company. But the job being offered by O'Connor's was a better job and it also meant that I could have a car.

In fact, when I took the job at O'Connor's, I went, overnight, from having no car (never having had a car) to having a Mercedes Benz 300 series model. It was so big that I couldn't even park it in Madden's Buildings because the street wasn't wide enough.

I loved every minute of my new job with O'Connor's. I found it very satisfying. It was a happy place to work, actually; that might sound strange but it's true. The O'Connor's were and are lovely people as were all the staff there.

Now, one situation where the job did impinge upon was my sporting life – my career as a footballer and hurler. All funerals at that time were walking funerals. So, for example, if there was a funeral in the southside, everyone would congregate at the funeral home (which was at North Gate Bridge) and they would walk with the remains to the church on the southside or where ever they had to go.

That often happened in the evenings (all removals had to be after 6:30 pm) and my training sessions also took place on evenings and sometimes I couldn't go to training as a result of having to work. I was the manager and it was my responsibility to make sure everything was done properly and correctly, so I had to oversee all of that.

I was happy in the job at O'Connor's but on the night of the All-Ireland final of 1969, I met Barra O Tuama, who was a Glen Rovers/St Nicholas man; he had played for both teams in his time. I knew him well.

He later became a famous impresario bringing international tenors and operatic singers to Cork, but at that time (September, 1969) he had a company called Cork Fertiliser Distributors (CFD). They were based in Cork and they were the agents for Albatross Fertilisers, the big company based in New Ross.

Barra told me that they wanted a representative in the south, driving around to all the creameries and companies that sold fertiliser, and he asked me would I take the job. Which I did, after some reflection, and it was a great decision. Ten very happy years of my working life followed.

The job was very sport-friendly – in the sense that I would always be back in Cork in time for training. It also gave me a lot of stability; I was due to get married the following April and Margaret and I wanted to buy a house.

◄◄◆►►

MY MEDIA WORK began in earnest in 1973 and it came about through the iconic commentator Michael O'Hehir.

Cork Fertiliser Distributors owned the Barleycove Hotel, which was a very popular summer destination, down in West Cork. They owned another company in Dublin which ran commercial warehousing. And I was a director of those companies and was involved in their management.

We also had the Irish agency for a high-class English horse feed called Pettifers. I used to travel around the stables in Kildare and other places where horses were bred and trained. I also travelled around the UK selling it, especially around Lambourn, near Reading, where a lot of stables are located. Promotion of the feed was built around the famous racehorse, Grundy, who won the Irish Derby and the Epsom Derby in 1975. And we wanted to advertise this product on the radio and television, so we had to find a well-known person to do that.

Now, there was no voice in Ireland better known than that of Michael O'Hehir, and after a National League match I approached the great man and he agreed to do the adverts for us. So, I got to know him fairly well, and I'd often meet up with him and have a chat about games and the adverts. And he asked me to co-commentate on games with him, which I was happy to do.

Through Michael, I was also invited to an interview for a job with RTÉ in Dublin. They were setting up a sports programme on television for Sunday nights and it was to be called *Sports Stadium*. It was a general sports programme, covering all sports. It was a round-up, basically, of all the sport that took place over the weekend and it was to be broadcast at 10pm on Sunday nights. And they were looking for a presenter for the show.

The interview was more of a mock presentation, really, and I had to do it in front of Michael O'Hehir, Fred Cogley and Tim O'Connor, who later went on to become Head of Sport at the station. They filmed me presenting various mock details about sports and it was an interesting experience being in front of the camera like that.

Before the interview was actually completed, I told them that I would not be interested. I had no great ambitions in that whole area; I was quite happy with my own 'day job' in business. When I 'retired' from county hurling and football in 1974, I began to commentate on more games with Michael and it was very enjoyable because I had so much free time, not playing for Cork.

I really enjoyed the commentating through 1975, climaxing on the first Sunday in September, at the All-Ireland final, which was between Galway and Kilkenny. Galway had beaten Cork a few weeks previously and the world of hurling was buzzing with the possibility that they might win their first All-Ireland hurling title since 1923 (having lost in the final seven times since then). As it happened, Kilkenny broke their hearts and they had to endure more heartbreak in 1979 (again, having beaten Cork) – finally making the magical breakthrough the following year.

I got to Croke Park at my appointed time of 12.30 pm to prepare with Michael. I was also keen to watch the minor match, which involved Cork. I immediately noticed that there were a lot of Americans in the press area. ABC's *Wide World of Sports* were doing a special report on the final and were filming the match for their viewership in the United States – a viewership in the tens of millions, the show being broadcast at weekends.

After a while somebody senior in RTÉ asked me would I 'transfer' to ABC for the day – would I help them out because they didn't really appreciate what was going on. They wanted me to co-commentate with the legendary Jim McKay, who was one of America's most famous sports commentators and who was the voice of ABC's *Wide World of Sports* for 37 years.

As I was briefing McKay about the match and the day, the producer got the idea that I should go down on the pitch and be interviewed on film with a hurley and ball, and demonstrate the skills of the game. My interviewer was a famous NFL running back by the name of OJ Simpson, who was playing for the Buffalo Bills at the time and was being groomed as a broadcaster by ABC.

OJ later became a famous actor, starring in over 20 movies and TV series. He subsequently became notorious when he was tried for and acquitted of murdering his ex-wife, Nicole Browne Simpson in 1994. He was later jailed for other offences, including armed robbery, in 2008.

But when he interviewed me on the pitch in Croke Park in 1975, he was still a hero to many Americans and was one of their most famous sports people at the peak of his career. He asked me several questions about the game of hurling and I showed him some of the skills, how to pick up the ball, how to strike it and so on. All the time being filmed by the cameraman.

A fairly surreal experience, especially when I look back on it, now. Me in my suit with a hurley and sliotar on the pitch at Croke Park being interviewed by a man who would later become probably the most infamous former sports star of all time.

Funnily enough, I met OJ again a few years later when I was on a tour of California with the Cork hurling team. In LAX Airport in Los Angeles I was waiting for a flight with a few other players when we noticed a commercial for Hertz Cars being filmed. Who was doing the advert, only OJ – who was by now playing for the San Francisco 49ers. I told the lads that I had been interviewed by him in 1975 but they didn't believe me. So, I made a bet with them that if I went over to him, he'd remember me and the interview we did in Croke Park.

During a break in the filming, I went over to OJ and he did remember me. I wanted to talk to him about the 49ers and some of his films, but all he wanted to talk about was hurling – he had become fascinated by the game. I won my bet, but I'm not sure if they ever paid up. I'm naming no names but they know who they are.

I also commentated with Michael O'Hehir the following year, in 1976, even though I was back playing hurling for Cork. That was a bit strange, especially when I was working on the two All-Ireland semi-finals between Galway and Wexford, both of which were held in the new Páirc Uí Chaoimh. This despite the fact that I would be playing for Cork against the winning team – which turned out to be Wexford after a replay.

Long after my playing days, when I was also finished as manager of the Cork footballers in 1986, I was approached by Billy George to do a series of articles previewing and analysing hurling and football games for the *Evening Echo*. I did it for a few years. I would go to all the assigned games and Billy would interview me on the following day and the piece would be on the back of the *Echo* on the Tuesday.

The funny thing about those articles and those games is that I never made any notes during or after the game because I could remember almost every detail of the match afterwards. While I never had aspirations to become a full-time commentator or to have a long-term involvement in media, I did enjoy my time doing that work – especially when I was on my 'gap year' of 1975.

◄◄◆►►

I WAS APPROACHED in 1979 to head up an insurance brokerage company on the South Mall in Cork city. This was my first experience in insurance, so I was a bit unsure, but I felt I could give it a go. I was 34 and I had been working on the road for 10 years and had enjoyed every minute of it. But it was the right time for a change too, and it was a dream job. Still, change is hard and I do remember telling Margaret about it – how nervous I was.

The company was called DEFK – Drumgoole, English, Flood and Kennedy which was Dublin-based. It was John Drumgoole who approached me first and he was involved with the Dublin club St Vincent's. His brother, Noel had been the hurling full-back for St Vincent's and Dublin and went on to manage Limerick and set up the club Na Piarsaigh in the city. Noel was also a member of the Sports Council, that's how I got to know him, and himself and John were keen to open an office in Cork. Although I didn't know the insurance business, they trained me up and we opened the office on the South Mall.

I asked Jack Lynch to open the office, but he wasn't available, so Ronnie Delaney did the honours for us, for which I was very grateful. Ronnie's family used to come to West Cork for the summer those days and sometimes they would be down in West Cork before him and if we had a Sports Council meeting in Dublin, he and I would travel down to Cork together afterwards. He kindly opened the offices on one of those Fridays.

I enjoyed the work and we began to do fairly well immediately. So much so that there was another company on the South Mall called Dwyer Life and General who approached me a few years later to know if we would amalgamate. Which we did and we called it City Life and General Limited and it was also based in the Citibank building on the South Mall. In that company we had about 18 people, between life insurance and general insurance (relating to industry and business). So, it was a busy time for me, but also very rewarding.

That went well for me until 1996 when myself and another director of City Life, Brendan Coleman decided to go out on our own. Later, we took on board another director, Johnny Hughes and the company became Coughlan Coleman Hughes. We moved the business to Trinity House in George's Quay and it is still very much in business with the same name although I no longer have an involvement, since my retirement in 2004.

Just as I was in sport, I feel that I was very lucky in my business career. I worked as hard as I could without ever being a workaholic or anything like that. I always tried to keep things balanced. I would always be into work early and stay until 5pm, when I might have a game of squash or pick up one of the lads and bring them home.

IN THE 1960s I have to say there was a lot of work available and because I had become well-known through sport, I had a lot of opportunities and I was happy to take some of them and move on – stepping up into new and more responsible and challenging positions. I'm the kind of person who thinks things through and gets all the information lined up before making any decision and, of course, Margaret was a rock of sense always and a great support.

But as it turned out I wasn't fully finished with business. One day after I'd retired, I was in Cork Golf Club and I was chatting to a member whom I didn't know that well – Norman Baker is his name – and he was interested in my retirement, he had heard about it. I told him what had happened but also that I was still dropping into the office occasionally to help out – that had been our agreement.

And he said that he'd love to have the same arrangement for himself – that he could wind down but not fully finish in a jolt going from 100 miles an hour to zero, overnight. So, we got chatting and to make a long story short I ended up buying his company. He had a blinds manufacturing company called Charisma Blinds which was very successful.

And my son, Jonathan who had been working in the bank at the time took over managing the business and he's doing a great job of it, I must say. We talked about it at length before the acquisition and he was happy to take over the business. He is much more skilled with his hands than I ever was – but he's a great manager too, and is very good with the customers and the staff.

That has been another fulfilling chapter in my business career, although in reality it's Jonathan's time now. I'm not really involved.

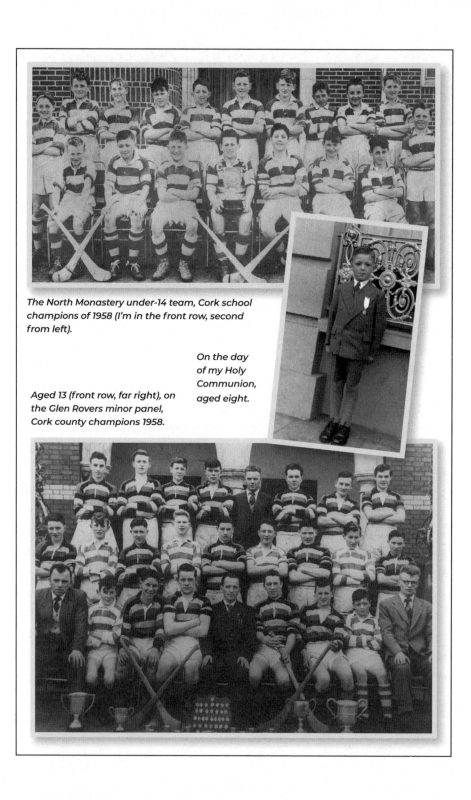

The North Monastery under-14 team, Cork school champions of 1958 (I'm in the front row, second from left).

On the day of my Holy Communion, aged eight.

Aged 13 (front row, far right), on the Glen Rovers minor panel, Cork county champions 1958.

« CHAPTER 3 »

The Glen, St Nicks and Cork

AS I SAID earlier, I played for four years on the Cork under-21 football team (1963-66), mostly at centre-back. Cork's track-record in under-21 football All-Ireland championships is very good – we are leading the roll of honour, with 12 wins, to Kerry's 10. But I was never to be part of any of those.

In 1964 Kerry got their revenge in the under-21 football – they tend to do that. They beat us in the semi-final in Killarney, 2-7 to 1-1. They went on to win the All-Ireland – they tend to do that too.

But in 1965 we bounced back. Amazingly, Clare beat Kerry in the first round and Tipp beat Clare, so our Munster final opponents were Tipperary. Tipperary are often overlooked in terms of their football, but they produced some great players and teams and I had the honour of playing alongside some mighty Tipp footballers when I togged out for Munster: people like Babs Keating, Gus Danagher, Paddy O'Connell, Dinny Burke, John O'Donoghue, Sean Kearney and Jim Kehoe.

The final was played in Castletownroche on the 8th of August and we were too good for Tipp on the day. In the end we ran out easy winners, 2-14 to 1-6.

In the All-Ireland semi-final against Galway I scored a penalty to win the game and we qualified for the final against a brilliant Kildare team. They were hot favourites to beat us because of their progress through Leinster and their win over Down in the semi-final had been so impressive. They had some great players, people like Ollie Crinnigan in goal, John Donnelly, Tommy Carew, Pat Dunny, Pat Morgan, Pat Nally and Sean Kelly.

The final was a wonderful occasion and to play in Croke Park was such a thrill, especially in front of over 18,000 fans. We began the game well and were winning 1-6 to 1-4 at half-time. But a combination of some bad misses by our forwards and a lucky goal for Kildare pulled them ahead. We pegged them back level again and then there was a tremendous period of play, with score after score, tit-for-tat up and down the pitch. But eventually we couldn't maintain it and Kildare drove on to win, 2-11 to 1-7.

ANOTHER ASPECT OF that under-21 final was that I played centrefield the same day. So, already I was being moved from position to position, even at underage. I played minor at corner-back; then I was centre-back for the under-21s, and now I was centrefield. That's a trend that would run and run in my career.

I started off as a corner-back in 1963 with the Cork junior footballers and I played in that position all year for them. But I never played corner-back for my club and it always interested me how I could be put in different positions. Often, I couldn't understand the positioning, but you played where you were told those days and that was that.

I played in almost every position except goalkeeper, especially in football. In 1964 I was corner-back with the Cork senior team and then in '65 I was centrefield. You almost never see that now when there is such specialisation, but it happened those days. Then they put me into the forwards in the Cork senior team. I played in all five lines for Cork in senior football, that's for sure.

In hurling my favourite position is very clear: it was left half-back. About half of my career – more than half probably – I was playing centrefield with Glen Rovers. The first-half of my career with the Cork hurlers I was at centrefield, too.

But the strange thing is that while left half-back was always my favourite position, it was only in my last few years that I got the chance to play there for Cork.

Funnily enough, my father played left half-back on the Cork junior hurling team in 1934. I played left half-back for Cork from 1976 to '80. My son, Jonathan played left half-back on the Cork under-21 team, my grandson Donagh is now playing left half-back on a Cork development squad, and my granddaughter, Beth plays wing-back for the Glen in camogie. So, there must be something in the blood there, when it comes to left half-back, if four generations were so drawn to it and have represented their club and county in that position.

◄ ◄ ◆ ► ►

FROM THE AGE of 12, I was waiting with bated breath every Saturday from 2pm on Great William O'Brien Street for the Cuchulainn lads to arrive from Gurranabraher, I loved to play football for St Nicholas Football Club – St Nicks. I was always proud to don the black and white hooped jersey, whether it was at underage, junior or senior levels. Always and ever. And whenever I played for Cork or Munster, I felt I was representing St Nicks too, and that spurred me on. The sense of belonging I feel in the club – to this day – is something I have always treasured and will forever hold dear.

I grew up hearing about the 1941 and '54 wins and the great feats of derring-do by famous St Nicks men like Jack Buckley, Bobby Buckle, Dan Moylan and Jack Lynch in 1941. And the heroes of '54 including Christy Ring, Donie O'Sullivan, Donie O'Donovan, Vincie Twomey and Dave Creedon, whose scoring feats in the final against Clonakilty went into Blackpool folklore. Dave Creedon deserves special mention because he had also played in 1941, and as well as playing for St Nicks in '54, he also trained the team. I would follow in his footsteps in that regard (player-manager), but without the same success. In 1952 when Dave was retired from county hurling, Cork's first three choices of goalkeeper all got injured and he was persuaded to come back into the Cork fold. Three years later he had been part of a three in-a-row – I would end up having that in common with him too.

St Nicks also attracted wonderful footballers from other counties, who were based in Cork, the most famous being Jas Murphy, who captained Kerry to an All-Ireland championship in 1953. Another was Jack Cosgrove of Galway, who won an All Star in 1971; Jack and I were on opposite teams when Cork beat Galway in the All-Ireland football final of 1973.

Luckily for me, the 1960s – when I did a lot of my footballing – was a golden period for St Nicks. As well as reaching two county finals in 1963 and '69, which we lost, we also won two county championships back-to-back in '65 and '66. As a result of that St Nicks had the captaincy of the Cork team the following two years.

against Askeaton to begin. The win against Clonmel Commercials in Dungarvan was anything but easy, but we sneaked through 1-5 to 1-4. Never underestimate a Tipperary footballer.

The final against John Mitchels of Tralee was played in Killarney on July 19th, 1967 and it was another dramatic affair. Andrew Flynn goaled for us early on and we dominated the first-half – even if we had a lot of wides. Myself and Patsy Harte were going well at centrefield. We were 1-3 to 0-1 up at half-time and looking good. All the more so after six minutes of the second-half when a Finbarr O'Neill goal put us eight up. But Kerry teams never give up – never. They moved Niall Sheehy to centre-forward and he caused havoc. They pegged us back, score after score, until they were just one point behind.

We were under siege until the final whistle and Teddy Dowd very nearly goaled for the Kerrymen with seconds left. The ref blew full-time from the kick-out. St Nicks 2-4, John Mitchels 1-6. St Nicholas were the Munster champions. And we were the first Cork team to accomplish that – something that can never be taken away from us.

That year we took part in an unofficial All-Ireland club final too. In 1967 Galway were on the crest of a wave in football, going for three in-a-row. Their county champions were Dunmore MacHales and they had several of those Galway players on their team like Pat and John Donnellan, Seamus Leyden, John Keenan, Bosco McDermott and Gay Mitchell. They contacted St Nicks to know would we be interested in playing in an unofficial All-Ireland club final on a home and away basis. So, we did. We played in Cork first, in the Mardyke and it was a draw – a great game with 5,000 people cheering us on. The second game was in Tuam and they beat us that day. The enterprise was so successful that it led immediately to an official All-Ireland club championship and St Nicks were also proud to have played a part in that.

After we'd beaten John Mitchels that day in Fitzgerald Stadium in Killarney – a place I would be revisiting many times over the coming years – I remember watching our captain, Tom Corbett accept the cup and thinking… *Wow. St Nicks are the Munster football champions and I am part of it. This is everything a footballer could ever hope for, everything a club could hope for.*

Everything.

◄ ◄ ◆ ▷ ►

GLEN ROVERS WAS founded in 1916 and so 1966 was a big year for us, our Golden Jubilee. And the main commemorative event was to be a tour of the United States in September. We desperately wanted to do that in style and one way to achieve it would be to travel as the champions of Munster.

The Glen had won its 20th county title in 1964 as I already said. Then we went forward into the Munster club championship which was played in 1965. But it dragged on and the final didn't take place until the 5th of December in Cashel. There were doubts about the game going ahead because of a snowfall the week before, but it did, unfortunately. It was a horrible day, completely unsuitable for hurling. There was rain, sleet, snow, driving winds – you name it. Despite that, a great crowd from Blackpool travelled up, busload after busload making the mid-winter journey.

And what followed was the most bizarre match I ever took part in. As a spectator or a player, I never saw anything like it before or since. We had a great team with Christy Ring, Finbarr O'Neill, Patsy Harte, Jerry O'Sullivan, Joe Salmon – a great blend of experience and youth. But so too did Mount Sion. They had several players on the Waterford senior team, some of whom had won the All-Ireland in 1959.

The pitch was in a desperate state, especially around the goalmouths; it was a pure mud bath. The whole match was a joke really, you couldn't play hurling. One sportswriter the following day said that it was more of a poking match than a hurling match, and he was right. With a gale force wind behind us, the Glen were 11 points up at half-time but sure enough Mount Sion whittled away at that in the second-half.

With about 10 minutes left, the Glen were still ahead but only by a goal – 3-6 to 2-6 – and Mount Sion were pressing hard. Next thing, the ball landed in the Glen Rovers square. And one of our players – I won't say who – stood on the sliotar. Deliberately, now, I have no doubt about that.

And, basically, the ball was never seen again.

A few players started tussling, trying to get at the ball and they ended up rolling around in the mud. Then a crowd of spectators, from both clubs, started to crowd around the goal and they were shouting at each other and at the umpires and the ref.

One of them ran onto the pitch (maybe he was a Glen man) with another hurlers was in July, 1965 when I had just turned 20. That was an Oireachtas Cup game and we were beaten by Kilkenny. In late 1965 and early '66 I also played a couple of National League matches. But then two things happened.

Firstly, I got injured, I hurt my knee. The second reason had to do with Glen Rovers' trip to the United States in late September. In order to be allowed to travel to the U.S. at that time you had to be vaccinated against smallpox and that had to be done several months in advance. It would then be marked on your passport and checked on entry.

The problem was that the vaccination affected some of us badly, including me. I got very sick and I missed out on the first round of the senior championship in 1966 against Clare – I was too sick to train and I couldn't play. Finbarr O'Neill from the Glen was the goalkeeper and he was also too sick to play in that game. Paddy Barry got on the team in his place and although Finbarr was brought back on the panel, he remained the substitute goalkeeper; but I wasn't brought back in. Jerry O'Sullivan wasn't affected by the vaccine, thankfully, because I remember he played against Clare in that match. Three other Glen men were involved with Cork in 1966: Mick Lane, Patsy Harte and Denis O'Riordan.

Cork were very lucky to beat Clare in that first round match in June. In the dying moments, Justin McCarthy got a goal from a free about 35 yards out. In fairness to him, he went for it and that allowed Cork to draw the game. We won the replay handy but that was a very close-run thing.

Now, I have to add that I didn't feel I lost out on the senior All-Ireland that year. I can't say that I was disappointed not to be playing, however strange that may sound. I was on so many other winning teams, and I was still only 21.

On the contrary, I was just as excited for all the lads on the team as anybody else on the sideline. The last time Cork had won an All-Ireland was 1954 so there was enormous joy and great celebrations at the homecoming which I enjoyed just as much as anyone else.

I probably also felt that I was going to make up for missing out in 1966 and that Cork would be in finals in the hurling for several years to come. But, of course, it didn't work out like that.

THE GLEN ROVERS trip to the United States in 1966 came about mainly because of Christy Ring. It was for the Cardinal Cushing Games – he was a prominent cleric in the United States and had games called after him. The American Irish used to invite teams linked with famous Irish sports stars – celebrities, really – and there was no bigger name in hurling than Christy Ring. But I remember teams associated with Mick O'Connell, Ollie Walsh and others travelling out in later years. A big group was going: 160 people in a specially chartered plane.

Being only 21, it was an exciting trip for me, but it was a huge event for all of Blackpool. Four busloads of people went with the travelling party to Shannon just to see us off and have a look at Shannon Airport, which we had never seen before. CIÉ ran special buses for the day and my mother and father were on one of those.

The trip was for three weeks which was another big deal. We played a Cork selection in Boston, first, then we went to Chicago and played there. But the big game was in New York City in Gaelic Park and 8,000 people turned up just to see Christy Ring. It was a real game too, because New York had a serious team with county players from all over Ireland.

This was in the autumn of 1966 and with Cork as under-21 and senior All-Ireland champions, and Glen Rovers as champions of Munster, it was the icing on the hurling cake for us.

From my own personal perspective, I think this is the moment that I first established myself as a serious Glen Rovers player. People said that to me afterwards. But on that trip I reached a standard of hurling that I could be proud of, coming of age, really.

IN 1967, I WAS a sub for the Cork hurlers in the first round of the Munster championship when we were beaten by Waterford in Walsh Park. They beat us by eight points, 3-10 to 1-8 – we didn't play at all well on the day. That was on the 4th of June, which meant no more county hurling that year – by now I was 22 and over-age for the under-21s.

I was playing well for the Glen in 1967. It was another great year for us because we won the club's 21st county title and now I was an established player on the team. That '67 final was Finbarr O'Neill's best ever game, I think. He was incredible, especially on such a wet and windy day.

I played for the Cork hurlers during the National League in 1968, cementing my place on the team, and I was starting in every game. We got to the Munster final that year and met Tipperary. Tipp were a powerhouse of hurling in the 1960s, and they beat us well in the final in Limerick, 2-13 to 1-7. Babs Keating had a great day, scoring 1-3 and he played havoc with our defence.

Tipperary had Donie Nealon and PJ Ryan at centrefield that day and I loved playing against established players like Donie. I did well against Donie in 1968, so much so that Tipp moved Liam Devaney to mark me in the second-half. I grew up admiring great Tipp players like Donie, so it was very exciting to be playing against him. I loved it.

In those days it was up to yourself who you would mark playing at centrefield. It sounds strange but that's the way it was. Everybody had a job to do and you did your job, and that was that. Instructions were few and far between. This was county and you were supposed to know what you were doing.

◄◄◆►►

TO SAY I had a baptism of fire the day I made my debut as a Cork senior footballer is an understatement. This was in the semi-final of the Munster championship in 1965. It took place on the 20th of June in Fitzgerald Stadium, Killarney, when Cork played Limerick, and I had just turned 20 two weeks before. Although this was my first senior championship game, I had been on the panel the year before, having been propelled in directly from the minors. I was probably too young to be playing senior county championship football, but there I was anyway in the dressing-room before the game, all geared up to do a job in my position of corner-back.

I didn't know anybody well on the senior team that year. There were no other St Nicks players, even though we had been beaten in the county final of 1963 and we would go on to win the county in '65. And my place on the team would have raised questions so I was a quiet man in a dressing-room containing several veterans. Having said that, everybody has to start their county career some time but I was nervous before the game – who wouldn't be? Suddenly – and this was just minutes before we were due to go out on the pitch – the players were called together in the dressing-room by the chairman and the secretary of the county board, Weeshie Murphy and Con Murphy (Weeshie was my friend, Dr Con Murphy's father – no relation to the other Con). These were very well respected, very senior men.

Formidable men. You knew your place with those men and I certainly, as a rookie 20 year-old just on the team, knew my place in the order of things.

And they announced there and then that Flor Hayes from Clonakilty, who was playing corner-forward on the team, was dropped – he would not be playing. Now, we were all togged out at this stage, we all had our jerseys on and they were saying that Flor was not playing and another player would be playing corner-forward instead. To be honest, I can't remember if they took Flor aside first and told him privately or if they just announced it. But it was certainly the first that any of the other players knew about it. Flor was told in no uncertain terms to take off his jersey and to give it to the other player.

They gave the reason. They said that somebody had told the county board or a message had come through to the county board that morning – that very morning – that Flor had allegedly played a soccer match that week below in Waterford. Except the word 'alleged' was not used. As far as they were concerned, Flor had played the game and he was off the team, off the panel, in fact. I doubt if the word 'Ban' – the infamous GAA Ban was mentioned either. Every player knew what it meant if you were accused of going to a soccer or rugby match, let alone playing one, in 1965.

But when it was put to Flor by the shocked group (to say we were all shocked is an understatement) he said he had not played soccer that week. He was adamant, it hadn't happened. And immediately the senior players in the squad backed him up. If Flor said it never happened, it never happened as far as his teammates were concerned.

The chairman and secretary said that they had evidence to the contrary. The senior players were resolute and it became immediately clear that there was a strike situation now in place. If Flor was not playing, then nobody was playing. Cork were not playing. Limerick would get a walk-over and everybody there could go home. Some of the senior players sat down and one of them said, 'We're not playing without Flor and that's that'.

The chairman and secretary got around them with the following argument. They said that if Flor played, Limerick could object and the result would be rescinded. Flor was – de facto – ineligible to line out and if Cork played him, they would be disqualified from the championship and there would be a huge controversy.

We eventually went out on the pitch (minus Flor) and were sensationally beaten by Limerick. I remember little about the game except the scoreline… Limerick 2-5, Cork 0-6. It was a shocking result, probably the biggest shock of the decade. Limerick had not beaten Cork in football since 1897 and would not do so again until 2003. That's not to say the Cork team were world-beaters at the time. We had not won a Munster senior championship ourselves since 1957, but we did go on to beat Kerry the following two years and get to an All-Ireland final in 1967.

How or why did we lose? I can't say. I'm certainly not saying that some of the Cork players didn't try as hard as they should have. But that accusation was made in the ensuing fall-out and is still made to this day. And while I did my best, I was marking Éamonn Cregan and he ran rings around me. But if you can think of a worse way to prepare for a championship game in the dressing-room, it would be good to hear it.

As an addendum to this story: poor Flor was suspended and he missed out on Clonakilty's championship that year. Worse still, he missed out on playing for Cork in the under-21 championship and if we did have him against Kildare in the final, who knows? In fairness to him, he came back after the suspension and starred for Cork in two great wins against Kerry in the coming years, narrowly missing out on an All-Ireland medal in 1967.

So, we drove home from Killarney to Cork with our tail between our legs, waiting for the criticism to follow – which it did. But those days, games were quickly followed by other games, especially if you played hurling and football like me. If you were fit and there was a match, you played it and that was that. We just got on with it, nobody was precious about playing sport those days.

THAT VERY SUNDAY evening, for example, after we got back from Killarney, I played a hurling match with Glen Rovers against St Finbarr's in the Mardyke in the annual Eucharistic Procession match.

Those annual matches were very big occasions. There could be up to 10,000 people at those games in the Mardyke and they were seriously contested – they weren't like challenge matches. It was the same two teams every year so there was great rivalry and if one team lost the previous year, they would be determined not to lose this year.

It's hard nowadays to imagine 10,000 people packed into the Mardyke on a sunny summer's evening for a non-championship club game. In hindsight they were extraordinary events and we will never see the likes of those days again.

◄ ◄ ◆ ▷ ►

ON THE WEEK of the All-Ireland football semi-final against Cavan in August, 1967, my father's sister, Mary died in Cork. He felt that, even though I was captain, he should not go to the game – it would not be appropriate.

The game was on television and television was really only beginning to show live sport – before, we always would have listened to matches on the radio. Television was only in black and white that time and that influenced the jerseys and togs that teams wore. For example, Cork wore black togs to differentiate us from the Cavan players in 1967. RTÉ only televised semi-finals and finals so it was a big deal. Not everybody had a television, so people would crowd into neighbours' homes to watch matches.

At this time, I had known Margaret for three or four years and she was living in Dublin. And the only times I could really get to see her were when I was visiting Dublin. By 1967 it wasn't really on for me to go to rugby internationals anymore because of the Ban – I might be recognised. So, the game against Cavan was a great opportunity to meet. Margaret hadn't come to Cork yet by that time and so those visits were rare and precious to us both.

On the day before the game, the Saturday, the Cork panel travelled on the train and we arrived into Heuston Station at around 6pm. I had arranged to meet Margaret at Nelson's Pillar on O'Connell Street. One of the lads took my gear to the team hotel which was the Lucan Spa Hotel.

Margaret and I went to the pictures. Amazingly, (53 years later) I can still remember the film. It was a Steve McQueen film called *The Sand Pebbles*. It was a kind of a war film set in China and Dickie Attenborough was in it too.

When the film was over, I took Margaret back to her family home in Rialto on the bus. I dropped her home and then I began to walk to the team hotel in Lucan. I didn't know how far it was. I thought it was maybe a few miles but it turned out to be a long walk, especially with the match the following day. I think it was seven or eight miles.

So, I walked out to Lucan and I didn't get to the hotel until about midnight.

When I arrived there several men were waiting for me in the foyer. What they had to tell me was not good.

I knew things were serious when I saw the expressions on their faces. As well as the three selectors, who else was standing there only the chairman and secretary of the county board, Jack Barrett and Con Murphy, looking very stern. They demanded to know where I had been.

Despite being shocked I remembered that my aunt had died during the week. Maybe I had this in the back of mind, in case I was caught. I told my 'welcoming committee' that my father's sister had died during the week and that I had to go to visit another aunt (her sister) who was living in Dublin to pass on my condolences and that we went to Mass together. I don't know where that came from but, in any case, they said it didn't matter.

There had been a meeting earlier that night of the players and selectors to plan out the game the following day, and as captain I should have been at it. They told me that I wouldn't be playing for Cork on the following day because I had missed the meeting. Then they sent me off to bed like a small boy.

In my defence I have to say that at no stage up to then in my sporting career had there ever – ever – been a players' meeting on the night before a match. It just didn't happen those days. Nor did we have meetings on the morning of games – it wasn't the done thing, unlike today. So, I had no way of knowing that there would be a meeting the night before the Cavan match since there had never been one before. If I had thought I would be needed, as a player, or especially as captain, I would of course have gone straight to the hotel from the train station and stayed there all night.

So, when I went on the date with Margaret, I had no worries that I would be missed or that there would be an issue for me. I thought there would have been some food or fellows might go to their rooms, or watch television, or they might play cards or something like that.

Now, the moment they told me I wasn't playing the following day, I took it as gospel. They were adamant – there wasn't a question about it – I would not be playing in the semi-final against Cavan. And when they dismissed me to go to bed and I went to my room I knew that I would not be lining out the following day. What I didn't know were the long-term implications with regard to future selection. It didn't matter that I was captain – for them, that made my indiscretion more serious. And these were very respected people and very influential men when it came to the GAA in Cork. And I remembered well what had happened to Flor Hayes a couple of years earlier, too.

Furthermore, players did what they were told those days – the place of players in the hierarchy was much, much, lower than it is today. Players were there to be seen and not heard, as people used to say about children. And you took the word of the selectors at that time – what they said went and that was that.

It was a long night – I can't say I slept well. But what would happen in Croke Park the following day wasn't my main worry. My biggest worry was the fact that the match was being televised and my father would be at home watching the television and I would not be on the team. And I did not know how to explain this to him. What would he say and what would I tell him? Amazingly, this was the main reason for my sleepless night. But there was nothing else to do except await my fate.

ON THE FOLLOWING morning I doubt I had much of an appetite for breakfast. I went to Mass with some of the other players. After Mass, the selectors called us all together again because they wanted to finalise some of the details of the game such as who would take frees in the back line and in the forward line. Since I wasn't playing, it didn't really concern me but of course I went to the meeting along with everybody else on the panel. I was at the meeting but I was not really a part of it. I was waiting for the announcement that I would not be playing and why; along with who would be replacing me as captain and who would be on the team in my place. I kept my head down.

They started to outline who would be taking the frees and 50s and letting those players know. Then there was a bit of a lull and I was waiting for my fate to be confirmed. Suddenly, out of the blue, somebody asked what would happen if we got a penalty – who would take it? Now, in those days, penalties were few and far between. You nearly had to decapitate somebody for a penalty to be given against you.

And for some unknown reason (I still don't know why) I said I would take the penalty. I don't know where on earth this came out of. Especially because I had not been taking penalties regularly. I had not been practicing penalties – in fact, we did not practice penalties at all in training; it was never part of the conversation the way it would be nowadays when every single thing is planned in advance. I had taken one penalty in my career against Galway in the under-21 All-Ireland semi-final two years previously and I don't know why I ended up taking that, either.

It was actually very difficult to score a penalty in football at the time. The ball didn't travel as fast – it was heavier (often muddier) and there was no swerve on it, as there is today. Boots weren't a patch on what they are today either.

When I said that I would take the penalty there was no reaction from anybody. There was a kind of a silence or at least I thought there was a silence, because, of course I was waiting for someone to say you won't be playing... what are you talking about? Instead, nobody spoke for a while, and then somebody said, 'Okay, so' or something like that. And the meeting continued and was wound up.

Only at that moment did I realise that, in fact, I would be lining out after all. Whether they changed their mind, or they only wanted to give me a fright the night before, or if somebody interceded on my behalf, or what else might have happened – I will never know.

The only things I did know were that I would be playing and I was still the Cork captain and – most importantly – that I wouldn't have to explain anything to my father. Best of all, the chances of there actually being a penalty were astronomical – there was no fear I'd have to come good on my 'volunteering' to take it.

But, with two minutes to go in the game and with Cork two points down, what happened? We got a penalty. I was centre-back so I ran nearly the length of the Croke Park pitch to take it, knowing full well that if I missed, we would probably lose.

That was a long run. There was a lot going through my head. But I had to take it, I said I was going to take it – albeit in unusual circumstances, let's put it like that. Luckily, I managed to score which put us a point ahead.

But the game wasn't over, and Cavan went on the attack from the kick-out. They won a last minute free to draw the game but Charlie Gallagher – Cavan's top player, in fact Ireland's top scorer in 1967, a wonderful footballer who died tragically young – missed the free. He just barely put it wide. So, we survived and made it into the final against Meath.

What a turnaround. The night before I was facing the prospect that I had possibly disgraced myself, disgraced my family and disgraced my club. At the age of 22 my whole career with Cork could even be at an end. I had no idea what was in store for me and I had no idea what I was going to say to people when the team was announced on the Sunday with me not on it for disciplinary reasons. I suppose I would've told them the truth – I honestly don't know.

◄◄◆▷►

THE ALL-IRELAND FINAL wasn't for another seven weeks, so I was able to go on a motoring holiday to England with my friends for seven days.

Finbarr O'Neill had relations in Birmingham so we drove there first, four of us in his Mini. Our plan for the holiday was to drive to all the soccer grounds we could in England. A remarkable thing in hindsight but that's what we planned and that's what we did. The soccer season had already started but our plan wasn't to go to games; instead we wanted to see some of the famous grounds we had read about and heard about so much since our childhoods.

I'm not sure of the order of the grounds we went to, but we visited stadiums in Birmingham (Villa Park), London (Highbury), Blackpool (Bloomfield Road) and Manchester (Old Trafford).

Blackpool was a big club, a famous team in 1967, and they played in the First Division. They had some of the great players of the 60s like Jimmy Armfield (who went on to manage Leeds United). and Alan Ball also played with them – and, of course, Stanley Matthews had played for Blackpool all through the 50s and into the early 60s. We went into Bloomfield Road to watch the first team training – you could do that those days.

Eventually, we made our way to Manchester. Strangely enough, or maybe not so strangely, (given I had an All-Ireland final in a few weeks' time) I brought my gear with me. I was training during the week – doing a bit of running and so on. I had a good run on the beach in Blackpool one day, I remember.

We strolled into Old Trafford. We walked through an open gate under a stand and there was the pitch and the famous 'Field of Dreams' arrayed around it. Now, this was the Manchester United of Matt Busby. They were the league champions, for starters, and were about to have the season of all seasons, winning the European Cup. This was the club of Best, Law, Charlton, Kidd, Foulkes – the names just roll off the tongue and, of course, there was a strong Irish contingent, including Shay Brennan, Tony Dunne and Cork's own Noel Cantwell.

When we got inside the ground, we saw that a group of players were training at the other end of the pitch and we made our way up towards them and watched them kick balls around and do various drills. I told the lads that Noel Cantwell's brother used to work with my mother in Cohen's in Cork city. That's the thing about Cork – there's always a connection.

Anyway, we got close enough to one of the players and he asked us where were we from. We said we were from Cork and he said, 'Noel is from Cork you should talk to him'. So, Noel came over and we were chatting away to him for a while and I told him about the connection between my mother and his brother in Cohen's.

I must admit I also told him that I was playing in the All-Ireland final for Cork in three weeks' time, and his eyes widened. Whatever possessed me, I asked could I do a bit of training because I needed to get ready for the match against Meath.

'Come on, boy,' says he, and I had my gear with me so I changed and I did a bit of training on the pitch at Old Trafford. There I was kicking a ball around with the Manchester United players in preparation for the All-Ireland football final of 1967.

WHEN YOU THINK of all the trouble players got into over the infamous Ban (including Flor Hayes) – not even for playing but merely attending games – and there was I, the captain of Cork, not only playing a foreign code, but with foreign players, on a foreign pitch, in the heart of the old enemy, England. If the county board ever found out, they would have had my guts for garters.

◄◄◆►►

THE BUILD-UP TO the All-Ireland final against Meath in 1967 was very exciting and very new. This was mainly because none of us on the team had ever experienced a senior All-Ireland football final before. The last time Cork had been in a football final was 10 years before in 1957 when we were beaten by Louth. The last time Cork had won was in 1945, the year I was born, the year Jack Lynch starred, in between winning five hurling All-Ireland medals.

And I was only 22, one of the youngest players on the team, if not the youngest.

There was a seven-week build up to the final, but in the meantime you were allowed to play away with your club, in hurling and football – that's what we did in those days. In the county championship that year Glen Rovers went all the way to the semi-final – in August we played Muskerry in Bandon and that was a draw, so we had to play them again. This was between the All-Ireland semi-final and the final and, again, that would never happen nowadays.

The All-Ireland final against Meath was played on the 24th of September. It was an amazing occasion for me personally and for the other players too. Cork and Meath developed a bit of rivalry later, contesting several semi-finals and finals, but that match in 1967 was the first time the two counties had ever met in a championship game, so there was a certain novelty about it, too.

When I was young, I really never thought that I would play senior football for St Nicks. But I certainly never expected to play senior football for Cork or to be involved in an All-Ireland senior football final. And here I am at 22 years of age not only playing in a final but captaining my county. It really was beyond any kind of expectations that I ever had – it still amazes me, if I'm honest.

You never got a telegram those days unless somebody died. But I got a telegram – sent to the house in Madden's Buildings – and again, in hindsight, this sounds funny but it was from the showband *The Dixies*. I didn't know *The Dixies* or any of the band members. Like everybody else my age I had danced to them but whatever possessed them to seek out my address and send me a telegram, they did.

One thing for sure about the final was this: I was not going to go missing on the night before the game. I'd learned my lesson about that. When the team got the train to Dublin, I stayed with the group and went from Heuston Station to the team hotel like everybody else. The hotel was in Dame Street and was very close to the Olympia Theatre. We all trooped along to the theatre the night before the game to see a Jack Cruise and Jimmy O'Dea show – they were two famous Dublin actors at the time.

I WON THE toss and we had decided beforehand we'd take the strong wind first. We controlled the first-half of the game completely and at half-time we were winning four points to one. And the only point Meath got in the first-half was literally a minute before half-time. In reality we should have been out the gate by that stage – the game should have been well over. Four points was a very poor tally for our possession and dominance. Eight wides didn't help the cause either.

We were still in a great position to drive on and close out the game in the second-half but it didn't happen. In fairness, Meath were never going to go down without a fight – on the contrary, that was never their way. With the wind behind them they came back at us, and the second-half was very competitive. Meath were tough and it was a very physical game. Our defence was going well, but our forwards couldn't make any headway.

The deciding goal for Meath was unusual. They got a 14-yard free and the free-taker, Tony Brennan was going for a point but he failed to raise the ball high enough and Jerry Lucey caught it – it was more of a save than a catch, really, he did very well. He caught it right in front of the goal and kicked it out to the wing – an excellent clearance.

The Cork midfielder, Mick O'Loughlin (who had a great game) and Meath's Mattie Kerrigan tussled for the ball on the wing. Kerrigan won it and kicked it back in, and Terry Kearns who had moved in towards the goal punched it over his head in the air and somehow (it very rarely happened) the ball caught Billy unawares. There is a great photo of the moment, with me looking on in horror as the ball is about to enter the net. It was a lucky goal, really, but it happens.

It was a crucial score and they beat us 1-9 to 0-9. To this day (over 50 years later) that goal is a bit of a stickler. I probably should have cut it out, but Billy called for it and between the two of us, it ended up in the net and we lost. That's sport.

When you lose an All-Ireland final (or any final) all you want to do is go home and get away from everyone and lick your wounds. But with an All-Ireland you can't do that until the Monday night – there is a banquet and all sorts of events. And, as captain, I had to be heavily involved in those, making speeches and so on. It's the last thing you want to do and the last place you want to be but that's part and parcel of the process, and you have to get on with it. It wouldn't be the last time I captained a losing team in a final, unfortunately.

But, again, the most amazing thing was that on the following Tuesday evening – that's the day after the homecoming – I had hurling training with the Glen because we were playing in the county final against St Finbarr's on the following Sunday.

It doesn't mean you're not sick about losing an All-Ireland final (you are) but the games go on – there's always another game and another game. Those days, too, no player ever complained about having to play again or needing a rest or anything like that. You just played the next game or trained for the next game. If you were fit and you could play, you played, and if you were fit and you could train, you trained, and that was the way it was.

◂ ◂◆▷ ▸

IN NOVEMBER 1968 MY father went into hospital for a gallstones operation – a fairly common and innocuous procedure. But that night we were called into the hospital – the Bon Secours – and they told us he was very ill.

My mother said, 'Look, let you go up to the Bons and come back and let me know how he is'. Anne, my eldest sister, was in England, so it was down to me. It was a night-time phone call and we had no car in the house, so I walked over from Blackpool to the Bons on College Road.

On my way into the hospital I met a doctor, Jim Brosnan coming out against me. He was a famous footballer with Kerry. Years later myself and my friend, Brian Hurley used to have great talks with him when we went to Ballyferriter to the Gaeltacht there.

'What are you doing here?' he said. He probably saw that my expression was not good.

'I'm visiting my father,' I said.

'What's wrong with him?' Jim said and I told him.

'He'll be grand,' Jim said.

And it was with that belief I went in to see my father – thinking that he would be okay. But he was seriously ill after having had a heart attack and I got a terrible shock. I couldn't believe it. He was semi-conscious and I remember him telling me to look after my mother.

Early the following morning word came through of a phone call for us in a shop up the street from our house. I went over to take the call and I was told that my father had died during the night.

The upsetting thing is, up to that time, my father's health had been very good. He had been working away in the brewery and just developed this gallstones problem that they said an operation would cure. He would have been 60 years-old on the following day. I was only 23 and my sister Catherine was only 21. My mother had been widowed at only 51.

IN THE 1960s ALL the old traditions still held, especially in Blackpool. So, the blinds in the house were down for 12 months which meant that most areas in the house were dark. My mother also wore black for 12 months. Widows did, those days.

And everything was very sombre, really, and this was true of every house that suffered a bereavement. That was how it was.

My sister, Anne came home from England for the funeral. And she stayed about a week and then she had to go back to her job. Catherine was still at home all the time – and I was still in Madden's Buildings living with Nan.

The loss of my father was a huge blow for me. He was such a major presence in my life and the emptiness left behind by his absence hurt me deeply and created a void that could never be filled. If there was anything I was ever not sure about I would have talked to my father about it and he was always there for me.

I would especially miss him after matches. When the Glen won the county in September the following year, for example, he wasn't there to share the joy with me. He wasn't there to travel with me to the match and to talk about it in the following days. He wasn't there to hug me after the final whistle on the wet grass of the Cork Athletic Grounds. I would never again see the light in his eyes when Cork and Glen Rovers won.

St Nicholas, Cork county champions, 1966 (top left) and the Glen Rovers team of 1966 in Gaelic Park, New York City, versus New York. I'm front row (third from left) beside Christy Ring.

Scoring a penalty against Cavan in the All-Ireland semi-final, 1967 (left).

Jack Cruise and Chris Curran (centre) the night before the 1967 All-Ireland final. From left: myself, Jerry Lucey, Brian Murphy (Crosshaven), Con Paddy O'Sullivan and Mick Burke.

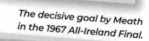

The decisive goal by Meath in the 1967 All-Ireland Final.

Leading the Cork team for the 1967 All-Ireland football final.

« CHAPTER 4 »

Christy Ring

WHEN I WAS a child, people like Jack Lynch and Christy Ring were gods.

I remember Garvey's Bridge, it was halfway between Blackpool and where the old Glen Rovers pitch used to be – in the country, really. Some of us, when we were boys, would go up there on summer evenings and we used to wait under the bridge just to see the senior Glen players coming up. They would walk up or cycle up to the pitch to train.

In fact, Christy Ring was the only person with a car, mainly because he was living in Cloyne at the time and it was the only way he could get to training. His car was an old Ford Anglia. So, he might leave his car in Blackpool and then walk up with another player – all the players would make their way up the hill to the Glen field in twos or threes.

And myself and my friends used to ask them if we could carry their hurleys up to the pitch. I'm sure they were embarrassed by this – I know I would've been embarrassed when I became a senior hurler – but we did it anyway and they humoured us. It was a big treat – that's how innocent children were those days. And then we used to go behind the goals while they were training and hit the ball back out to them.

Of course, Christy Ring was the foremost hurler at that time, not only in the Glen, not only in Cork but in Ireland, so you had to be very brave to ask Christy to carry his hurley. But that was only because we were shy of him – it wasn't anything to do with him – it was our shyness.

I ended up playing with Christy for four years, and he was at the end of his career and I was at the beginning of mine. But I felt very privileged to have hurled alongside him for Glen Rovers. The first occasion I was on a team with him was in 1964 and I played with him up to '67 – I think his last game for the Glen was against UCC. And, of course, I watched him closely in training and in matches to learn as much as I could. But I didn't really know him that well when he was a player – we never really had a meaningful conversation, to be honest. It was only later that I got to know him better.

When I did get to know him, years later, I realised that he was a very shy person. If you didn't know him, he could appear aloof or haughty, but in reality it was shyness.

In all honesty, Christy was also one of the nicest people I ever met – you couldn't meet a nicer man. And he was the kindest man as well. Christy used to talk about himself in the third person but it was in no way egotistical, it was just a habit he had.

He looked at things differently from other people, hurling especially. He saw things that other people didn't see. He saw something in me that I didn't see – that was for sure. And he knew me so well.

WHILE THERE IS much said and written about Christy the hurler and Christy the mentor (and I do my share of it in this book) it was Christy the man who meant the most to me. From the time we became good friends in 1972 to the moment he died in '79, it meant so much to have him in my life. He was like a second father to me.

In 1975 I was offered a very good job before the county final against Blackrock. One day I was training with the Glen in the Mardyke (where the game was due to be held because the Park was being renovated). As I was coming out of the dressing-room, Christy called me aside and asked what was wrong. He knew that there was something on my mind – I was preoccupied.

And I told him I'd had a job offer and I didn't know what to do about it. He didn't want to know anything about the job, what it was or who the company was. He just asked me if I liked the man I was currently working for. I said I did, very much – he was very honest and straight. Then he asked me if I liked the man who had offered me the new job.

And in that moment, I had my decision made and it was a great decision. If another person had pointed out those simple facts to me, I might have resisted. But when Christy did it, I knew he was right. 'Go with your instincts,' was what he was saying. And I did, and I was glad I did and I had another thing to thank Christy Ring for.

◄◄◆►►

MY RELATIONSHIP WITH Christy changed in 1972 in unusual circumstances. That year I was playing with the Cork hurlers and we were in the Munster final against Clare. And on the Friday before the match – this would have been late in July – I pulled into the garage at the top of the Monaghan Road to get petrol. And Christy was in the garage before me getting petrol as well. It was around one o'clock in the day. That time I was living in Blackrock and Christy was living in Ballintemple just up the road. My office was not very far from where Christy was working.

Those days you could go home from work for what we called our dinner and I guess myself and Christy were doing just that when we met in the garage. He had a red Cortina at the time, 25 DRI.

While we were both getting petrol, he said to me, 'What kind of a hurley do you have for Sunday?'

And for some strange reason I had my hurley in the boot of my car. This was unusual because I was very finicky about my hurleys. I minded them religiously and I wouldn't have my good hurley in the car for love nor money in case anything happened to it – my hurleys were that important to me.

I said, 'Here, I'll show you,' and I took my hurley out of the boot and handed it to him. And whatever he did to the hurley, he broke it in half. His own hurleys were heavy as far as I remember and strong whereas my one was light – I preferred them light – and he must have misjudged its strength. I think he might have been testing the spring or something, but whatever he did, the hurley ended up in bits.

'Christy!' I said, in shock. 'What are you after doing?'

This was three days before a Munster final, remember. And as soon as I spoke, I regretted what I'd said. He was very upset, I could see it in him. He went pale when the hurley broke.

'Don't tell anyone,' he said, the two bits of the hurley in his hands.

'No, of course I won't,' I said, shame-faced.

'Do you know what you'll do?' Christy said. 'Go on away home and have your dinner and I'll sort this out.'

I said I couldn't, that I'd have go and get a hurley for the match straightaway. I used to get my hurleys handmade to my own specification by a Mr McCarthy in Glanmire. Coincidently he used to make Christy's hurleys too, but Christy wasn't playing any more by '72. Now, Mr McCarthy used to make only 10 or so hurleys a year so I thought I wouldn't have a hope of getting a good one in time for Sunday – a total disaster.

'Go on away,' says Christy, 'Go down home and then back to work and I'll call to your office at four o'clock and I'll have a new hurley you can use on Sunday.'

I didn't have the heart to contradict him, so I drove home to Blackrock and Margaret was there with my dinner ready. I told her I couldn't eat anything, I would just have a glass of milk. I told her I had to leave immediately to go straight down to Glanmire and get a new hurley because I broke my own and I needed to get a replacement.

So, I went back out the front door and who was standing there only Christy.

'I thought I told you to stay at home and have your dinner and I would bring your hurley to your office at four o'clock?' says he.

Didn't he follow me home without me knowing it. He knew I wasn't going to do what I was told and I got caught. Now, when Christy Ring told you to do something related to hurling, you did it. I had no choice but to nod and go back into the house, and eat a meal I didn't have the stomach for.

But he was as good as his word and at four o'clock he arrived into my office with a hurley identical to the ones that I always used. It was perfect, in fairness. Panic over.

'There you are, now,' says he. 'That will bring you luck on Sunday.' And I said thanks very much and I was very grateful.

WE PLAYED CLARE on the Sunday, two days later, in Thurles and we were on fire. I think Charlie McCarthy, Ray Cummins and Seanie O'Leary all scored two goals each the same day. We were well ahead in the second-half, and the game was as good as over long before the final whistle. Michael Ellard said the next day that if it had been a boxing match, the referee would have stopped it long before the end. I wish he had.

I think we were winning by 18 points – it was that one-sided – when disaster struck for me.

I was playing centrefield and midway through the second-half Séamus Durack, the Clare goalkeeper, pucked the ball out and it landed between myself and my marker in the middle of the field. We both went for the ball in the air and we both missed it. As the ball hopped on the ground and rose up again, I turned to flick it, and I made contact with the ball. But my hurley, in the follow-through, struck my opponent on the head. I think he was one of the few players on the pitch (if not the only one) wearing a helmet the same day and I could clearly hear the sound of my hurley hitting the helmet – it made a kind of a plasticky sound. And he went down.

It was beside the sideline and the nearby Clare mentors and officials immediately made a bit of a fuss. The referee was Sean O'Grady from Limerick. I think it might have been his first Munster final. Now, Sean is a very nice man and he was a very good referee. And he saw what happened and he said to me, 'Denis that's okay, that's an accident. I saw what happened'.

But the Clare player stayed down and the Clare officials convinced Sean to send me off. So, he changed his mind and he did send me off. The only sending off of my career. In fact, I think it might have been the only time I was ever spoken to by a referee. I don't think I was ever booked, either. Anyway, off I had to go and of course the lad I was marking got up immediately and played on. But I was gone.

Immediately after the Cork-Clare game, Glen Rovers were due to pay Thurles Sarsfields in a challenge match. And Cork were winning by so much that the Glen players didn't even wait for the game to end before going into the dressing-room to tog off for their own game. And they missed my sending off as a result.

When I went into the dressing-room after being sent off, they started slagging me that I should be playing for the Glen in their game too. 'Who do you think you are, boy? Put on that jersey there,' – that kind of thing.

I was totally deflated. This was a new experience for me and one I was not enjoying. I didn't get what they were on about for a while. When they persisted, I said that I couldn't play.

'Why not?' somebody said.

"Why not?' I replied. 'Because I was just sent off... I'm suspended for a month.'

They thought I was joking – especially with Cork winning the game at a canter.

But it wasn't a joke and I was suspended for a month – that was the automatic suspension those days. It didn't really matter why you were sent off. You were suspended for a month automatically from all games and that was that. No suspensions were ever rescinded in the 60s and 70s, whatever the referee's report. However, suspensions could be longer and there was a minimum six-month suspension for 'striking an opponent with a hurley'.

So, I had to sweat it out until I would know whether or not I'd be eligible for the All-Ireland final. And that's if we got to the final in the first place. But the county board secretary, Con Murphy still had to make a case to Croke Park and try to ensure the minimum suspension – which is what I received. In fairness to Sean O'Grady, he didn't accuse me of deliberately striking an opponent.

Besides the suspension, which would mean missing out on the All-Ireland semi-final against London and important club games, there was another potential implication for me because that was the second year of the All Star awards. One of the main eligibility rules of the awards was that if you were sent off you could not be put forward for selection. But for some reason they either made an exception for me or they dropped the rule that year because I was picked as an All Star at centrefield in 1972 despite having been sent off.

◄◄◆►►

BESIDES THE BROKEN hurley event in 1972, the first time I had a long conversation with Christy was in 1974. Margaret and I had taken a house in Fountainstown for a month during the summer. It was to give the children a holiday. Jonathan and Mags were quite small.

During that time – in fact it was in May, 1974 – Cork had just won the National Hurling League. We played Limerick in the final and they were All-Ireland champions and it was a fantastic match. I was working in Dublin and the final was played in Limerick on the 5th of May. So, I took the train down. In the dressing-room before the game we discovered that four players had cried off injured, including Ray Cummins and Mick Malone. This greatly depleted our team. There were over 25,000 people at the game. Limerick were flying high and there was a huge crowd there to support them, but – depleted or not – we beat them by 6-15 to 1-12. Éamonn O'Donoghue from Blackrock got three goals the same day, and the whole team just clicked.

As a result of that win we were immediately installed as favourites to win the All-Ireland in 1974 and we were playing Waterford in the first round of the championship. The match was below in Walsh Park in Waterford which was always a very difficult place in which to perform. It's a tight pitch and Waterford are a very different proposition playing there. Waterford were always an enigma to me, because you never knew what to expect – which Waterford would turn up – but they were always very physical (in a good, clean, way) and I felt we could never play to our best ability against them. Somehow, they could prevent that, especially in Walsh Park, and they did that in 1974 and beat us – deservedly so.

It was a very tight game on a sunny day and with about 10 minutes left, the teams were level. A low ball came into the Cork goalmouth and our goalkeeper, Paddy Barry moved out to block it on his hurley. But didn't the Waterford forward, Martin Geary get there ahead of him and flick the ball into the goal, breaking Paddy's hurley in the same movement. Paddy picked up the broken end of his hurley and in disgust he flung it into the net. Or so he intended. Didn't the umpire walk in front of the goal at the same time to wave the green flag and Paddy's hurley-end hit him on the thigh. The man had to be taken off and brought to hospital. And Paddy was sent off – by Sean O'Grady, would you believe, who had sent me off two years previously.

With the extra man Waterford held their lead and beat us by four points – a major shock. Cork, the favourites for the All-Ireland, were gone, sensationally beaten in the first round of the Munster Championship. That's the way it was before the so-called back door.

I had travelled that morning to Waterford with Christy Ring because he and his family were also staying in Fountainstown for the summer. He had picked me up outside our front door and driven me to the match. He wasn't a selector or anything, he was just going to the game.

We headed back to Cork immediately afterwards, crestfallen. And in the car, I said something like, 'You know, now that we're gone, I hope Waterford win it out now... win the All-Ireland'.'

Christy shook his head. He believed that it was just as important that the 'strong' counties kept winning All-Irelands, in order to keep the standard of the game up.

I didn't actually agree with him at the time but subsequently I have changed my view and I can see the truth in what he said. If hurling is lost in the heartlands it will fade away. Since hurling does not have that many counties – certainly not as many as football – it needs to be vibrant in the traditionally strong counties.

That isn't to say hurling should not be developed and promoted in the so-called weaker counties, and I was delighted when Offaly, Wexford and Clare made their breakthrough in subsequent years. But it must stay strong in Kilkenny, Cork, Tipperary, Limerick and Galway or it will come under threat. Arguably it is already under threat, to all kinds of forces, inside and outside of sport – in Cork, particularly.

ANYWAY, FROM THAT day on Christy and I became great friends. We just clicked. And I think it actually changed my life.

Christy Ring was our greatest hurler because of his fearlessness. He had a tremendous will – he was not afraid of anything on the pitch. And then there were his physical attributes such as his speed and strength, the power of his wrists, his skill and his hand-eye coordination. He was also very tough – you had to be very tough in the 40s and 50s to survive as a hurler.

Generally, Christy was a very soft spoken man, but in the context of hurling, in the dressing-room – where I got to know him very well for the Glen and for Cork – he could come alive, especially if things weren't going well. I remember many memorable speeches he gave in dressing-rooms but the one that had most impact on me and the team was at half-time at the Munster final against Clare in 1977. Because of it, we went out in the second-half against all the odds and won. He also had an incredible knowledge of the game and his knowledge, his presence and his will that Cork would win, *must win*, were the foundations of the three in-a-row later that decade.

And although I had been playing hurling for a long time at that stage, between 1974 and '79 I learned more about hurling from Christy Ring than I had in all the years beforehand.

I was far closer to Christy Ring the man than I was to Christy Ring the player or selector. I never witnessed or experienced him being anything but gentle, thoughtful and kind – and he was especially so to me.

◄◄◆▷►

IN 1975 CHRISTY WAS involved with Cork as a selector. This was the first time many Cork players from clubs like St Finbarr's and Blackrock had any close-up experience of Christy Ring the man, and not Christy Ring the legend. The only interaction they would have had with him before that was in playing against the Glen – having Christy as an opponent, which was no easy task. So, a lot of those men got to know Christy between 1975 and '79.

And I think it brought Christy out of himself too, because he enjoyed the training; he enjoyed working with different players with different skills, from different backgrounds and different clubs. He enjoyed the matches and – most of all – he enjoyed Cork winning All-Irelands. And we enjoyed having him there and we all learned so much from him.

He made a huge difference to us all collectively and individually as hurlers and there is no doubt that the success of the three in-a-row was very much part of Christy Ring's legacy to Cork. And he was very good to everybody no matter what club you were from or where you played, or whatever your background. And he was *Christy Ring*.

Ringy, as he was popularly known (but he was always just 'Christy' to me) made the 1952-54 three in-a-row happen on the field. He captained Cork in 1953 and '54. And he made the 1976-78 three in-a-row happen too. I have no doubt about it.

In the autumn of 1975, I wasn't playing hurling for Cork and my dreams of winning All-Irelands were over. I was retired, having called it quits in 1974. The story of how that changed and how I came back into the Cork hurling fold I'll recount later in this book. But the man who made that happen was … Christy Ring, in his own very inimitable way. The fact is that without Christy I would never again have played hurling for Cork after 1974. The fact is that I would never have been part of the three in-a-row, never have won three more All-Ireland medals, three All Star Awards, never have won a Texaco Hurler of the Year award. I owe him all that, along with so much else.

◄ ◄ ◆ ▷ ►

I REMEMBER MY father taking me in to MacCurtain Street – it used to be called King Street – when Cork came back after the three in-a-row in 1954, on the day after Christy Ring had won his eighth All-Ireland medal. I was nine years-old at the time.

As a child, I used to keep a scrapbook, of all different sports. I used to cut articles out of the newspaper. And I had an article and a photo of Christy Ring with his medals taken somewhere. I was clutching the picture like a treasure on the side of MacCurtain Street that evening waiting for the homecoming of the heroic Cork team.

The place was packed – thronged. As a child I had never seen anything like it. The excitement, the joy, the anticipation. The word went up… 'The lorry is coming! The lorry is coming!' My father held me up and I held up the photo. And as the truck passed, I could see the cup and the players waving. And there was Christy Ring, suddenly, looking right down at me. At me.

I know he was looking at everybody but he actually looked straight at me. I have no doubt about it, to this very day.

'Christy Ring looked at me, Dad,' I said. 'He looked at me.' And my father smiled.

'Christy Ring looked at me,' I told my mother, when I got in home.

And I never thought in my wildest dreams – never – that I would go on to know Christy Ring and to play with him and to later call myself his friend.

He meant the world to me, he really did.

When Christy died on the 2nd of March 1979, it was like the light had gone out of that world. And it was a terrible time in my life personally – the details of which I'll share later. What was the point of a world without Christy Ring, anyway?

I'm sure that's what the thousands who paid their respects to him in Forde's Funeral Home were feeling on the night after he died, as they filed past his coffin, weeping. And the tens of thousands (up to 60,000 people, imagine) who lined the streets and roads of Cork as his cortege passed by the following day – most of them weeping too.

But thinking about a world without Christy Ring isn't the way to look at it, at all. The way to look at it is how blessed we were to have *ever* had him in our world. And how amazing it was to have lived in a world where such a wonder as Christy Ring was possible, imaginable, let alone true.

In a world like that, anything was possible. Everything was possible.

Everything.

Myself and Christy Ring lining out for the Glen in Gaelic Park New York City, 1966.

Winning my first All Star award in 1972.

« CHAPTER 5 »

Bad Days and Good Days

ON SUNDAY JULY 28th, 1968 Glen Rovers played UCC in the quarter-final of the county championship and it was a tight game. UCC had a very good team including Ray Cummins, Billy Morgan, Tom Field, Paddy Crowley and John O'Halloran. With about a minute to go, we got a '70'. It was the duty of the wing-backs to take the '70s' that time, depending on where the ball went out over the line. If it was on the left, the left half-back would take it and if it was on the right the right half-back would take it. It's very different nowadays.

Our man mis-hit the '70' and I caught the ball – I was playing centrefield – and I put it over the bar. So, we were two points up practically on the final whistle. When I ran back to my position and turned to face the puck out, I noticed a schmozzle in the college goalmouth, which left one of the UCC players injured.

There was a dispute afterwards whether or not a Glen Rovers player had been sent off before the final whistle; but whether or not he was, everybody was shocked a few weeks later when the county board expelled him from the association. His previously exemplary record – he was also on the Cork panel at the time – counted for nothing. Three other Glen players were also suspended for six months and three months, but to have somebody actually expelled from ever being involved in the GAA again as long as he lived, shocked and angered everybody in the club – as far as I know he was the only person ever to have been expelled from the association. Now, I'm not forgetting the player who was injured, and whom I still know to this day and I play golf with him from time to time; and it was a serious injury too.

A factor in the decision of the board was the fact that Con Murphy, who was secretary of the county board, and Seán Ó Síocháin, who was secretary general of the GAA, were both at the match and saw what happened. The club was also severely reprimanded by the board about the behaviour of its officials in the investigation of the incidents during the game.

It was such a severe punishment that the Glen felt very aggrieved. The club called an extraordinary general meeting which Jack Lynch, who was Taoiseach at the time, attended. It was the largest meeting ever held in the Glen Hall. At the meeting, Jim Young, who was the president of the club, said that the sentence was, 'most severe, unjust and savage'. He spoke of a 'personal vendetta by certain members of the county board against the club which has been carried on for many years'. The club chairman, Theo Lynch (Jack's brother) said, 'The findings of the board had dragged the name of one of the most famous clubs in the country in the mud and instead of benefitting the association, they had done great harm to it.'

It was unanimously decided, in the meeting of over 200 people – completely unanimous – that the Glen would pull out of the Cork county championship, even though we were through to the semi-final. Glen Rovers players would not play for Cork, and any of the club's selectors for Cork teams would resign. Glen Rovers players would not attend any Cork games or any club games organised by the county board – the county final included. As far as I remember, St Nicks followed suit, but it was decided that underage teams would not be affected and would continue to play.

I think the only dissenting voice at the meeting was Jack Lynch and he was making the very sensible point that at some time in the future the club would want to return to playing. How long would the withdrawal last, and how would the Glen move forward in future years? And how would the club seek permission to get back into the championship? It was a fair point, but emotions were running very high. Taoiseach or not, Glen Rover and St Nicks hero or not, the proposal to withdraw was passed unanimously.

OF COURSE, THE club also appealed the decision of the board to the Munster Council, but that was not expected to be successful and the withdrawal stood. In

September, the Munster Council rejected the appeal and the expulsion remained in place. And the Glen and St Nicks remained outside the Cork county board hurling and football fold.

Now, some players were affected more than others by all this. Myself, Denis O'Riordan and Jerry O'Sullivan were all playing hurling for Cork at the time. I was also playing football for Cork, so I was very seriously affected. How badly affected I wouldn't know for some time, but I would find out to my bitter cost.

The extraordinary thing was that everyone – every single person – obeyed the club's decision. We didn't go to any matches, we didn't play with Cork in the National Leagues – Cork were out of the championship at the time. And I remember distinctly where I was on the day of the county final, which I had never missed up to that day.

Myself and 10 others went off down to Carrauntoohil, and we climbed up to the highest point in Ireland. So that's where we were, instead of possibly winning a county championship with the Glen.

It was a strange time for us, being so inactive and not playing games. And an uncertain time too. There was talk that the club was going to actually disband at the next AGM the following December and some newspapers ran with that story. Thankfully that didn't happen. In fact, the opposite was decided. The club decided to resume all GAA affairs in the county, and agreed to re-affiliate all teams in all grades of championships, while at the same time pressing at every opportunity to have our player's expulsion from the association revoked.

Again, this was decided unanimously. At that AGM, Jack Lynch said that the action taken by the club was fully justified, that the club always had the best organisation of any unit in the association and down through the years those in authority were envious of the club's success and spirit.

The extraordinary thing was that the lifetime ban that caused the whole furore was subsequently rescinded. Firstly, in 1972 it was, on appeal, reduced to 10 years. Within a year of that, congress decided that the maximum suspension for any offence would be two years and so our player was – thankfully – reinstated, and he did play again for Glen Rovers.

A SMALL FOOTNOTE about 1968.

Between 1963 and '80, for 18 years, I won at least one championship with St

Nicks, The Glen, Cork or Munster, in football or hurling every single year. Apart from one year: 1968. That year Cork got to the Munster final in hurling and football but were beaten in both – within the space of a week.

How lucky I was to have been on all those teams in those years and to have won so much. In sport, as in life, you have bad days and good days. I was blessed to have had so many good days.

◂◂◆▸▸

THE GLEN BEING the Glen, we bounced back in 1969. We felt we had to. In Glen Rovers there is always a cause and the cause that year was our teammate who had been wronged. And we were Glen Rovers. Being honest, we wanted to put it up to the county board too.

Now, we had to reapply to the county board to play. There was no truce or coming together or agreement or anything like that. We had to eat humble pie and reapply. There was no backing down by the board; we had to send a formal letter from the club – which is exactly what Jack Lynch had foreseen the previous year but he wasn't heeded at the time.

We were men with a mission in 1969. It was always drummed into us in the Glen how important it was to win the county championship and we desperately wanted to win our 22nd title that year.

We played UCC in the final on the 22nd of September and remember it was against them the previous year that all the trouble had happened. They had Ray Cummins, Seamus Looney, Pat McDonnell – and the best of players from other counties too. The so-called 'College Rule' was in place those days which meant that all senior hurlers had to play for UCC and not their clubs, or they would not be allowed sit their exams. Thank God it was withdrawn later or UCC would have won a lot more.

But we had good players too and our captain was Denis O'Riordan. The game was billed very much as a veteran-laden team versus a talented array of youngsters. And it looked for a long time during that game that the UCC youngsters would come out on top. After 20 minutes they were leading by 0-8 to 0-2. Then Mick Kenneally got a great goal from a free. But we were still down by four points at half-time and then UCC started to pull away.

With 10 minutes of the second-half gone, UCC were well ahead, by 1-12 to 1-4 but we rallied and drove on, our momentum building minute on minute. We won the game by an amazing 12 points, 4-16 to 1-13, a 20-point turnaround in 20 minutes.

We always had great team spirit in Glen Rovers but we could hurl too. This was our 22nd county title and I think that was one of the very best we ever won. It was certainly one of the sweetest and it was very important for us. It also marked a transitionary period for the club. By the time we won our next championship, several players had retired or emigrated; people like Bill Carroll, Maurice Twomey, Mick Kenneally, Mick Lane, Jackie Daly and Seanie O'Riordan. So, we had to build another team. Which, being Glen Rovers, we did.

THERE WERE ALMOST 18,000 people at that hurling match in the Athletic Grounds in Cork. But there was one man missing – the man I most wanted to see me winning championships for the Glen. The man who had brought me down to the Athletic Grounds when I was a child. The man who had hugged me on that same pitch two years previously. But he wasn't there.

But in a way he was too. I knew I would probably never have played hurling or football to such a level without my father. I knew that all the games he brought me to, all the support he gave me and all the love he had for me, were the reasons I was playing for Glen Rovers on the 22nd of September, 1969. And even though this was the first major championship I'd won since he died, I kept him close and I felt him close. I always would and still do, to this day.

OF COURSE, ST NICKS were on a mission too in 1969. Because the Glen had done the business in September, we were determined to do the double the following month. We had won the championship in 1966 and we really felt we could do it again. We had played some great football to get to the final, beating the holders, Carbery and then hammering Clonakilty by 3-12 to 0-4 in the semi-final on the 18th of October.

Who were we facing in the final the following Sunday? None other than UCC. And again, they had the likes of Ray Cummins, Seamus Looney and Eric Philpott from Cork; Brendan Lynch and Mick Morris from Kerry, and Mick Power from Waterford. Again, many of our players were coming to the latter end of their careers, even though I was still only 24. Teddy O'Brien was also very young and Martin Doherty was only 17. In fact, that match split the Doherty household, with Martin playing at centre-back for us and his older brother Pat (thanks to the College Rule) playing centrefield for College.

It was a tough, dour, low-scoring game and UCC were leading 0-6 to 0-3 at half-time and they were four points up with 15 minutes to go. But we rallied, we had great spirit, and when Patsy Harte drew us level with a point with a few minutes to go, I was sure we would win or at least draw the game.

Instead we were robbed. At least, we felt we were robbed, there was a very bad decision made against us. I'm not saying it was deliberately done for us to lose, or UCC to win, but it did have that effect and we felt very aggrieved. I still feel it to this day because I was personally involved.

The match was a draw with a few minutes to go after Patsy's point. We were attacking and the ball went wide. I was centrefield and from the kick out I caught the ball – right in the middle of the field – and I have to say this was one of the best catches I ever made in football; I had no business getting the ball but I managed it all the same. And when I came down, the ball in my hands, I was surrounded by at least three, maybe four, college players, who were all over me.

And just like that, the referee blew the whistle and everybody – everybody now – thought that the free was being given against UCC, that I'd been fouled. But no. He gave the free the other way – what for, I have no idea, it couldn't have been over-carrying, not nearly enough time had passed and I'd taken hardly any steps away from where I'd landed.

College took the free quickly.

This was in the Athletic Grounds, near to where the covered stand is now, where the teams come out. And Brendan Lynch, who was playing right half-forward for UCC, got the ball. And he was fouled – that was a genuine foul, Jerry O'Sullivan fouled him. And he was 40 yards out by the sideline – a long way out, now – and he was a left-footed kicker. But didn't he kick the ball straight over the bar from the free, a brilliant kick, in fairness, and one worthy to win any championship. But it should never have happened.

That loss was devastating. We wanted to win that championship so badly and to add to our great wins in 1965 and '66. We wanted to win the double as well, and to come so close was galling. We really wanted to put it up to the county board, too. But it wasn't to be, and we were bitterly disappointed.

And once again, the man I would have loved to meet most after the final whistle and who would have consoled me – that man wasn't there.

◀ ◁ ◆ ▷ ▶

CORK HAD A good start to 1969, winning the National Hurling League final against the All–Ireland champions, Wexford in Croke Park on May 4th. I have more to say about that match, later, because I didn't play in it. Nevertheless, it was my first National Hurling League medal but it was also the first time Cork had won the league since 1952. We were about to rectify that poor record. Cork would go on to win six National Hurling Leagues between 1968/69 and 1980/81, and I was involved in four of them.

A week after the league final in 1969, the Munster Hurling Championship began rockily when we only managed to draw with Clare in the first round. I came on as a sub that day for Gerald McCarthy and the *Irish Press* were kind enough to say that my arrival *"inspired Cork"*. Whatever about that, we won the replay well, 3-8 to 1-4. I played centrefield that day with Roger Tuohy, my old buddy and teammate from primary school and I had a point to prove to the selectors, as I'll explain later.

The Munster semi-final was a novel pairing when we played Galway – yes, in the Munster Championship – and again we won, this time by a score of 3-15 to 1-10. Again, I was playing centrefield.

The Munster final was set for July 27th in Limerick against Tipperary. Margaret had moved to Cork by now, so we drove to the match together for the first time – and it was very exciting. I was really keen that Margaret would share in this aspect of my life and this was her very first game.

Cork had lost the football the Sunday before against Kerry; they beat us well, so our inter-county season depended on the match against Tipp. This was the first year my father was not there to watch me play, and I felt that keenly after every game. I remember well the year before, when he had come out on to the pitch in Limerick after Tipp had beaten us. And I remember saying to him, 'Crikey, imaging losing two Munster finals in a week'.

Well, even if my father wasn't there in 1969, I certainly didn't want to repeat the dose. Especially against Tipperary. I was brought up on Cork and Tipperary matches; they were an integral part of my childhood. Those were the games my father used to take me to in the 1950s and I might only see a bit of the match unless he lifted me up on his shoulders, which you couldn't do, really, in a packed ground.

But I was there and I felt the excitement of the crowd, it ran through me like electricity and I loved every moment of it. I felt my father's excitement too, he was lit up on those glorious days. Tipperary always played a big part in my life. Tipp was the team I always wanted to play against in hurling.

That time, players and selectors went together in cars and I had access to a car myself, now. It was a big car – a Ford Zephyr 6 – the bonnet seemed to go on forever. It wasn't my car, of course, but I could borrow it if O'Connor's Funeral Home didn't need it that day.

Margaret and I brought two friends with us, there was so much room in that car we could have fitted the whole Cork forward line. Tom Buckley who is a doctor in Australia, now, and George Murphy, who lives in Ovens and is involved with Cloughduv Hurling Club, came with us. They were both playing with the Glen at the time and they were in the back of the car and Margaret and myself were in the front.

That time, the road to Limerick was much slower than it is today and you had to go through a lot of towns and villages; the traffic would be terrible on match days – especially a Cork-Tipp Munster final. The worst traffic jam was always in Croom, since all the Cork cars built up on the road, funnelling into the town. And there was a huge crowd headed to Limerick that day – the attendance was over 43,000.

We got as far as the outskirts of Croom and we had to stop with the stationary line of cars in front of us. I looked in the rear-view mirror and I saw this fellow coming up behind and he was flying. I knew immediately he wasn't going to be able to stop and sure enough he slammed into the back of us. And he was flying, now. He rammed us into the car in front, so we were concertinaed between two cars.

All four of us got out and by the grace of God none of us were hurt. If it was a smaller car, I'd say we'd have been in right trouble. After the dust settled and my horror at the state of O'Connor's lovely Zephyr had subsided a bit, I realised that I had no way to get to the match. We pushed the car into the side of the ditch by the road – and it was a ditch. We just pushed it in there, out of the way.

And we left it there – there was nothing else we could do.

We then split into two groups – we knew that four of us would never get a lift – and the lads and myself and Margaret began to hitch to the game, me with my hurley and gear. This, now, a few hours before the Munster hurling final.

Everybody could see us because the traffic was either stopped or crawling, trying to get through Croom.

A CAR PULLED up and we got in. When I saw who it was, I couldn't believe it. It was Eamonn Young, who was very famous – he was on the Cork football team that won the All-Ireland in 1945, a living legend, really. And who was with him only his nephew, John Young who was playing with the Glen and whom I knew well.

Well, my life wasn't worth living by the time I got out of the car in Limerick. They gave out stink to me the whole way there. I can't remember a longer journey, it felt more like 120 miles than 12. Not only were my ears red by the time we got to the Gaelic Grounds, my whole face was like a beetroot with the giving out stink I got from the lads.

I shouldn't have been driving and I shouldn't have been this and I shouldn't have been that. A litany the whole way in and Margaret listening to every word, shocked – what an experience at her first match. And I was mortified in front of her, a woman I really wanted to impress.

How can this day get any worse? I was thinking to myself in the back of the car and the two boys reading me from a height all the way into the city.

As it happened, it turned out to be a great day.

Cork beat Tipperary in a Munster final for the first time since 1954, and lo and behold, I had the game of my life. Of my life, now.

Literally this was the best game I ever played for Cork and I played many, and I played well in a fair few but I couldn't do one single thing wrong on the pitch that day. To top it all off, I was marking the best player in Ireland, Mick Roche, at centrefield.

We had a great first-half. Cork were winning well by half-time, we were six or eight points up. Which was huge against Tipperary. Then Tipp started coming back at us. They were coming and coming and coming, and the Tipp crowd were getting louder and louder, and louder. 'TIPP... TIPP... TIPP' was all you could hear during parts of that second-half.

They got it back down to two points and we didn't score for the first 20 minutes of the second-half; we were hanging on, really. And the next thing was, I scored two points one after the other. The first was right-handed and the second was left-handed.

Now, scoring from centrefield was a bit unusual those days, it wasn't like today. You normally just let the ball in quick for the forwards to do their stuff, but whatever happened I scored the two points and we went on to win.

Well, there was great joy after the game and I had mixed feelings because while I was delighted that Margaret was there, I was also aware that my father was not. God, he would have loved that win in 1969 so much – against Tipperary of all teams. But it was a wonderful win and I still treasure it to this day.

When things settled down and I got out of the dressing-room, I realised that I had no lift home. And I couldn't travel with the other players because I had to get Margaret back to Cork too.

There was a priest at the time, a Father Ormond, he was above in St Peter and Paul's. He was originally from Shandon Street – his family had a bakery there, Ormond and Ahern. He brought myself and Margaret home, along with a brother of his. And I remember when we passed the car outside Croom, it was still there in the ditch looking forlorn. I didn't know what to expect but I was half-afraid somebody would have robbed it.

The following day, myself and Val O'Connor went down and got it and he was very good about it; he didn't mind a bit, in fairness. His beautiful car and it was a kind of a violet colour and it was the height of luxury those days, lying there in a ditch outside Croom.

AS A RESULT of beating Tipperary we were installed as favourites to win the All-Ireland but Kilkenny had other ideas. They beat London in the only semi-final and we went straight through to the final on September 7th.

That wasn't one of my better days, I have to say. I was marking Frank Cummins and Frank was a real handful to mark, he was a great player – one of the best all-round hurlers in the history of the game. I didn't really know him at the time, I'm not sure if he had arrived in Blackrock in Cork yet – he went on to play with them for years and to play with great distinction.

Kilkenny beat us by a score of 2-15 to 2-9 and it was very disappointing. It was my second All-Ireland final and we had lost both – the football in 1967 and now this, two years later. Sport is cruel. I was beginning to wonder if I would ever win a senior All-Ireland medal in hurling or football.

◄◄◆►►

IN THE FOOTBALL in 1968 we reached the Munster final but we were beaten by Kerry. Nothing new there. But in football there were two highlights for me that year.

The Munster final was in Killarney and Ray Cummins scored two goals the same day. That was his first senior football game for Cork. The first of many, thank God. He was playing full-forward and he scored his two goals in the first couple of minutes of the game so it was a huge introduction for him. His debut and the impact he had that day reflected what a wonderful player he would become – he was a truly outstanding forward in football and hurling, one of the best I had the good fortune to play with.

But Kerry are Kerry and although we were actually eight points up after six minutes of that final, by half-time we were a point behind. Imagine that. And that incredible turnaround was mainly because of Mick O'Connell who was playing centrefield. I was playing centre-back for Cork and I was able to observe him closely.

I can still see him so vividly, some things you never forget. No matter where he got a free – and he was fouled a lot, needless to say – he never placed the ball on the ground. He just rolled the ball on the ground and hit it straight over the bar with a sweet stroke of the boot, every single time. He was the most beautiful striker of a football you could imagine and he had an amazing leap too – you'd pay money just to see him catch a ball.

That same year marks my establishment as a dual county player, and I felt comfortable in both teams in a way that I hadn't really before. Although we lost both Munster finals, I knew I had a lot to contribute and that I could improve year on year and play regularly in the championship in both codes.

In 1969 we also lost the Munster football final to Kerry and the strange thing about that game was that I was picked right half-forward. I don't know why. I couldn't understand it because I was mostly playing centrefield and I was very comfortable there. Either there or centre-back, which I loved as a position too.

The match was in Cork and when we arrived at the dressing-room, we learned that Dan Dineen, the centre-back, was injured and had to cry off. So, I was moved from wing-forward to centre-back.

The game was tight enough for a long time but we got a penalty in the second-half and, as I said before, they were scarce enough those days.

I went up to take it. Johnny Culloty was in goal and I took the penalty and Johnny went to his left and I struck the ball low to his right, my left. But didn't it hit the butt of the goalpost and come back out. One of the Kerry defenders picked it up when he was running back in but he picked it up off the ground inside the square. Another penalty.

The relief! I was sure I'd score this time.

So, I placed the ball down and stepped back. And I couldn't make my mind up what to do, which side to go for. Should I go for the same side – would Johnny go to his left again, or what? And on my run up to kick the ball, didn't another Cork player go past me. He passed me on my right and he struck the ball. He was a left-footer so we didn't clash or anything but I was totally shocked. He missed it and Kerry went on to win the game, 0-16 to 1-4.

A lot of people afterwards thought this must have been pre-planned, that we had arranged it to put Johnny Culloty off. I often talk to Johnny about it when I meet him. In reality, this Cork player had done what he did off his own bat completely. There was no consultation, no hint; we never talked about it or he never took a penalty in training. Nothing.

IN 1970 THE CORK football selectors played me at corner-forward and I was really relishing it. Not least, I suppose, because I was scoring so much. We may not have had the best full-forward line in Ireland that year, but we probably had the tallest – myself, Ray Cummins and Declan Barron.

In the Munster semi-final against Tipperary I scored a goal and 10 points. I think it was the most anybody scored in a single game in 1970. Amazingly, Babs Keating scored 3-1 against us the same day, which he likes to remind me whenever we meet. And I remind him back that I scored three points more.

In the Munster final against Kerry I scored 2-4, and I was being marked by Sean Murphy who was a very good corner-back. That's an average of over 11 points per game in the championship (admittedly for only two games), which was the highest in Ireland for the year. I loved corner-forward, it was a novelty for me. It was so different to centre-back or centrefield.

I drove down to Killarney for the match on my own but there was such a crowd that I was forced to abandon the car in a little place near Barraduff, a few miles outside Killarney. I had to walk the rest of the way to the grounds, Fitzgerald Stadium, with my gear bag over my shoulder, chatting away to Cork and Kerry fans heading for the game.

And, even though I scored 2-4 the same day, we only managed 2-9 altogether and Kerry beat us out the gate, nearly a score a man. They went on to beat Meath in the All-Ireland final – they had great players those days like Brendan Lynch, Mick O'Connell and Mick O'Dwyer.

I was really enjoying my football in the late 60s and early 70s, even if we had just lost three Munster finals in-a-row to Kerry.

◄◄◆►►

THE RAILWAY CUP is another great feature of hurling and football that is now lost and I think our games are very much the poorer for it. It was a childhood dream of mine that I would play for Munster alongside and in opposition to great players from many other counties and thankfully that dream came true.

The Munster jersey was a lovely blue with the three famous gold crowns on its crest and I remember the first time I was selected and got to wear it in 1968 when I was only 23. It was in January and the team was called out on the radio. Those days there used to be a lot of 15-minute radio programmes in the middle of the day and there might be a sports report between them. I was at home with my mother and father, having our dinner. So, when the team was called out on the radio (on RTÉ no less, there were no local radio stations), my father was there beside me, listening. He was getting ready to go out on the 2 to 10 shift and the Munster football team was called out with my name on it. I'll never forget my father's expression when he heard that – the joy in his face that his son would be playing in the Railway Cup. And my own expression probably mirroring his joy and pride on the same day. It's funny the things you look back on.

There were eight Corkmen on the Railway Cup team in 1968, which isn't strange when you remember that we nearly won the All-Ireland the year before. The other Cork players were Billy Morgan, Jerry Lucey, John O'Mahony, Frank Cogan, Mick Burke, Mick O'Loughlin, Con O'Sullivan (captain) and Johnny Carroll. There were only two Kerry players on the team, I'd say that's the lowest number before or since.

It's hard to imagine how popular the Railway Cup was when I was playing in the 1960s – you could get 40,000 or more at Railway Cup finals those days. The reason I think that there were so many people at Railway Cup hurling and football games was that it might be your only opportunity to see great players in the flesh; players like Christy Ring and Mick O'Connell. There were almost no games on television and many people might not be able to afford to go to Killarney or Thurles to a game, so if there was a Railway Cup match in Cork or Limerick, there would be throngs to watch it. And the novelty of seeing people like Ring, Mackey and Doyle on the same team would be too good an opportunity to miss.

And the players took it very seriously too. This was never truer than in 1972 when Mick O'Connell and Mick O'Dwyer took over responsibility for training the team. Munster had not won a Railway Cup in football since 1949 – it was the one medal that had eluded O'Connell and O'Dwyer, and they really wanted to rectify that omission and to bridge that gap of 23 years. Although Cork were the Munster Champions in 1971, the two Mick O's along with Donie O'Sullivan from Kerry organised the team's preparation.

And we trained very seriously. There were only 20 on the panel – which was selected by the Munster Council – and we trained in Cork. All the Kerry lads travelled to Cork in February and March of 1972. When you think of the distances they had to drive you can see the importance of the Railway Cup. We beat Connacht by a goal in the semi-final and went on to play Leinster in the final in Croke Park on St Patrick's Day.

I remember that match very well. I was playing centre-forward. Offaly were the backbone of the Leinster team that year because they were All-Ireland champions – they had beaten us in the All-Ireland semi-final the previous August. I think they had 10 players on the Leinster team and I was marking Nicholas Clavin, who become a priest afterwards and went to America.

Mick O'Connell was centrefield and I recall that we were one point down with one minute to go and we were awarded a free a long way out. Maybe 55 or 60 yards out under the Cusack Stand and we were playing into the Canal End, and into a strong wind. And Mick O'Connell threw the ball down, stood back and … BANG… straight over the bar to draw the match. It was a magnificent kick of a ball, I'll never forget it.

The replay was in Cork in April and we beat them well, 2-14 to 0-10. O'Connell was imperious that day too, and himself and Frank Cogan dominated midfield and our captain, Donal Hunt scored two goals. Babs Keating played well – he was a great footballer – and John O'Keeffe from Kerry was brilliant at centre-back and we never looked like losing at all.

It was a sweet win, all the sweeter to win it in Cork and although I played on the Munster football team for four years (1968, '72, '73 and '74) 1972 was the only time we won the Railway Cup in football.

IN LATER YEARS, it was as a hurler only that I represented Munster. We got to the final in 1977 but we were beaten by Leinster, 1-13 to 1-7. But we won it in 1978 which was lovely, it really was. We beat Connacht, 0-20 to 1-11. My last year playing Railway Cup was 1979 and Connacht got their revenge.

Attendances at Railway Cup finals had reduced maybe to 20,000 but it still mattered. I loved playing with great hurlers who I'd normally be opposing: people like Ger Loughnane, Mick Moroney and Séamus Durack from Clare; or Nicky Cashen and Mossie Walsh from Waterford; or Éamonn Grimes and Pat Hartigan from Limerick; or Jim Keogh, Tommy Butler and Tadhg O'Connor from Tipperary; or Pat Moriarty and Johnny Bunyan from Kerry.

I played four years on the Munster hurling team (1973, '77, '78, and '79) and the win in 1978 allowed me to complete the set of Railway Cup football and hurling medals, of which I am very proud.

◄ ◄ ◆ ► ►

AFTER THE ALL-IRELAND final of 1969 and the subsequent Oireachtas final, I wasn't feeling well and the doctors told me I had a blood infection – a virus of some kind – and they advised me to take a break from hurling and football.

They suggested six-months but, while I did take the winter off (missing the National Leagues before and after Christmas), I was back training for the Glen and St Nicks in early March and I was feeling great, raring to go. I was 25 and the break had done me good, and I was straight back training with the Cork footballers.

But I wasn't welcomed with open arms by the Cork hurling selectors. I just got on with it and eventually I was brought back into the hurling panel.

Although Glen Rovers had won the county championship in 1969, we had only two players on the Cork championship panel in 1970, myself and Jerry O'Sullivan. That in itself, was a travesty, but I wasn't on the team, either – I was a sub. Since Jerry was the only Glen player on the team, he was automatically the captain.

So, Jerry captained Cork in the Munster semi-final against Limerick which Cork won by 4-13 to 3-6 in Thurles – a big win. That was on the 28th of June. I was an unused substitute. Then the bombshell: Jerry was dropped off the panel – *the panel* – for the Munster final against Tipp three weeks later.

Can you ever remember a captain of a county team being dropped off the panel for a final, having won the semi-final so well? I can't.

Of course, this meant that when Cork beat Tipperary in the final by two points, Paddy Barry of St Vincent's, as the longest serving player, was captain and received the cup. The fact that I had been Man of the Match in the previous year's Munster final didn't impress the selectors, either. I was not given a run that day, even though it was a tight game.

Perhaps this was when Glen Rovers people began to wonder what was happening with the county board and its selection committee for the Cork hurling team in 1970. Remember that this is less than two years since Glen Rovers had defied the board and withdrawn from all board activities after the UCC match. And Glen Rovers were now county champions. But we weren't even represented on the pitch the following year in the Munster final.

The reprisals against Glen Rovers had begun in 1969 when I was playing in the National Hurling League semi-final against Tipperary in April. This is how one newspaper reported what happened next... *"Coughlan had a brilliant game that day (against Tipperary) at centrefield but, shortly before the end, was pulled out of the game by the selectors and replaced by Gerald McCarthy who only a few hours earlier had been considered unfit to play. This shock change is still one of the most controversial arguments in Cork GAA circles. Many regard it as a retaliatory dig against Glen*

Rovers by the Cork GAA board."

What made matters worse was that the 60-minute game was right in the balance when they took me off, prompting Mick Dunne, in the *Irish Press*, to write... *"When Tipperary took back the lead for those three second-half minutes Cork were still unsettled following the 52nd minute withdrawal of Denis Coughlan … Coughlan had been such a dominant figure at centrefield … that Tipperary were never happy around the middle".*

Then they dropped me for the league final a few weeks later against the All-Ireland champions, Wexford, prompting no less a sportswriter than Paddy Downey to write in the *Irish Times*... *"Surprise of the Cork team to play Wexford in the National Hurling League final at Croke Park on Sunday is the omission of the Glen Rovers man, Denis Coughlan, who was one of the outstanding members of the side which beat Tipperary in the semi-final at Thurles on April 13th."* He added that my substitution against Tipp was... *"to the astonishment of nearly every Cork supporter at Thurles Sportsfield".*

The *Sunday Press* (on the morning of the game) went further, saying... *"Five famous men of Cork hurling go on trial at Croke Park this afternoon. [the article goes on to name the Cork selectors, which I don't want to do] For these are the five men who sat down last week to name the Cork side. And once again they stepped right into the judgement box by consigning the brilliant Denis Coughlan to the substitutes. Their thumbs-down was, in my opinion, a direct snub to Coughlan and to his club Glen Rovers. This youngster put on a spectacular display against Tipperary in the semi-final in Thurles, particularly in the first-half when he dominated the centre of the field with an almost incredible mastery. Everyone in Thurles, including Tipperary's diehard supporters saw and appreciated this. But not the Cork selectors. With five minutes to go, at a see-saw stage in a tremendous battle, they pulled Coughlan out of the game, replaced him with a man who only a few hours earlier had been deemed unfit, and then made the feeble excuse that they considered Coughlan to be tiring."*

Now, I'm not putting in these newspaper reports to big myself up, but rather to show that all this wasn't a Denis Coughlan/Glen Rovers/Blackpool conspiracy theory, but something that was widely known and accepted in GAA circles – even outside Cork. Me being dropped for the National Hurling League final of 1969 was no surprise to anyone. But what happened the following year was far worse.

FOR THE 1970 All-Ireland semi-final against London on the 16th of August

I was picked to play at centrefield. And I was captain – I had to be if I was playing. My inclusion was a surprise, not only to myself but to the newspapers. One article went... *"The surprise is no reflection on Coughlan's ability. It comes because of the continuous running battle between the Cork selectors and the county champions Glen Rovers, disagreement that had meant that appearances by Glen members on the Cork team being few and far between".*

When it was put to me if I had any ill-will to the selectors because of what they had done, I was quoted as saying,... *"All I am concerned with is hurling itself and the fact that I have now got my place back on the Cork team. This is my only chance of playing in this year's All-Ireland final. On this game alone I will be judged and I have to make the best of it".*

And, even though I say so myself, I played well, and Cork won well on the day.

But the board and the selectors had other ideas for the final, and when the team was named I was dropped. Jerry, the captain of the team, had been dropped for the Munster final and I, the captain of the team, was dropped for the All-Ireland final. The only two Glen Rovers players on the panel. The only two players who would have been captain on either day to raise the cup for Cork. Two captains dropped for two consecutive finals, both from the same club. To rub salt in the wound, how I learned I wasn't playing in the final was also unpleasant.

I got a phone call from the journalist, Val Dorgan on the Tuesday night before the final. I knew Val, he had played for the Glen himself.

'Do you know you're not playing on Sunday?' he said.

'No, Val, I didn't know that, this is the first I've heard of it,' I said.

'And,' he said. 'Did you know that if Cork win on Sunday it will be the first time ever that Cork have won an All-Ireland that there wasn't a Glen Rovers man on the team?'

'No,' I said, gutted. 'I didn't know that, either.'

The following morning the team was confirmed, with the headline... *"Cork Restore Four Players for Final: No Glen Rovers Man in Team".*

The article also confirmed that 1970 would be the first time, *"since 1929 when Paddy 'Fox' Collins became the first Glen Rovers player to wear a senior jersey in an All-Ireland final that the Blackpool club will not have a representative on an All-Ireland team".* Grim reading.

Now, while I may not have known about the Glen always having had a player on Cork All-Ireland final teams, I'm sure others inside and outside the club did know it. And the club wasn't happy; everybody knew what was going on – what the board was up to – that this was revenge for what Glen Rovers had done two years previously.

SO, THE CLUB ordered its representative on the selection committee (yes, there was one since we were county champions) to resign, but he refused. While everybody knew what was happening, nobody – least of all Glen Rovers – could do anything about it. The board said the selectors were independent and the selectors said they were picking the best team.

The final went ahead against Wexford and Cork won easily.

I sat on the sideline watching. The game was extraordinary from a few perspectives. There were four Quigley brothers on the Wexford starting team, Dan, John, Martin and Pat – that must have been a very disappointed household the following day. But I was delighted that Eddie O'Brien scored a hat-trick of goals for Cork, a record that stood until Lar Corbett equalled it for Tipperary exactly 40 years later.

It was obvious mid-way through the second-half that Cork were going to win in a canter. With six minutes to go, we were ahead by an extraordinary 17 points. And this was the first ever 80-minute final, where, to bring on subs would not only have been expected but almost essential. But I wasn't brought on, anyway, and that was always the plan.

I was never going to be presented with the Liam MacCarthy Cup that day and Glen Rovers were never going to be represented on the team.

When we went up to collect the cup afterwards, I must admit that I wasn't feeling particularly well because I knew in my heart and soul the reasons behind what had just happened. I can't say I experienced any consolation that this was not a personal campaign against me – that I was, as it were, collateral damage. And, of course I was not the only victim of what was going on; Jerry O'Sullivan had been treated shamefully, too.

Jack Lynch was Taoiseach and of course he was there, both in his official capacity and also as a proud Corkman. And we all had to go up on the podium – Paddy Barry first, as captain. When I reached the podium, Jack was about six feet away from me. And he made a bee-line for me; he had to go past people to get as close to me as he could. I remember this as vividly as if it were yesterday.

He shook his head angrily and said, 'The so-and-sos didn't even give you a taste of it'.

Except he didn't say 'so-and-sos' but I don't want to repeat the word he used – it was a word that you wouldn't often hear from Jack Lynch, but everybody knew what was going on.

Now, I didn't write this book to settle old scores. Anybody who knows me knows that I'm the one most likely to be trying to stop the fight rather than start it. And there was a lot more I could have put in this book that wouldn't show people at their best – about this particular incident, too – but I didn't. Nor, you will notice, am I naming names which I could have if I wanted to, they're all dead now. Despite the bitterness shown towards Glen Rovers at that time, I'm not going to return the compliment. No, life is too short.

On the other hand, I did decide when I started the book that I would tell the truth – that's the way I was brought up. And the truth is that politics was rife in Cork hurling and football those days, with people using positions of power to further their own personal ends and that of their clubs rather than Cork teams. It was especially prevalent in Cork minor teams, unfortunately.

Luckily for me, all that was about to change in Cork hurling and football, and luckily for Cork, too.

My last word on the hurling of 1970 is this. Once it was over, I forgot about it and got on with playing hurling and football for Munster, Cork, St Nicholas and Glen Rovers. In his book, *Three Kings, Cork, Kilkenny and Tipperary: the battle for supremacy*, Ralph Riegel writes about me being dropped for the All-Ireland final of 1970. And he contrasts my reaction to that of Charlie Carter, the Gowran forward, who, even though he was captain of Kilkenny in 2003, could not get his place on the team. Charlie walked away, never to return to the Kilkenny fold, whereas I stayed put.

I never considered quitting, it didn't enter my head, to be honest. I never let it fester and I never looked back, that's just the way I am. There was always another match, another championship, another challenge, another opponent to overcome. And I loved them all and I applied myself to them all as best I could and as positively as I could.

IT WAS ONLY when I sat down to write this book that I really looked back on it all; I never did when I was playing. Again, life is too short and when I look back on 1970 now, I think of it as a wonderful year because that's the year that Margaret and I got married.

When I was thinking back about 1970 for this book and I mentioned it to Margaret, she told me an interesting story; her memory of my hurling that year. When she took up her job with John O'Meara in December of 1969, she mentioned to him that she and I were getting married in early April the following year and she would need some time off.

'Are ye taking a honeymoon?' John asked her.

'We are,' she said.

'Where are ye going?' he asked.

'Well,' she told him. 'If Cork win the National Hurling League, we're going to New York, but if they don't, we're going to Scotland.'

Now, I must have told her that the National League final in 1970 was due to be played in New York. Which it was, against New York. As it happened, Cork did win the so-called 'Home Final' against Limerick in May and the team did head out to New York straight after the All-Ireland final in September.

But I wasn't on that flight, and neither was Margaret. I suppose this was the final twist of the knife. When the panel to contest the two league finals in New York was announced immediately after the All-Ireland final, I wasn't even on it. I wasn't going. They didn't even give me that.

But it was low on my list of priorities, because at that time Margaret and I were expecting our first child. And when Jonathan arrived safe and well in February, 1971, league finals and being selected or not selected for teams became completely and utterly immaterial. What a blessing we were given in 1971 – the gift of a new life, a healthy baby boy. A gift surpassing anything, surpassing everything.

◄◄◆►►

1971 WAS MORE of a football year for me because Limerick beat Cork in the first round of the Munster Hurling Championship – a major shock as Cork were All-Ireland champions but uneasy lies the head that wears a crown. The Glen had a poor enough year too, as did St Nicks.

In the first round of the football Munster championship we played Clare. They brought us all the way up to Doonbeg – about as far as they could. I was corner-forward and I scored 1-6 from play out of the 2-10 that we managed overall. I was scoring for fun at the time, I really was flying as a footballer. Or was I?

Munster finals were played in Cork on the odd years those days and in Kerry on the even years, so the Munster final was fixed for the Athletic Grounds on the 18th of July, 1971. We were training away for that and the week before the game I went out to Blackpool for a visit. My sister, Anne was home from England and staying with my mother in the Buildings. It was the Wednesday morning, and I picked up Anne from the airport and dropped her down home. When I went in the door, my mother took a look at me and said, 'What are you after doing now?'

'I didn't do anything,' I said, alarmed.

'You're all over the papers,' she said. 'You're not playing again on Sunday.'

I shook my head. I knew I'd been dropped for the Munster football final, but I hadn't seen the newspapers. I apologised to her for being all over the papers (not a good thing). Even though I was a grown man, now married and a father, there I was saying sorry to my mother for being dropped off the Cork football team.

I found out I was dropped the night before at training. I went into the dressing-room and Billy Morgan, who was togging off, looked at me. A few other players were looking at me too – there was something wrong, the place was too quiet.

'Did you hear the news?' Billy said.

'No,' I said. 'What?'

'You're dropped for Sunday,' he said. 'But it doesn't matter because we're not playing. We're going on strike.'

I was shocked. I was shocked about being dropped after scoring 1-6 in the previous game, and 7-41 in my previous nine games for Cork – I was the leading scorer in Ireland at the time. But I was also shocked that the other players were going to refuse to play. It was my first game against Limerick in 1965 all over again, when the players told the board they wouldn't play without Flor Hayes. It was the All-Ireland hurling final of 1970 all over again, too – I thought to myself… *Here we go again. First the hurling selectors drop me, now the football selectors do the same.*

I talked to Billy and some of the players, trying to convince them to play. I was shell-shocked, I must say, but I didn't want to be the cause of a strike, I'd have hated that.

'You can't do that, Billy,' I remember saying.

'No… we're not playing,' said Billy. 'We had a meeting, our minds are made up. This is ridiculous. We're not playing and that's that.'

I begged Billy and the others not to do anything and eventually I convinced them. They settled for sending a letter of complaint to the county board demanding that I be reinstated on the team or else the selectorial committee should be sacked, and the picking of the team should be left to the players. I was delighted to hear that all 13 of my teammates who were present signed the letter. Thankfully, there was no all-out strike for the Munster final. I made up my mind immediately that I wasn't going to do anything – I came under fierce pressure from several journalists to make a comment. Maybe it was because of my experience with the hurlers the year before – I don't know – but I decided not to do one thing, not to say anything to anyone and to just get on with it.

I wasn't going to question it. Nothing.

I was gutted I must say, and unlike the previous year I didn't see it coming. I had been completely blindsided. In hindsight maybe I should've been expecting the football selectors to do the same as the hurling selectors the year before, but I wasn't.

The papers were full of it the following day – me being dropped was big news. There was a furore really and a lot of questions were asked. The county board said the selectors were completely independent and they couldn't interfere. The selectors said they only ever picked the best possible team for Cork – exactly what the hurling selectors had said in 1970 when the same questions had been asked of them. News of the letter from the players also leaked out and there was I in the middle of the whole thing – the centre of all attention for all the wrong reasons and exactly where I hated to be.

IT WAS A long few days until Sunday. Everywhere I went – at work or anywhere – people were asking me why I was dropped and telling me it was a disgrace. I wanted to hide away to be honest, even though I hadn't done anything wrong. I didn't want to look at the selectors, let alone get an explanation. You weren't told anything in those days, anyway. Things are much improved now.

Kerry were All-Ireland champions and National Football League champions so they were favourites to win the game. It was a lovely sunny day – I do remember that. I also remember walking down to the pitch from our house in Blackrock and people looking at me, and telling me that I should be playing. I felt almost ashamed, although I had done nothing wrong. But it was a long and painful walk down to the grounds knowing I wouldn't be getting a game.

One thing about that day makes me smile now. I was very finicky about my food on the day of matches. I was fastidious. I might have something very small for breakfast or nothing at all. And that would be it. I mightn't eat after the game either, until the following day. Against all the modern nutrition rules, but that's just the way I was.

But, because I wasn't playing and the game was just down the road from our house, I decided to have lunch on the day of the match. What we used to call a proper Sunday dinner. So, I had plenty of food, whatever it was – roast beef or something – and I remember having strawberries and cream afterwards, too. If I wasn't playing, sure I might as well.

When I was a child, as I said earlier, I used to go to the Athletic Grounds with my father on the day of big matches. And Jimmy O'Rourke used to take me up to the scoreboard and I could see everything from way up there and all the players looked so small.

Well, that day in July, 1971 as I took my place on the subs bench, I felt very small. The dugout and the subs bench was right beside the pitch and surrounded by fans. I sat down and kept my head down as the teams got ready for the throw-in. I was miserable.

To say that Kerry got a flying start would be an understatement. Mick O'Connell and Din Joe Crowley were lording it at centrefield and delivering scoring chance after scoring chance to their forwards who were tapping the ball over the bar like there was no tomorrow. After 15 minutes Cork were losing by seven points to one and it looked very much like we were going to get an unmerciful beating. Which is when they told me I was being brought on.

I thought it was a mistake – they're sending me on after 15 minutes? Did you ever see a sub being brought on – barring injury – after 15 minutes? I don't think I ever did, but before I knew it, I was being put in at centre-forward on John O'Keeffe, possibly the best footballer in Ireland at the time, and Cork were losing by six points to Kerry in a Munster final.

I think it was the good start that gave me the confidence to play the way I did.

With my first ball I scored a point, and with my second ball I got another. *Tús maith* … Of course, I had a point to prove, too.

And, bit by bit we just turned it around. Frank Cogan went centrefield and Donal Hunt went wing-forward and we were holding our own. I scored two more points from frees and at half-time the scoreboard looked more respectable at Kerry 0-8 Cork 0-5.

In the second-half we gave an exhibition of football. We crushed the mighty Kingdom, All-Ireland champions or not. Within five minutes of half-time myself, Ray Cummins, Ned Kirby and Donal Hunt kicked points to level the game and when I scored again from a free, shortly after, for us to take the lead, I don't think I ever heard the like of the roar from the crowd at the Athletic Grounds. I'd swear the big old stand by the Marina shook with the noise.

And we were only getting better as the game went on. Ray Cummins was outstanding, he gave Paud O'Donoghue a torrid time of it – if only we'd had Ray in 1967 I'm convinced we'd have beaten Meath the same day. As for myself, I ended up scoring 10 points, having come on as a sub. Did I feel vindicated? Yes, I bloody did. I don't think we ever had a sweeter or more comprehensive victory over our old rivals. Cork 0-25, Kerry 0-14 – a record winning score against the green and gold. Our total of 25 points was also a first for Cork. My score of 10 points was also a record for an individual against Kerry in a single championship match and a lovely balance to my 2-4 in the final the year before.

FROM THAT DAY to this I was never given an explanation for why I was dropped for that Munster final, just as I was not given an explanation why I was dropped for the All-Ireland hurling final the year before. One letter to the papers proposed some reasons why I was dropped, despite being the leading scorer for Cork, saying... *"rumours circulating behind the city goal during the game were many and varied. Some said he marched on the 12th in the North; more said he visited Peking lately; while one more vicious than any of the others said it was because he was a Glen man"*. I can confirm that two of those accusations are not true and I'm not going to speculate either as to why I was dropped in 1971. Luckily for me – unlike in 1970 – it turned out well personally.

Although I did feel vindicated, I just took my own advice and I said nothing to anybody. I could've gone to the newspapers; I could've done several things but

I didn't. Now, the dugout was very close to the pitch in the old Atlantic Grounds and whether, after 15 minutes, the selectors were getting stick from the crowd, or whether it was the fuss in the newspapers during the week, I don't know why I was brought on so early in the game. The main thing was that we had won, we had beaten Kerry – for the first time since 1967, too. And I was happy I'd done my bit.

Unfortunately, as so often happened, beating Kerry was the highlight of our year, our Mount Everest, and we didn't play as well against Offaly in the All-Ireland semi-final. I scored four points, which was scant consolation. I was glad after when Offaly went on to win their first ever All-Ireland, a famous win for them.

Nowadays, almost 50 years later, 1971 is the thing that people my own age most often remark upon when I meet them. Me being dropped for the Munster final and the great win we had against Kerry the same day.

◄◄◆▷►

FOLLOWING THE SENDING OFF in the Munster Hurling Final of 1972 (with Christy Ring's 'lucky' hurley) I was suspended for a month and I missed the All-Ireland semi-final against London which was played at the Cork Athletic Grounds. That was a terribly one-sided match with Cork winning by 7-20 to 1-12. In hindsight, the game didn't do us any good in preparing for a final against Kilkenny.

The day of the All-Ireland final was a beautiful day. I was marking Frank Cummins at centrefield again and Justin McCarthy was marking Liam 'Chunky' O'Brien. Kilkenny had a great midfield partnership between O' Brien and Cummins – they were two very different players but they complimented each other really well. My instructions before the game were simple and succinct.

'You take the big fella.' That's what passed for tactics those days.

It was a brilliant match full of amazing hurling – one of the classic All-Ireland finals. Eighty minutes of incredible scoring and tension, and ebbs and flows. But, as Christy Ring said to me a few months later, 'You know, Kilkenny always win the classics'. I didn't know whether he meant that if it's a classic, Kilkenny will win it; or if Kilkenny win it, people will call it a classic.

You often weren't exactly sure what Christy meant when he said something.

The issue of 'classics' and Kilkenny would come up again in 1978 when we were about to take on the Cats again, that time in search of the three in-a-row. But this was 1972 and in the weeks preceding the final I was acutely aware of my track record in Croke Park in All-Ireland finals and semi-finals. I was injured for the hurling in 1966, missing out on that win. We then lost the football final in 1967 and the hurling final in '69. I wasn't playing in 1970 when we did win the hurling and then we lost the semi-final in the football to Offaly in '71 when I was playing.

So, in five recent occasions that Cork were involved in championship matches in Croke Park I had either not been playing when we won, or I had been playing when we lost. Not good. Not good at all, and I wanted 1972 to be better – to finally be my year.

One of the striking things about 80-minute games is how often one team would dominate for a period and then the game would swing, and the other team would have its period of ascendency. You could almost never be on top for the whole game, it was simply too long. And the real trick was this: when you do dominate you put enough scores on the board to counter-effect the period when you are struggling.

Also, the aim is to be driving on at the end of the game, because if you are ahead at the final whistle, obviously you win. And those two tricks were exactly what Cork failed to achieve in the hurling final of 1972.

There were two really telling periods of play that have vividly stayed with me. And you always remember the ones you lost more starkly than the ones you won. About half-way through the second-half, we were four points up when Eddie Keher got a goal. One point up. Within a minute Ray Cummins scored a goal for us and within a minute of that, Seanie O'Leary got another. Three goals in two minutes – only in hurling. Seven points up.

Con Roche, the great hurler from St Finbarr's, was playing left half-back. And straight from the puck out he won possession under the Cusack stand. We were playing into the Canal End and he struck a great ball, he must have hit it 80 or 90 yards – BANG... over the bar. It was a wonderful strike and it put us eight points up (5-11 to 1-15) with the wind in our tails. Seven or eight points was a lead you always wanted because it meant that two quick goals would still leave you ahead.

Now, this was at the 67-minute mark – today you would be home and hosed with a lead like that, but not then, there were 13 minutes left. And amazing things can happen very quickly in hurling (which we have just seen), let alone in 13 minutes. Still, eight points up after an hour and a bit was always a good place to be against Kilkenny.

Not good enough, that day. We lost the match by seven points. In the next eight minutes we surrendered our lead. And in the following five minutes Kilkenny tacked on seven unanswered points to win by seven. I'll spare you the details. I certainly don't enjoy looking back at it. All credit to Kilkenny, they were a great team. As well as that wonderful midfield pairing, they had Eddie Keher (who scored 2-9 that day) and Noel Skehan (their captain) in goal.

But there was a turning point in the match which most commentators missed and it wasn't any of the great scores by Keher or Frank Cummins's goal. The turning point in that game was when Kilkenny took off Fan Larkin at corner-back and they brought in Martin Coogan. However he managed it, Martin shored up the Kilkenny back line in the last 10 minutes and we couldn't get through. It's normally forwards who turn games but that day it was a corner-back who broke our hearts, a man who never really got the credit he deserved.

An amazing thing happened 25 years later. I was at a business function in Dublin and a man came up to me and introduced himself – a very well-known man, as it happens. He was very friendly with the father of a business partner of mine. We were just chatting about the connection and other acquaintances in common and he was telling me a bit about himself. Suddenly he said, 'God, I'll never forget the final in '72… it was an amazing game'.

Here we go again, I thought, *the famous 'classic'.*

I was blue in the face from hearing about it. And then he said, 'Do you know what the turning point in that game was?' I had my opinion, but I said nothing.

'I think,' says he, 'That it was Martin Coogan coming on at corner-back for Kilkenny. God ye were flying until then.'

I was shocked. I asked him was he at the game?

'At it?' says he. 'Sure wasn't I one of the umpires behind the goal only yards away from it? I saw the whole thing.'

On the positive, I had established myself as a dual inter-county player by 1972 and was playing in all Cork games and, I felt, holding my own, putting '70 and '71 behind me. But that wasn't much consolation on that September Sunday in 1972 with the black and amber celebrating yet another win over us. And me, enduring yet another miserable day at Croke Park where everything matters most.

◄◄◆▷►

MARGARET SAYS I asked her twice to marry me. I disagree. She says I asked her first in a letter and she has the letter to prove it, but I think that was more of a hint or a suggestion. But I did ask her (eventually) in person over dinner.

She said yes and we picked a ring later in Dublin where she knew the jewellers. That was Christmas 1969.

Soon after there was a badminton social out in Blarney and we got our photo taken and it appeared on the front page of the *Evening Press* the following day, with an announcement of our engagement. Those days you could get the *Evening Press* as well as the *Evening Echo* in Cork.

I remember that evening well because Christy Ring was at the social too, and he was very uncomfortable. Can you imagine Christy at a badminton social? He was a very shy man and he never drank, either.

My only regret around that time was that Margaret didn't meet my father more often. The only time she met him was after the All-Ireland final in 1967, and that wasn't a good day for me. By the time she came to Cork he had died, which was a pity, they would have gotten on so well.

We picked a date for April 3rd the following year, so that was a lovely end to 1969 and the decade, which had been a momentous 10 years for me.

In fairness, Margaret organised almost all of the wedding, I didn't have much to do with it. She's a really organised person and the wedding was going to be in Dublin and she did a great job in only a few months. Her family – who I was always very fond of and who were very good to me – were a great help to us too with all the arrangements.

Margaret's mother, Kitty was from Carrickmacross, County Monaghan and she was a nurse in Dublin. Margaret's father, Jim was from Broadford in County Limerick and he was a guard in Dublin and that's how they met. They were lovely people altogether, the nicest you could possibly meet.

Margaret also has two sisters, Jeannette and Kathleen, lovely women. And two brothers, Pat and James, both of them were in the guards like their father. They originally played football with Rialto Gaels who were a senior football club. That was where they lived – in Rialto. Pat then went on to play with St Vincent's and with Dublin. I actually played against him once in the National Football League.

All of Margaret's family made me very welcome whenever I visited and with my own two sisters away it was lovely to have a second family, in a sense, in Dublin. It was like going from home to home.

THE WEDDING TOOK place, as I said, on Friday 3rd April, 1970 in the Church of Our Lady of the Holy Rosary of Fatima in Rialto. It was the Friday after Easter. Back then weddings took place early in the day; ours was at 12 o'clock – I remember it was the latest time we could get. A local priest married us but I had a friend who concelebrated the Mass with him – Father Owen Murphy from Crosshaven. He was one of five brothers who were all priests, imagine. I met him originally in Chicago in 1966 when the Glen travelled there. He was based in Loyola College in Chicago and we got very friendly. It was lovely of him to travel all the way back to be there at the wedding with us and to concelebrate the Mass.

I had a black-eye for the wedding. I had been training with the Glen on the Friday beforehand and I got a bang in training. Great timing, but what can you do? Poor Margaret, she has to put up with a lot from me.

BEFORE MARGARET AND I married, I was still living in Madden's Buildings. After my father died, I moved back in with my Mam when Catherine moved away. The main reason for that was because my mother was on her own and was lonely in the house. But my Aunt Lily, who had been living in Farranree, was also ready to move into Nan's house with her. As a blood relative the house would go to Lily when Nan died, but only if she was living there. All the houses were corporation houses and if you didn't occupy them, you'd lose them, which would be a disaster.

Margaret and I had bought a house in Blackrock. It was strange looking back that we were able to buy a house because I had no savings at all, I was only 24. And I was probably only 23 when I bought the house in Berlingford Drive. It was a brand new house, a builder from Mayo had built about 20 houses there – right beside the Blackrock hurling club, ironically.

Those days you could get a mortgage from the City Hall and it was £3,300 to buy the house. A three-bedroom, semi-detached house in Blackrock, and the mortgage was £23 per month. I was getting paid between £4,000 and £5,000 a year that time so when you think of how much cheaper a house was those days, it's amazing really and Margaret was working too.

Funnily enough, we decided to move five years later, in 1975. And in only five years the value of the house in Blackrock had gone up to £12,000 – it had almost quadrupled in value in only five years. Amazing when you think about it. We saw a lovely American-style bungalow – one of three just built – in Carrigtwohill and bought one of those for £16,000 and our repayments went from £23 a month to £80 a month, almost four times the amount.

Money and houses aside, I was the happiest man in the world. I thought that all my dreams had come true, and I was right. Having Margaret by my side was all I'd ever wanted, all I could ever have imagined.

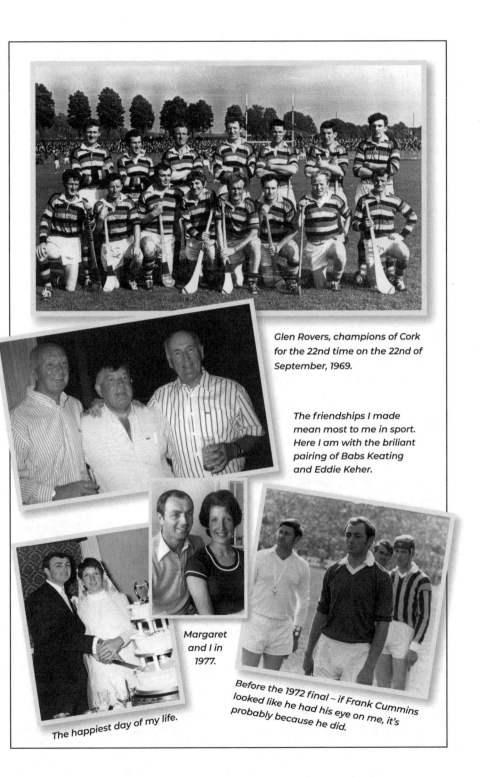

Glen Rovers, champions of Cork for the 22nd time on the 22nd of September, 1969.

The friendships I made mean most to me in sport. Here I am with the briliant pairing of Babs Keating and Eddie Keher.

Margaret and I in 1977.

The happiest day of my life.

Before the 1972 final – if Frank Cummins looked like he had his eye on me, it's probably because he did.

« CHAPTER 6 »

Sport Life Balance

IN AUGUST 1968, ABOUT a month after Glen Rovers pulled out of all competitions, a man called Amby Fogarty contacted me. He had played soccer for Sunderland and Ireland, and he was the manager of Cork Hibernians at the time. And when he got hold of me – I can't remember how – he asked me would I play for Cork Hibs.

Now I had never played soccer and I put this to him when we spoke.

He said he knew that but he saw me playing in the Munster football final against Kerry in July and he felt that I would make a good soccer player. He went further (I realise he was trying to persuade me to play) and said that with his own connections in Sunderland, he would have me playing professionally in England within 12 months.

So, he badgered me, really, into playing a pre-season soccer match for Cork Hibernians against St Patrick's Athletic, down in Flower Lodge. Now, even though the Glen's decision meant there was no hurling or football at the time and I didn't know when or if there would be again, I had serious misgivings about playing in that pre-season game. I said I'd play on one condition, not thinking for a moment that Amby would agree to it. I said I would play if they closed the gates – if I could play behind closed doors with nobody watching. I was shocked when he agreed to that and then, of course, I had to go through with it. I'd given my word.

So, I went down to the Boreenmanna Road and played in the soccer match for Hibs. But I had three dilemmas. Firstly, I was afraid that the Glen and St Nicks would hear about it – I'd be killed if that happened. Secondly, I was afraid the county board would find out – if they did, they would throw the book at me, especially because I was from Glen Rovers and they were in dispute with the Glen.

But my biggest dilemma – and this sounds strange, but it's true – was getting my football boots out of the house to play in the game. And this is why. My father used to clean and polish my boots before every game I played. I never had to do that myself even though I was well into my twenties now. It was something my father wanted to do and I didn't want to take it from him. Sometimes it was actually an embarrassment because my boots would always be beyond clean – shining – when I'd take them out in the dressing-room and I'd often get a bit of a slagging about that.

And after I played in Flower Lodge, I lived in fear from that evening on that my father would hear about it. Which of course – Cork being Cork – he did. About two weeks after the game my father came in from work one night, from the 2 to 10 shift and I was sitting inside in the kitchen with my mother. In he arrived about a quarter past 10 and he was looking at me and he said, 'Come here, did you play a soccer match for Cork Hibernians?'

And I said, 'No, Dad, I didn't… why?'

'They were saying it below in the brewery,' he said, 'that you did.'

'But I haven't used my boots since the Glen match against UCC.'

'That's what I told them. "Sure his boots are still there, how could he have played a game?" They said you did… well they *heard* that you did.'

'No,' says I, 'I didn't… It wasn't me, anyway.'

And it would be very rarely now I didn't tell the truth to my father. To be honest, I nearly died. And to be fair to my father, after that conversation, as far as he was concerned, the match never happened, that was an end to it.

Of course, then it got out to the newspapers, but only that I'd been approached by Hibs. There was one article that a Cork footballer had been training with Hibs and showed promise – but they didn't name the player. Then it was put to me and I had to publicly deny that I was moving to soccer – which was true – and the newspapers had a bit of a field day with that for a while. But it never got out about the match I had played behind closed doors. Nor did my father ever mention it again; the poor man was dead in two months, anyway.

I HAD TO laugh when I saw an article in the *Sunday Times* a few years later in February, 1971. Amby had fallen out with Hibs and he moved to Drumcondra. And he said that he hoped it would be easier to attract local talent in Dublin than in Cork. He said, 'For one thing it should be easier to get local players without meeting the GAA Ban opposition like we did in Cork. I had one boy who wanted to sign but his father wouldn't let him.' [I may have used that excuse, but I can't honestly remember. Maybe it was a different player.]

It gets better. He also said, 'Doors were slammed in my face because boys were afraid neighbours would see them and report it to the Glen.' I had to laugh at that.

In truth I don't really know how I did in the game itself against St Pat's. Because I knew I was never going to play for Hibs and give up hurling and football, I played with abandon and I just tried to enjoy it. Flower Lodge was a lovely pitch to play on and Hibs had some great players at the time. To be honest, I would have had to leave Ireland, let alone Cork, if I was to take up soccer in 1968 and that was never going to happen.

◄◄◆►►

ANOTHER THING ALSO happened in 1968 when the Glen and St Nicks pulled out of the championship. There was suddenly no training, no matches – nothing – and that was very strange for us, it felt wrong. And by sheer accident in the Glen Hall didn't we find a few badminton rackets and a shuttle in a cupboard there.

We had never seen badminton rackets before; we didn't even know what they were. But we started playing – we were desperate for something to do. And we formed a badminton team and began to play other teams. In fact, the Glen premises – which had been built and completed in 1953/54 – was ideally suited to indoor sports such as badminton. They often had bingo there, too, and it could seat up to 1,000 people for concerts – which they used to have during Lent, because dancing was not allowed during Lent. Those were the days!

We really began playing badminton just to keep ourselves occupied in 1968. We weren't used to being idle, we had never been idle in our lives. But soon we were hooked – we loved it. A great thing about badminton is that it is a mixed sport, so we put together a team of four men and four ladies, got some coaching, and off we went. Another great thing was that the Ban didn't cover badminton for some strange reason.

Within four years – 1969 to '72 – we had won the Cork badminton championship at minor (any age), junior, intermediate, and senior levels. It was unheard of at the time. And the team consisted of all lads from the Glen, all hurlers. Finbarr O'Neill, Tom Buckley, George Murphy, Pat Horgan, Paudie McCarthy and myself. Plus, the ladies who were all hockey and camogie players. Some of us played badminton at inter-county level, for Cork, while Pat Horgan went on to play at international level for Ireland – a great honour. We played in all the open championships throughout Munster in singles, doubles and mixed-doubles. I came across many other hurlers and footballers playing badminton on my travels, which was lovely – including the great Jimmy Doyle and his brother Paddy (both beautiful players) at a Munster championship event.

When Margaret and I got married and started our family, I had to give it up – it wasn't physically possible to keep it going. But I loved badminton.

◄ ◄ ◆ ► ►

I STARTED SQUASH seriously in 1976, when I was winding down from football. I just loved the competitiveness of it and I would play four times a week those days without any trouble whatsoever – I enjoyed it that much.

Funny thing is that one of the first squash lessons I got was from Christy Ring, who was a great player – it just goes to show how many areas of my life he influenced. His games with Eamonn Young were legendary and although he was 25 years older than me, he was still very competitive and still had great strength in his wrists. He played in the Orchard Club, in Ballinlough, as did I.

Squash was the opposite of badminton in the sense that you could plan your game – it was far more family-friendly, especially in terms of home life. You could play a quick game for 40 minutes after work at 5pm in the Orchard or someplace nearby and be home by six.

I continued playing squash very actively after my county hurling career wound up. In a way it was like another career for me and it gave me great satisfaction. When we moved house to Carrigtwohill we played for Watermans Squash Club.

Squash courts were being built all over Cork at the time, it was very popular and growing rapidly.

Eventually we ended up in The Sunday's Well Club, and I have to say that I've probably got as much if not more enjoyment out of squash as I did from hurling and football. I absolutely loved it.

Margaret was a brilliant squash player, and we used to pass like ships in the night because we had a young family when we were most active at the game. So, for example, I could play a game at 5pm and be home by six. Margaret might have a game then and she'd head out and I'd mind the children.

Squash is a very sociable sport and we were also part of teams and that could get quite competitive. There were seven divisions of squash players to ensure you'd be playing against opponents at your own level. The highest I ever got was the second division, which was quite a high standard. Margaret played first division and she went on to play at Inter Pro, representing Munster, which is one of the highest standards you can reach. And although there weren't any mixed games, it was lovely to be in the same club as her and, at least at some level, to be sharing a sport with her.

I played squash for over 25 years, into the 1990s. Then I hurt my knee and I couldn't really play pain-free any more so I had to say a reluctant goodbye to the game. From then on golf took over.

I had been playing golf in the 1980s and a business colleague, Ted Dwyer was coming in as captain of Cork Golf Club. He encouraged me to apply for membership and I did, and I was accepted. And I'm still there to this day almost 40 years later.

Cork is an excellent golf course and a great club. I became club captain myself in 2001 which was a great honour and I enjoyed it thoroughly. And, of course, Margaret is a very keen golfer and she became lady captain in 2009 so we both feel that we've done our bit in terms of giving back to the club, considering how much we have gotten from it over all those years.

We have made so many friends and have had so many wonderful experiences, and such a great time golfing.

It's very fulfilling and very good for your mental health to be part of a community and a golf club is a great community. I can't speak highly enough of Cork Golf Club, it's a wonderful club full of wonderful people.

BESIDES MY GAME for Cork Hibs at the insistence of Amby Fogarty in 1968, I had another soccer experience – a more enjoyable one, if I'm honest. St Mary's AFC is a well-known junior soccer club in the north side of Cork and a lot of their players and supporters would also be connected with the Glen and St Nicks. And there was one particular family involved in St Mary's in my time: the Geaneys.

Michael 'Baba' Geaney was a very good soccer player in his day – he played League of Ireland and in the early 70s he was one of the main people running St Mary's. He was a great supporter of the Glen too, and I used to meet him and some of his family at matches. And he'd often be on to me to play for St Mary's when there wasn't any hurling or football in the winter.

That time I was living off Church Road and there were some soccer pitches right there, just across from the Blackrock Club grounds. And if I had nothing to do on a Sunday morning in the winter, I used to go over there and watch a junior soccer match or two. They had brilliant games with big crowds watching them on Sunday mornings, generating a fantastic buzz.

Eventually, Baba talked me into playing a game. It must have been 1972 or '73 – after the Ban was lifted in 1971, anyway. And it was probably in January, when I didn't have any GAA matches. When I look back at how much I loved those winter breaks, I realise how badly I was overdoing it with all the matches I was playing.

At the time there was a famous referee, Eddie Mullins who used to officiate at games in Cork. He was a League of Ireland referee for many years and he refereed at international level, too. Eddie had a very deep voice and he was a great character, full of personality. He was in total control of the game at all times.

There were four pitches in this complex and I'm sure a lot of the people there would watch whatever game Eddie was refereeing, no matter who was playing. He was that entertaining. And, of course, spectators would also join in the banter. For some reason the interaction between supporters and players was always better at soccer matches than GAA. Maybe it's something to do with the pace of the game or the proximity of the spectators. And with this particular referee the craic was absolutely brilliant – you'd be splitting your sides. Eddie always had control over that, too, you couldn't ruffle him; he was like an experienced stand-up comic dealing with hecklers.

There's a famous story about Eddie refereeing a match at one of the old pitches in Blackpool. One day a player was giving out to him, disagreeing about some decision. Eddie gave him the eye and said, 'Player! Come over here!'

He would never walk towards a player; you would have to go to him. So, the player goes over.

'What's your name?' says Eddie taking out his book.

'Roy,' says the player.

'Roy who?'

'Roy Rodgers.'

'Is that so?' booms Eddie, the whole place delighted with the show. 'Well, Roy, hop up on your horse Trigger there like a good lad and trot off to the corral. You're gone.'

So, I togged off for St Mary's anyway on Church Road and I was playing in the old position of inside right. At one point, St Mary's got a free kick about 30 yards out and I can still hear Baba shouting from the line… 'Denis, you take that!'

Over I went and placed the ball, and I took the free. I was used to taking frees in football but of course there's a wall in soccer, but I managed to lift it over the wall and score. Roof of the net.

Well if I did, Eddie Mullins took a good look at me – he probably knew who I was too, but he wouldn't let on. His big deep voice reverberated around the grounds, 'Player! Take that again.'

Of course, all the St Mary's mentors, fans and players erupted, but Eddie wasn't having any of it. 'Take it again,' shouts Eddie and blows the whistle. He didn't give any reason either; his word was law, no matter what dogs' abuse he was getting from the sidelines.

So, I had to take it again and, lo and behold, didn't I do the same thing – roof of the net. And the place went ballistic. Eddie was caught – he couldn't disallow the goal twice. He looked over to the Guineys on the sideline and boomed, 'Where did you get that player?'

I ALSO HAD a short stint playing rugby. Barry McGann, the Irish rugby international, was living beside us in Blackrock in 1972. Even with all my matches, being a dual player and everything, I still had time off in the winter.

Barry invited me up to Cork Constitution to do some training and I went there with him – it was only over the road. Before I knew it, I was playing rugby with Cork Con – some junior matches. And I really enjoyed it. Eventually wasn't I picked for the senior team and by now, it was getting a bit close to the resumption of the National Leagues when I'd have to go back playing hurling and football. The senior match was against Young Munster in Limerick and I think I was a bit relieved to have to tell Barry that I couldn't play because I had a hurling match the same day. Playing against Young Munster was a serious proposition and maybe I wasn't quite ready for the physicality of that.

To be honest, my favourite sport to watch as a child was rugby. If I went to a different school I'd have played rugby, I'm sure. Before I became too well known to be recognised, I used to go to Irish international rugby matches in Lansdowne Road – when I was old enough to afford them – but I had to stop doing that when I began to play for Cork.

◄ ◄ ◆ ► ►

MUSIC IS SOMETHING else that has given me so much joy and has greatly enriched my life. I suppose my love of music traces back to my family; my father playing the gadget and the sing-songs that we used to have in the kitchen. And, as I said, it was part of my primary school experience, too. So, at an early age, I became proficient and comfortable singing, either as part of a group or on my own. It doesn't matter if you are a great singer or not (I'm not); as long as you are happy to stand up and you know a song; it gives you a lot of satisfaction, and that has stayed with me all through my life.

I am involved in two gramophone societies, one in Cork Golf Club and one in Collins's Barracks. There are many of these societies all over Cork and several are attached to public libraries. The one in Collins's Barracks has about 40 people, and Margaret and I have been members for about 30 years. At each gathering (maybe once a month or once every two months), one of the members presents a show or a piece of music, says something about it and everybody listens to it. Everybody gets a turn but it might only be once every few years. You learn a lot about the music and the people from these talks and it really enhances your appreciation of it.

Music is very personal and it's so subjective that I think the type of music you like really reveals the type of person you are. The character of the people in the groups really comes out in their choice of music and while you learn a lot about the music, you also learn a lot about the people too – which is so interesting.

These events are really enjoyable, and I've got so much pleasure out of them over the years. My own favourite type of music is light opera – not the heavy serious opera. The kind of music that you hear from Pavarotti and Andrea Bocelli and the Three Tenors.

I also have a great love of poetry and I don't really know where this came from. But I find myself composing poetry in my head, I don't know why. And I'm part of a group of about 18 people and once a month we come together in Leo and Anne Brownen's home and we listen to poetry, and people will read poems by famous poets or by themselves. From time to time, I do write down my poetry but I never show it to anyone and I probably never will. But music and poetry have enriched my life more than I can say.

◄ ◄ ◆ ► ►

I'M 75 NOW and obviously well on in years, but I'm trying to be as active and involved as I can be. I play a bit of golf and go for a walk with our dog, Frasier up the Glen and I always looked after myself as best I could with my diet and habits. I was a Pioneer until the summer of 1979 and I'm still fairly abstemious and I eat well. I've never put on weight and I don't eat much sweet food.

But like most things in life, you have to work at keeping your health. It doesn't get easier as you get older and, of course, COVID-19 was a big scare for everyone over 70 and we had to conform to special safety measures. But when you get older you have to protect your mental health as much as your physical well-being. Volunteering, staying in touch, meeting people, getting involved and getting out as much as possible are vital. That's why clubs – of whatever kind – are so important to people, including the elderly. They provide a great local outlet and source of well-being.

In 2019 I became involved in the 'How to Age Well' campaign, which was an initiative by the GAA, TILDA and Irish Life. TILDA is The Irish Longitudinal Study on Ageing – a large-scale, nationally representative, longitudinal study on ageing in Ireland, the overarching aim of which is to make Ireland the best place in the world to grow old.

And, because it was about health and well-being, I was immediately interested – this is something I have always felt strongly about. When I was asked to be an ambassador for the programme I immediately said yes. I was one of five ambassadors – representatives, essentially – from the world of Gaelic games. I went to the launch of the GAA involvement in the programme in Croke Park and myself and the other ambassadors also visited Trinity College, where we learned about the work of Professor Rose Anne Kenny, who heads up TILDA.

The other ambassadors are: Claire Egan, former Mayo footballer; Mícheál Ó Muircheartaigh, legendary commentator; Anthony Molloy, former Donegal footballer (who captained Donegal to their first ever All-Ireland in 1992); Maria Devenney, another former Donegal footballer; and Eamonn Rea, the former Limerick hurler.

Then there was a series of seven seminars on 'How to Age Well' held around Ireland, one of which was in Cork and I was happy to speak at that. It was very well attended, with over 200 delegates. It was great to be involved in something positive around ageing, being active into old age – something we all have to face, if we're lucky, and something I'm certainly facing into now, as best I can.

Cherish and protect your health – it's everything.

SPORT IS NO guarantee to well-being – on the contrary, it can be damaging if it's not done in a well-adjusted way. I think it's a shame these days that many elite sportspeople can't achieve a better balance in the games they play. They are not experiencing anything like I had with badminton, squash, soccer, rugby and later, golf. Their schedule doesn't allow it. It seems that every part of their day and their lives is monitored and only relates to their one sport. This is really unhealthy, in my opinion.

Hurling and football are great but, if overdone, they can be damaging to your welfare. I think the games have completely taken over players' lives to the detriment of everything else. If they're not training or playing games, they're in the gym with specific activities for their single sport. Dual players are a thing of the past – even at club level, players are specialising younger and younger. If you're a good young hurler, it's hurling, hurling, hurling and nothing else. If you're a good footballer, it's football, football, football and nothing else.

As a result, these young people are missing out on so much. Where is the sport life balance in that, and where will it end? It has stepped outside reality a bit and the obsession with status and winning is, frankly, bizarre. I'm reading a lot about the mental health concerns of players and that simply should not be the case. When I hear of young county players (men or women) giving up their jobs to concentrate on sport, it really worries me. Sport is there to enhance our lives, it isn't meant to be our lives.

And it's not good for the games either, or for the future of our sport. The dropout for young people playing hurling and football used to be between 18 and 21, but now it's between 14 and 16 and I can understand why. There is something seriously wrong happening here and I'm not sure the direction the games are going in is in the best interest of either hurling or football, or the young people involved.

Meeting Jimmy Doyle at the 1983 All-Ireland final, a great friend and hero.

The Glen Rovers badminton team, in white instead of green, black and gold.

TILDA ambassadors (from left) Eamonn Rea, Claire Egan, Maria Devenney, Anthony Molloy and myself at the 'How to Age Well: GAA and TILDA Partnership' launch at Croke Park in Dublin, 2019.

« CHAPTER 7 »

A Bit of a Rest

IN 1972 THE GLEN won the county again – our 23rd title. We went on to win the Munster club championship and then an 'unofficial' All-Ireland club championship, which was continued on into 1973.

Because of the 1972 Munster final sending off I missed a Glen Rovers match in the quarter-final of the county championship against Muskerry in Bandon. And in my entire 20 years of playing senior hurling with the Glen I think it may have been the only match I missed through injury or for any other reason.

We beat Muskerry in a tight match and then we played St Finbarr's in the semi-final and I was back for that. I think it was the week after we lost the All-Ireland final to Kilkenny. The Barrs had a brilliant team at the time; they had Charlie McCarthy and Gerald McCarthy, and Con Roche. Jimmy Barry Murphy might have been playing senior by then, too, even if he was only 18.

I was centrefield and I was marking Gerald which was strange because we were teammates the previous week against Kilkenny, but that's the way it is in sport. Your best friend can become your worst enemy on the day when it comes to such local rivalries.

Our win against St Finbarr's in 1972 was unexpected and the newspapers the following day were full of surprise. But the Glen never feared any team in championships, we knew on our day that we could match the best of them. Players like Denis O'Riordan, George O'Riordan, Jerry O'Sullivan, Joe Joe O'Neill, Ted

O'Brien and my midfield partner, Don Lynch could be as good as anyone on their day. The weather was bad for that match; it was windy and the Barrs played with a gale force wind in the first-half. The teams were level 1-3 each at half-time, Pat Doherty – the Limerick man – having scored our goal. They only got two points in the second-half and we won 1-8 to 1-5.

This win ensured that we were firm favourites in the final against Youghal, who had come through on the other side of the draw. We didn't underestimate Youghal; they had a very good team. They had Seanie O'Leary and Willie Walsh, who was possibly the best centre-forward in Ireland. He was the ideal centre-forward. They had Noel Gallagher, who played with Cork in the 60s and Robbie O'Sullivan, who played junior hurling with Cork. They also had Pat Hegarty, Willie Doyle and their goalkeeper, Pat Barry was excellent, too.

The match was played on the 12th of November and it was certainly no walkover. Jackie Daly, our coach, had us very focused – I do recall that. In fact, Youghal were leading in the middle of the second-half but we were able to overtake them and hold out until the final whistle. Patsy Harte was captain that year, so he had the honour of accepting the cup.

Now, at that time I think the Glen had a record that we never went three years without winning a county championship. We had won it in 1969 and then we were beaten in 1970 and '71 so it was good to win it again in '72. But while such records are there to be broken, you don't want it happening on your watch and we were always very conscious of the great history of Glen Rovers and the tradition that it was now our responsibility to uphold.

The win was a huge personal boost for me. After losing the All-Ireland final to Kilkenny in September, it was lovely to be on the winning side again and to close out 1972 with another county championship for the Glen.

We went on to play Roscrea in the Munster club final in Limerick and that was held in the following calendar year, in 1973, on April 23rd. That was a typical Cork versus Tipperary match – there was certainly no quarter asked for or given. I was playing centrefield and coming towards half-time I distinctly heard a mentor from Roscrea say something to my marker.

He said, 'You have five minutes to do what we told you to do.'

I had a fair idea what he meant by that stage because my marker was playing a good bit of the man and not the ball. But now I knew he was doing it under instructions. Anyway, they mustn't have been happy with him because he didn't come out for the second-half, which suited me just fine. I was delighted to score the first and last point of the game – the last being especially important because it put us two up.

The game was incredibly close; the teams were level five times during the hour. Francis Loughnane had a goal called back for a free in the first-half, which was lucky for us. We had the wind behind us in the second-half and we just hung on, 2-9 to 1-10. It was a great relief. Roscrea were excellent – they really were – and had won the All-Ireland club championship in 1970, so we knew what we were up against. For us, Mick O'Halloran and Teddy O'Brien were brilliant in defence; Liam McAuliffe, Pat Doherty and Patsy Harte were outstanding up front.

AT THE CONCLUSION of the game the presentation of the cup was just about to take place, and, since I was now captain for 1973, it was up to me to accept it – a great honour. At that moment, Christy Ring saw Mick Mackey on the pitch and he called him over and, instead of the chairman of the Munster Council, Mick presented the cup to me. You can imagine the pride I felt, to be presented a cup by one of the greatest hurlers of all time.

But I do regret that I don't have a photograph of the presentation, or a photograph of me with Christy Ring and Mick Mackey on that day in 1973. It's one of my very few regrets in sport.

This was also my first time captaining the Glen Rovers senior team so it was a great thrill because my previous experiences as captain (and some future experiences) were not so happy. I would go on to captain the club again in 1980 and I consider myself very fortunate to have done so.

We played Castlegar in the All-Ireland semi-final and we won by a large margin. The final, against St Rynagh's of Offaly, was supposed to be played in September or October of 1973, but it ended up not taking place until the second week in December. There was a dispute between St Rynagh's and either Croke Park or the Offaly County Board. Whatever the rights of that, it was decided to award the All-Ireland title to Glen Rovers but we refused to accept it and insisted on the game going ahead. The game was unique in that it was the first and only time the two clubs have ever met, and quite a small crowd turned out for the final on a cold mid-winter day in Croke Park.

St Rynagh's had won many Offaly county championships over those years. Pad Joe Whelahan (Brian's father) was playing for them – I was marking him. They had Padraig Horan and Barney Moylan as well. All those players had represented Offaly and Leinster many times in the 1970s – formidable opponents.

My friend, Finbarr O'Neill made some great saves in the first-half and we crept ahead and stayed there. St Rynagh's had a good few wides and our free-taker, Tommy Buckley hit a great run of form, he scored 1-9 in all, and 0-6 from frees. Patsy Harte got another goal, Red Crowley and Mick Ryan scored some great points and we were delighted to win by 2-18 to 2-8.

So, I got to receive an All-Ireland cup in Croke Park after all, and how fitting that I did so on behalf of my beloved Glen Rovers, in the famous green, black and gold jersey. That was a good day. Glen Rovers had won their first All-Ireland championship, adding to past glories. The fact that we, as a group of players, had upheld the great tradition of the Glen gave us a special pride on that December day in 1973.

Because, in Glen Rovers, tradition is everything.

ONE THING ABOUT club hurling or football is that it brings you back down to earth if you are an inter-county player. You lose your importance immediately when you go back to play with your club – everybody is equal and everybody is in it together. And this comes out very much at Annual General Meetings (AGMs) which usually take place late in the calendar year.

I have one very vivid memory of a Glen Rovers AGM which took place in the 1960s when I was still a young player. At the AGM, people were selected for all the club roles for the following year, from the chairman down. Those days much of this was decided on the night, but nowadays almost everything is all agreed in advance and the AGM rubber-stamps it to a certain degree. But more than one man would be nominated for positions those days and there would be a vote then to select who would get the role.

On that AGM night in the 60s, much to my surprise, I was nominated to be club captain for the following season. Along with four or five other players. I was shocked because I didn't think I was senior enough or mature enough compared to the other nominees who were all well-established players and a good bit older. And I stood up and I withdrew my name at the meeting.

I thought no more about it and I was happy enough I had done the right thing until I was coming out the door afterwards and a man took me by the elbow. I turned and who was it only Christy Ring.

He said, 'Don't ever do that again.'

'Do what?' I said.

'Don't withdraw your name if you are nominated for something at the AGM,' he said. 'This club is built on people wanting to be captain and to serve it in whatever way they can. In my day Lynch and Young and everyone else would contest for the captaincy of the Glen and we don't ever want that tradition to be lost.'

I never forgot those words. They left their mark on me. And if I was ever proposed in the following years – and some years I was, and I was not selected – I never withdrew my name again. And when I was selected as captain for 1973 and for '80 I accepted it graciously and served the club as well as I possibly could.

FROM A VERY early age I was well aware of what Glen Rovers meant to Blackpool, my home. I remember my father taking me up to the clubhouse one evening as a child. Even though my father didn't play for the club, a brother-in-law of his, Jack Leahy was a member of the very first Glen Rovers team to win the county championship in 1934, and he was a selector afterwards. He brought my father and myself in to see the new Glen Hall that had just been built in 1954. I was only nine years-old. It may have been the official opening but whatever the occasion it made a big impression on me. I never forgot it.

And I would have been aware, too, of the reverence in their voices in the way that my father and other men talked about the great Glen Rovers heroes like Paddy 'Fox' Collins, Paddy O'Connell, Charlie Tobin, Jack Lynch, John Lyons, Christy Ring and others. I knew about the great eight in-a-row team of the 30s and 40s, and how Ring had taken over the mantle of Lynch and all of that. It made a huge impression on me as a child and I was very mindful of the great history and traditions of the Glen.

Another thing I was very conscious of was that you had respect for the people who were older than you, who had gone before you and who served the club before you did. That was very much part of the culture of Glen Rovers and Saint Nicholas. Those people from earlier times were greatly esteemed and, in some cases, revered. Whether they were players or mentors or officials – they were all volunteers and that volunteerism was at the heart and soul of the club. In fact, it's what makes clubs so great and so important to cherish and protect.

And that was what Christy Ring was trying to get through to me on that night of the AGM in the 1960s.

◄◄◆►►

WE LOST THE Munster football final to Kerry in 1972 but it was a very good match in Killarney and I felt that this Cork team was heading in the right direction. I scored 1-1 that day, the goal coming from a penalty. Although I was still playing in the back line for St Nicks, I was more or less established as a forward for Cork by this time.

In 1973 our first game was the Munster semi-final against Clare in the Athletic Grounds in June and I was picked at wing-forward. I didn't play particularly well and I failed to score. I had to go to England for two weeks prior to that match on business and I trained on my own over there (not in Old Trafford this time). But I had to do a lot of driving around Liverpool and Aintree, and it was stressful. I do remember being genuinely tired for that game, from the travelling and the long journey home. Luckily, we won the game very easily, 2-14 to 0-3, but I was picked at centrefield for the Munster final against Kerry in The Athletic Grounds.

In 1973 we had a very strategic approach to matches and it was a bit ahead of its time. I remember in that Munster final, for example, we targeted the Kerry full-back, Paud O'Donoghue. He was a great full-back and a lovely man, quite a colourful character in his own way, and he was captain of Kerry in '73. But we put Ray Cummins in corner-forward instead of full-forward and Paud followed him there.

Jimmy Barry Murphy (who was on the team for his first year – he had come straight in from the minors, I think) played full-forward and his movement completely unsettled the Kerry full-back line and opened it up for us. As a result, we scored five goals the same day which was very unusual and it killed them, especially in the first-half when most of the damage was done. Jimmy Barrett scored two; Declan Barron, Jimmy Barry Murphy and Billy Field scored one apiece.

Myself and Denis Long dominated midfield, especially in the first-half against John O'Keeffe and Donal Kavanagh. I remember that distinctly. So much so that they moved Jackie Walsh on me after 28 minutes (this was an 80-minute game, remember). We were 12 points up at half-time before Kerry rallied (which, of course, being Kerry, they did) and they dragged it back to a mere three points – a kick of a ball. But we pulled away again, winning by 5-12 to 1-15.

The Munster final in '73 was a very sweet win, all the more so for having happened in Cork, and our fans really enjoyed it. Kerry were National League champions and they were in good shape with a very strong team. The win really set us up for the All-Ireland series and for once we were in no way happy enough to be 'just' Munster champions. Billy Morgan, as captain, drummed it into us that we had to go all the way, it was long overdue.

TOO OFTEN WHEN we beat Kerry in the Munster final (and I was lucky enough to have done this five times out of the nine finals I played in) we sat back on our laurels. Everything was geared in Cork to beating Kerry because they dominated us so much over so many years. It was as if that was our All-Ireland and it didn't matter what happened afterwards. I think Cork definitely under-achieved in football All-Ireland championships. We had a completely different mentality from the hurlers who would never be happy with a Munster title alone and would always want to go the whole way to September.

There was a seismic change that year in the football set-up and the approach. I really felt it and it came about because Nemo Rangers won their first ever county championship in 1972. Denis McDonnell from Nemo came in as a selector and to run the team, and he really broke the mould in terms of that attitude.

It was an open secret up to now that – at county level – footballers were effectively second-class citizens in comparison to hurlers in Cork. The board didn't treat them with parity of esteem at all. This would have manifested itself in many ways; for example, the food that footballers got after training would be inferior to what the hurlers got. And, as somebody who had played both hurling and football for Cork, I can attest to that. The footballers might get a sandwich while the hurlers got a hot and nutritious meal. Which was ironic because the footballers often had to travel much farther and had a longer journey home to West Cork than many of the city-based hurlers.

Well, in 1973 that all ended, and it was about time, and I have to give great credit to Nemo and to Denis McDonnell for that. Denis also went for Donie

O'Donovan from St Nicks as the coach and that was also very innovative – there was a real change in 1973 in terms of how the footballers approached things. Billy Morgan was a huge factor, too – he had trained in physical fitness instruction in Strawberry Hill in London and he brought a new type of analysing games and planning that we had not really seen before. A new way of preparing and thinking about how best to prepare.

There was a great improvement in atmosphere within the camp too, and Donie O'Donovan must take a lot of credit for that – he really had a great way with the players and it didn't matter who you were. I had been involved in the football set-up since 1965 and I really felt in '73 the sense of purpose and focus was at a much higher level. It made all the difference in the end. Attitude is almost everything in sport, it really is.

When you look at it, Kerry and Kilkenny have won far more All–Irelands than they should have. What is that down to? It's down to attitude, to approach. They feel they should be winning them, and so they make it happen – they find ways to make it happen. The Cork football set-up had that attitude and approach in 1973. I feel I should mention the other selectors of the 1973 football team too, who are often forgotten: Derry Gowan, Mick McCarthy, Seán Crowley and Paddy O'Driscoll.

We scored another five goals in the All-Ireland semi-final against Tyrone. That was a damp, dour day but our football lit up Croke Park. We had a great set of forwards that year. They all combined really well, so that if you could manage to mark two or three of them, the other three or four would still do fierce damage. Scoring 10 goals in two games of football was almost unprecedented in those days against top class opposition, even in 80-minute games, but we managed it. And we got another three goals in the final against Galway. Jimmy Barry-Murphy scored five goals alone in three matches that summer. He may have been very young, but when you're a genius age doesn't matter.

I CONTINUED TO play away for St Nicks and the Glen that summer but it very nearly cost me. The Glen (and I was captain in 1973) had a rip-roaring county semi-final against St Finbarr's on the 8th of July. That's a week before the Munster football final. Four players were sent off that day and Con Roche scored a last minute free for the Barrs to draw the match.

I escaped injury (barely) and I was able to play against Kerry in our great win. But I did seriously injure myself in a St Nicks game three weeks before the Tyrone All-Ireland semi-final. I fell badly and tore ligaments in my right shoulder. I had to have a lot of heat treatment and massage to get fit enough to play against Tyrone, with the help of a pain-killing injection. The following Sunday the Glen had our replay against the Barrs. As captain there was no way I was missing that.

This time only two players were sent off but I ended up in the wars. I tore the ligaments in my shoulder joint, got a chipped bone in my right elbow and got a nice slap in my nose for good measure. I had to go off after 20 minutes because of the elbow injury.

I wasn't worried about the nose – as Christy Ring once said to Seanie O'Leary, 'Nobody ever won an All-Ireland with his nose'. But the shoulder and the chipped bone were a real concern; there was every chance I wouldn't make the team for the All-Ireland final against Galway on September 23rd. Elbow injuries are notoriously slow to heal. But an X-ray gave me some good news and, though my preparation was seriously curtailed, I made it to the final.

In the final Cork had to wear white jerseys because Galway's maroon was so similar to our own red – especially on black and white televisions which was what people had those days. That's a stand-out thing about the 1973 All-Ireland football final and people still say it to me to this day. There was a toss-up to see who would wear their own colours and Cork lost – hence the white jerseys.

The attention to detail was so great for the Cork footballers in '73 that we didn't just want to play on the day in all white, we wanted to train in those colours, too. That's the level of innovation and progressive thinking that goes into winning an All-Ireland. But we didn't have a white set, so we ended up training in the Tyrone jerseys. They actually sent down their gear for us to train in, which was very impressive, given we had just beaten them in the semi-final. Can you imagine that happening nowadays?

I have seen photographs of us training in those Tyrone jerseys – I vividly remember the bright red hand of Ulster on the crest during training sessions, it's amazing the little details you retain, decades later. And whether or not such innovations actually helped us gain an edge on Galway, it built confidence and helped us to believe that we could.

A sense of excitement wrapped itself about the team and fired the build-up to the final. Our forward line in particular was so good and getting so many brilliant scores, there was a great feeling of expectation and optimism – belief, really. And that excitement was especially strong in the traditionally football areas of the county which are different from the hurling areas.

We hadn't been in a final for six years, and we hadn't won a final for 28 years – the longest time ever that Cork had gone without winning a football title. There were three of us left from the 1967 team: Frank Cogan, Billy Morgan and myself were the last relics. Having been captain in '67 I definitely wanted to right that wrong, and Billy being captain in '73 wanted it badly, too.

Whatever about the level of confidence in the county, the panel were certainly not over-confident. And, given my experience on the previous September against Kilkenny (and on other occasions) I was certainly not over-confident. I was 28 now, and I probably would not have many other opportunities to win an All-Ireland medal. We all knew how good Galway were, too.

I remember asking Billy Morgan a question on the final night of training. We were in the old Victoria Hotel in the city centre having something to eat. And I was sitting beside Billy and I was nervous and I asked him straight out, 'Do you think we will win on Sunday, Billy?' That's not a question you would really ask and I think it was the first time I had ever asked a teammate a question like that.

And he looked me straight in the eye and said, 'I do'. You know, it had a remarkable effect on me. It really calmed me down for some reason and helped me to believe more, and I was very grateful for it afterwards.

In the final I was marking Jimmy Duggan, who was one of the best footballers I ever saw. I was assigned to mark him – that was my job, essentially, for 80 minutes. But I have to say that to my great relief and joy I played well throughout the game; I really did my bit for the team. And the truth is that when you do play well, it makes the victory all the sweeter.

Dinny Long was a brilliant partner at centrefield, I can't give him enough credit. He did most of the attacking work of the partnership and I did a more defensive role and it worked very well for us both.

We also had another major incentive for that final. The esteemed Weeshie Murphy had given the team talk before the Tyrone game, and had spoken on behalf of the 1945 team – the last Cork team to win an All-Ireland. How it was time to pass the mantle on and how we were the men destined to wear it once more. Weeshie died suddenly two weeks before the final and so he never got to see Cork as All-Ireland football champions again. But he was there in spirit with us, that was for sure, and we felt his presence.

And – though perhaps I would say this – it was actually a very good game of football. It had everything. It was the type of football that people enjoy most. A simple, pure game. When you have the ball, you go forward; you attack, you pass and you shoot. Gaelic football at its best, really. Kicking, fast flowing movement of the ball – the ball doing the work all the time.

We won that All-Ireland on pure merit. Our football shone on that God-given day in September, 1973 and we shone too in our pure white jerseys. Every player was there by virtue of his talent and application alone. There were no cliques, no politics, none of the old rubbish that had held back Cork so often in the past. It was a tremendous win and a great credit to everybody involved.

AND THE CELEBRATIONS!

There must have been 30,000 people to welcome us back to Cork with Sam Maguire, our famous fellow Corkonian. It was especially joyful for true Cork football people. Whatever about hurling wins, football All-Irelands simply don't come around often in Cork. People had waited since 1945 for this moment, and they must have thought they would never get to see it. They didn't get to see it again until 1989, 16 years later, when the great Larry Tompkins strode the field.

Football people are often forgotten in Cork and their game is sometimes looked down upon in comparison to hurling. So, when we brought Sam back in 1973, I felt that it was a great day for those people, especially. They deserved it for keeping the faith since 1945 and keeping the lights on during dark times. I was especially happy for all the St Nicholas stalwarts down the years and I felt I was representing them and my club that day.

And, since I had been playing on Cork senior football teams for 10 years by then, and even longer for St Nicks, I counted myself among Cork football people, and I counted my blessings in September, 1973. I had everything I could ever want from football that day. Everything.

◄◄◆►►

ONLY A WEEK after the All-Ireland football final in 1973, Glen Rovers lined out to play Blackrock in the Cork county hurling final. Ray Cummins and myself did not have much time to celebrate. We were great teammates on the Cork team but when the Glen met the Rockies, it was a different story and to make matters more interesting I was captain of the Glen. This was a big one for me.

I was really anxious to win the county the year I was captain, but the Rockies had outstanding teams all through the 70s, one after the other, full of county stars from one to 15. But we were Glen Rovers.

It was a tough close game but they had just too much firepower in the end and they beat us by two points – a huge disappointment. To go from such a high one Sunday to such a low on the next was hard to take. I still remember it vividly – you always remember the losses more than the wins and feel a responsibility for the loss. At least I always did. What made it even more painful was that this was the first county final that the Glen had lost in a long, long time – since 1956, to be specific.

We won three in-a-row from 1958-1960, then we won the finals of 1962, '64 (my first), '67, '69 and '72. So, for us to lose on my watch, as it were, was a bitter pill to swallow and it added to my abysmal record as captain – a record that would come to a head in a few years for Cork, when the Glen won the county again in 1976.

CORK HURLING HAD a quiet year in 1973. We were beaten by Tipperary which was always tough, all the more because I was also captain of the team, the Glen having won the county the year before. We were well on top during periods of that game (the Munster semi-final) but, typical Tipp, they came back at us and Roger Ryan, their big forward, scored two goals in the last two minutes. In hurling, 1973 was Limerick's year.

The Cork hurlers won the Oireachtas Cup in 1973. And we won it the following two years as well. That was another trophy I was sad to see fade away. I always had a soft spot for it because it was in the Oireachtas Cup that I played my first senior hurling game for Cork, back in '65.

The strange thing about it is this: although it had been played since 1939, Cork had never won it. Even Christy Ring couldn't manage it – it was one of the very few hurling medals to elude him.

Initially, it was just one game between two of the top teams, but then it grew and some years it would involve the four All-Ireland semi-finalists but in reverse order. Anyway, Cork entered it in 1973 and it was a straight knock-out. I don't remember how many games we played but the final was against Kilkenny. I wanted to play in the final, in the Athletic Grounds in Cork, but Margaret was due with Mags so I wasn't sure if I would make it. Mags was born the day after the match, so I got to play and to be at the birth as well.

Of course, the safe arrival of our second beautiful child was all that really mattered in December, 1973. It wasn't just the most important thing, it was everything.

CORK WON THE National Hurling League in 1974 with a tremendous win over Limerick. The final was played in Limerick, and they were All-Ireland champions. They had a great team including Richie Bennis, Éamonn Grimes, Pat Hartigan and Joe McKenna.

We clicked on the day, May 5th – we put on a great display. A few of the lads had cried off just beforehand so we were short on players. Ray Cummins, Brian Murphy and a few others were injured at the last minute, which was unusual, so we had a different looking team. Myself and Con Roche were both lucky to play. Con had serious problems with a blood vessel in his knee, it had been troubling him for months. His whole leg was strapped up from the sole of his foot to his thigh and he was hiding it from the selectors. He'd had to have an injection that morning to reduce the fluid and he'd been having similar injections for 10 days. I had a chipped bone in my ankle which I'd incurred the previous Sunday for St Nicks. The whole ankle was swollen and black and blue, and I had been told not to play, but with so many missing I felt I had to give it a go.

Not that it did us any harm: Éamonn O'Donoghue scored three goals and we got six in all and beat them 6-15 to 1-12. The All-Ireland champions beaten by 18 points on their home patch in May. Remarkable. John Horgan was our captain but the awarding of the cup was a bit of a farce because (we were told) Wexford, the 1972/1973 winners, had not 'surrendered' the league trophy. So, John was presented with the same cup that had already been presented to the captain of the North Tipperary team in the final of the curtain-raiser – the All-Ireland Vocational Schools final.

That aside, it was a great win. In a way, it showed the tremendous potential of the Cork hurling team at that time and was a foretaste to what was about to begin two years later.

IN 1974 CORK WON the Munster football final in Killarney on a wet day in July and that was memorable. Firstly, it was great to follow up on the previous year and secondly, championship wins against Kerry didn't happen too often, especially down in their own patch.

I was also captain, being the longest serving player on the team. UCC had won the county championship in 1973 and they didn't have any representative.

An interesting thing about that match: after 1974, Kerry would go on to win the next eight Munster Championships in-a-row. Cork managed to draw two of those (in 1976 and '82) but lost both replays. So, we wouldn't win another Munster football final until 1983, which was long after my time.

I played centrefield in 1974; it looked like I had settled down in that position – in football anyway. Not that my football playing days for Cork would last much longer. I didn't know it that day in Killarney, but 1974 saw an end to my county football career and that match was my last Munster Football Championship final.

I think it was Mick O'Connell's last championship game for Kerry, too. He came on as a sub after about an hour. There was a sad looking picture of him sheltering from the rain on the subs bench in the paper the following morning, but there was nothing sad about his career – it was glorious, as was he.

I mention elsewhere in this book how lucky I was to have won all the championships and honours that I did and to have played on so many teams. In many ways, it's all about timing, but one of my most fortunate pieces of timing related to my record against Kerry. I played senior football for Cork for 10 years. My first year, 1965 was disastrous against Limerick, on the day of the Flor Hayes 'affair'. After that I was privileged to be involved in the next nine consecutive Munster football finals, five of which Cork won. I don't know how many Cork footballers had such a good ratio against Kerry, but if my time had been later, I could have been nought for nine, instead of five for nine. And I was also very privileged to have captained Cork to two Munster final wins against Kerry, in 1967 and '74. In fact, the last time Cork had beaten Kerry in Killarney before 1974 was in 1966 when Jerry O'Sullivan of St Nicks was captain.

But my year in football wasn't over yet, we had an All-Ireland championship to defend. Sadly, in that, my old Croke Park captain 'hoodoo' would come back to haunt me with a vengeance.

AS WAS THE case every year, the games came fast in 1974, one after the other with training in between. How we managed to make time for training at all, I sometimes now wonder, and I missed a lot of training sessions for my clubs because of my involvement with Cork in hurling and football.

Take 1973, for example. In August we had the match against Tyrone and the drawn match between the Glen and the Barrs. Then in September, the replay against the Barrs and the All-Ireland final against Galway.

Then the county final for Glen Rovers against Blackrock in October.

After that, both National Leagues, in hurling and football, recommenced. We had matches in October, November and December of 1973, in both codes. Sometimes the hurling and football teams would have games the same day and myself, Brian Murphy and Ray Cummins would have to be 'allocated' to one team or the other.

Then the Glen played St Rynagh's in the All-Ireland club final in Croke Park in December and following that, Cork won the Oireachtas Cup – in December too.

Now we're into 1974… and I had January off.

In February, the National Leagues resumed and I had matches in both hurling and football. The highlight of the football league in 1974 was beating Kerry in Killarney but we didn't qualify.

I played for Munster in the Railway Cup in February, too, and we lost to the Combined Universities.

In March, 1974, I travelled with the Cork football team to California to play a series of exhibition matches against the All Stars – that went on into April. Also, in April, I played a Kelleher Shield final for St Nicks. Followed by a National Football League match against Wicklow. Then Cork played a challenge hurling match against Blackrock to prepare for the league final.

On the last Sunday in April, St Nicks beat Clonakilty in the first round of the championship. I picked up an injury that day.

On the following weekend, the first Sunday in May, we beat Limerick in the National Hurling League final as I mentioned earlier. I probably shouldn't have played, with a chipped bone in my ankle.

On the following weekend, I had a game for St Nicks and we lost.

Then we played Waterford in Waterford on May 19th, I've recounted that match already – a disaster, especially after our win in the league final against Limerick.

On the following weekend the Cork footballers were due to go to London to play in Wembley Stadium against Galway. This was for something called the Wembley Games which was played annually on the Whit weekend.

On the weekend after that (we're into June, 1974 now), Glen Rovers played Nemo Rangers in the first round of the county club hurling championship. The less said about that, the better, Nemo beat us 5-8 to 2-14. To call it a shock result would be an understatement – we were the reigning club All-Ireland champions, remember, not that Nemo were impressed by it. That was us gone out of the championship – in June. So, Cork were gone and the Glen were gone in the hurling, it was to be all football from now on in 1974.

Then, on the 9th of June, we played Tipperary in the first round of the football Munster Championship in Fermoy. Thankfully we won that. Then on into July and the Munster final against Kerry.

THE REASON I give this litany of games is because of what happened on a flight to London in May, 1974, when I was sitting beside Michael Ellard. Michael worked for the *Cork Examiner* as had his father before him. He and I had been school-mates – we were pals in the North Monastery primary and secondary schools. We were always very good friends and we remained good friends.

So, we were chatting away on the plane (a Cambrian Airways flight – remember them?) and Michael said something like, 'Tough couple of weeks, Denis?' (Cork hurlers and St Nicks had both lost the previous fortnight).

And I said something like, 'It was, Michael. You know… I'm thinking of taking a bit of a rest from it.'

And we were just chatting like that and whatever I said, or whatever way Michael took it up, the whole thing just snowballed from there. I thought no more about it and I enjoyed the experience of playing in Wembley – how many people get to do that? I was captain of Cork, too, the same day.

Margaret picked me up from Cork Airport on the Monday night and on the way down into the city, she said, 'You never told me you were retiring'.

I was shocked. 'Why do you say that?' I asked.

'It's on the back of the *Echo* tonight, with your picture… that you're retiring from playing hurling and football for Cork.'

And that's how I learned that I was retiring for Cork in May, 1974, at the age of 28. I genuinely had no intention of retiring and I certainly had no idea that Michael had taken it up that way. But now, I had a real dilemma: what was I going to do? And when Billy George, the sports editor of the *Examiner* rang me a couple of days later, I had a big decision to make and I had to make it very quickly.

'Denis,' Billy asked me, coming straight out with it. 'Are you retiring?'

And I told him what had happened, how Michael had taken me up mistakenly.

'We'll retract it,' Billy said. 'Before it grows any more legs… we'll shut it down, it's no problem.'

But I said no. I didn't want to do that to Michael for starters. And the second thing was this: I was just a couple of weeks shy of my 29th birthday. I had been playing senior football for Cork for 11 years and senior hurling for Cork for 10 years – when you combine those, that's like 21 years of service.

I felt like I had been playing for 21 years, too. I'd been on the go, hell for leather at senior level since 1964, since I was only 19. And that's not including even longer with St Nicks and the Glen.

When I did a quick tally of the amount of games I had played in the previous year, 1973, between January 7th and December 19th – in less than a year, actually, 343 days – it came to a staggering 66 matches. That's about a match – a competitive match, mind you – every five days, week after week after week, over a whole year. And that didn't include training sessions. How many of them had I attended that year?

A hundred? More? I had no idea.

That was just for 1973, but what about the previous years? And what about this year and next year, and the year after that? Was I capable of really doing that, playing a serious game a week all year round? Year after year?

Did I want to do that?

It was true that the coming summer in 1974 would be quieter for me, but I had a business career to take care of, too, and we had just had our second child, Mags in December – which I nearly missed because of a game – an Oireachtas game at that.

One of the big issues for me was the toll that all the Cork and Munster games were taking on my club career. In 1973 I had only played four games for the Glen and three for St Nicks. I was captain of the Glen but I was able to turn out for just one single night's training before the championship semi-final replay against St Finbarr's because I was training for Cork for the Tyrone All-Ireland semi-final. The drawn game with the Barrs was a week before the Munster football final and the county final was only a couple of weeks after the All-Ireland. I've already outlined some of my itinerary for the early months of 1974. So, there's a match every Sunday – every Sunday – and four nights training every week in between.

IN HINDSIGHT, ALTHOUGH I hadn't planned it, I probably said what I said to Michael on that flight because I knew subconsciously that I was heading for a burnout. Things couldn't continue the way they were going. I may not have admitted it to myself – or to anybody else – but I badly needed a break. I couldn't keep pushing myself the way I was, playing over 60 competitive games a year, year in and year out. It had to stop.

And suddenly, the thought of having a quieter summer in 1974 was very appealing to me – playing six matches instead of 66. And the thought of being able to dedicate myself to my clubs in hurling and football was also very appealing, both as a player, and later maybe as coach and administrator – it was time to give something back. Not to mention being able to devote myself to my career and spend more time with Margaret and the lads.

So, I didn't take Billy up on his offer to rescind my retirement. Other newspapers were soon on to me for interviews and quotes, and I talked to people like Eugene McGee, Owen McCann, Aidan McCarthy and my retirement became official very quickly.

And then it was done.

My hurling days with Cork were over – and they had ended disappointingly with that loss against Waterford, but I'd done my bit over the 10 years or so. Losing the 1969 and '72 finals ('69 especially) were tough to take and being dropped unfairly in '70, but I'd had some great days, especially against Tipperary.

And so, that was that. I'd given it everything I could.

◄ ◄ ◆ ► ►

BUT IN THE meantime, there was another football All-Ireland to win. I was captain and I was determined for it to happen. I really felt it could happen too, after winning it out in 1973 and beating Kerry in the '74 Munster final. We were earmarked to play the winners of Leinster, Dublin or Meath. They were playing on July 28th, two weeks after we had beaten Kerry.

The Glen had a match the same day. It was an evening match and on my way there, the commentary of the Leinster final between Dublin and Meath was being broadcast on the car radio. It was a deferred commentary and when it became obvious that Dublin were going to win, my heart sank.

Now, I can't explain this. Dublin hadn't won a Leinster Championship since 1965 and I'd had a bad experience against Meath in '67. But whatever it was about Dublin, I just hated playing against them. It was like Waterford in the hurling, we just couldn't fulfil our football potential against Dublin. No matter where we had played them or in what circumstances (mostly in the league), we could never get going and beat them – I think we only ever beat them once in all the years we played them. It was a National Football League game in 1972 and we beat them by 1-9 to 1-8, and I scored 1-8 the same day.

Even though they hadn't won anything major in my time (up to now) they always retained their confidence and the belief in their own ability – which is a huge advantage in sport.

Another factor was Kevin Heffernan, who had taken over Dublin in late 1973. We didn't know what kind of an impact he would have, but we soon found out. Overall, I think Cork probably underestimated Dublin on the day and I probably overestimated them. On the day of the match I was quoted in the *Sunday Independent*: "*My one fear is that the pressure is on Cork because our own supporters think we haven't much to beat in Dublin whereas in Dublin it seems they have everything to gain and nothing to lose*".

Again, the old malaise of having beaten Kerry was high in our minds and having beaten them by double scores, we thought we would drive on. Dublin had been playing in Division 2 of the league and had stuttered their way past Wexford, Louth, Kildare, Offaly and Meath to get out of Leinster. They were especially lucky to have beaten Offaly.

None of that mattered, of course. What did matter was that Dublin completely unsettled us from the very start of the game. Our wonderful forwards couldn't get going. Early on, Jimmy Barry Murphy had a great goal chance but, very unlike him, he blazed it over. Seán Doherty, the Dublin captain and full-back, had a brilliant game against Ray Cummins, who had to be moved to centre-forward. Gay O'Driscoll and Robbie Kelleher were outstanding at corner-back. We brought Martin Doherty in at full-forward but he couldn't make any headway.

We were out-muscled all over the pitch. Humphrey Kelleher dropped a ball and Jimmy Keaveney grabbed it. Billy Morgan had no choice but to pull him down and although Brian Mullins struck the penalty poorly, it eluded Billy and crept in. It was that kind of a day. We ended up not scoring for a whole 35-minute period of the game and not scoring from play for 45 minutes.

I was marking a total unknown that day by the name of Brian Mullins. He was only 19, just coming on the scene. I was 29 with years of experience behind me – having just won an All-Ireland. It didn't matter. I can honestly say that Brian was the strongest player I had ever come up against in playing county football for 10 years; he brushed me aside. Tony Hanahoe, Anton O'Toole and Jimmy Keaveney also tormented us and Dublin beat us well, 2-11 to 1-8.

I said some words about my retirement after the game and that was that. Back to Cork with our tail between our legs, and me losing as captain in Croke Park again.

For the last time.

My final championship football game for Cork had ended in failure as had my final hurling game. That was it, I was finished playing football for Cork. I felt terrible about losing but I was reconciled with my retirement, even at the age of 29. Just like in the hurling, I'd given it everything I had.

A SMALL ADDENDUM to my football days with Cork. There were various efforts made to keep me on – I was approached by several people, players and others not to retire. I got letters – very heart-felt and kind. A lot of people I met that year tried to convince me to change my mind. But I knew I wouldn't.

For some strange reason Cork convinced me to play a final game against Kerry in the autumn of 1974 in the National League. Maybe they were stuck but I'm not sure why I agreed. This was in Cork, in the Mardyke – Páirc Uí Chaoimh was being rebuilt at the time. They put me in at corner-forward where I was marking another newcomer, a 19 year-old called Páidí Ó Sé, whom I'd never heard of. If my experience with Brian Mullins was painful, the one with Páidí was nearly as bad, he was all over me like a rash. He was inside my shirt from start to finish, I couldn't shake him off for love nor money. He would go on to be one of the greats too, but although aged only 19 he was already a formidable opponent even if I did manage a goal and a point against him.

I'd known I had made the right decision to retire even before those Dublin and Kerry games, but after them, I was certain. Football is a game for young fellas and their time had come; mine had gone.

◄◄◆►►

DID I ENJOY my free time in 1975, not playing for Cork or Munster in hurling or football? I did. Did I enjoy training with St Nicks and the Glen and all the time I had with my family? I certainly did. Did I revel in my club football and hurling, playing with a freedom and freshness I hadn't known for many a year? I did, indeed. Did I enjoy the media work I had begun with RTÉ? Was it challenging and rewarding? It was.

Did I miss the inter-county games? Not really.

Glen Rovers reached the county final in 1975 and I don't know if I was ever relishing my hurling as much. I felt liberated, I really did. We beat Avondhu in April and then Carrigdhoun in May. I was playing centre-back and I honestly had never felt as fresh as I did that year. The time off that winter and spring had done me the world of good. The semi-final was in August and thank God we got a bit of revenge on Nemo Rangers from the year before. We beat them 4-10 to 2-9.

And so, on to the final against our nemesis Blackrock on the 14th of September. We went into the game hoping for the best, and we had prepared well for it. We had a nice mix of players, young and experienced. Martin Doherty was our full-back and he was brilliant as was John Kennefick at corner-back. Ted O'Brien was playing well as was Jerry O'Sullivan, in his mid-thirties now. And we had the wonderful hurler, Pat Horgan in the forward line (although he was still only 18) and Tom Collins had a good year and a good final, too.

But we were no match at all for the Rockies on the day. They were on top all over the pitch and Ray Cummins and Tom Cashman gave displays in front of the 15,000 people crammed into the Dyke. John Horgan, Pat Moylan, Dermot

McCurtain, Frank Cummins – the whole team was packed with outstanding hurlers, but we were still disappointed with our performance. Losing with Glen Rovers never came easy.

At centre-back, I felt I played well. I was marking Brendan Cummins and Éamonn O'Donoghue (both county players) and I think I got the better of them both. Things just went right for me, it was one of those days, despite the result. And what happened shortly afterwards confirmed it.

Well, that's that, now, I thought, leaving the Dyke. *That's my season over.*

It was just as well too, because I had broken both my hurleys. Now, I almost never broke a hurley, I could hold on to them for years at a time. Or if you broke one, it wouldn't be so bad, you'd have a spare. I broke two on that day for some strange reason but I wasn't bothered. I wouldn't need a hurley until the following year. Plenty of time to worry about that after Christmas.

Nine days later, the phone rang on the Tuesday evening at home and I answered it.

'Hello,' I said.

'Hello, Denis,' a man said. 'This is Mick Dunne here from the *Irish Press.*'

'Oh, hello, Mick,' says I. 'What can I do for you?'

'I'm just enquiring,' says Mick. 'Did you know you're playing for the Cork hurlers against Tipp on Sunday, in the National Hurling League? Can you give me a quote?'

Silence. Eventually, I gathered myself.

'I'm sorry, Mick, but you're mistaken there. I'm retired from inter-county hurling. I'm afraid somebody has misinformed you.'

'No,' says Mick. 'I have it here in front of me from tonight's county board meeting and that's you on the team… at centre-back. It's there in black and white.'

'Well, I don't know anything about it, Mick,' I said. 'And I can tell you I won't be playing. For starters, I don't even have a hurley, I broke my two hurleys last Sunday week against the Rockies.'

I was living in Blackrock at the time, so I went straight out in a daze and got into my car and drove over to Ballintemple to Christy Ring's house. Christy was a selector for the Cork hurlers.

'Quick question for you, Christy,' I said, after he let me into the house. 'Am I playing for Cork on Sunday?'

'I dunno, boy,' he said.

'But you're a selector,' I said.

He shrugged. I played my trump card.

'I've no hurleys, anyway,' I said, lamely.

He looked at me and said nothing.

'What am I going to do?' I said. 'Mick Dunne is after ringing me to tell me I'm on the team. If it's on the paper in the morning it will look terrible if I come out and say I won't play. I can't do that.'

'That's up to yourself,' Christy said.

Now, I knew Christy well enough to know what was going on, and what he was telling me, without really telling me. It was something he often did.

Off I went home in a tizzy and sure enough the team was announced on the paper the following morning and there I was on it, at centre-back. Not only that, my name was all over the headlines and my picture was there beside them. My old friend, Mick Ellard had a big article with the heading, *"New Cork selectors pick Denis Coughlan"*.

Thanks a lot, Mick.

So, I had to go and get a hurley. This time Christy hadn't offered to get one for me. In fairness, he'd done enough.

I also had to publicly justify my comeback; the newspapers were on to me in a flash. And I had to make it clear that I would be playing inter-county hurling only – that I couldn't go back to being a dual player except for my club. While I stuck to my guns about there being too much pressure on players and too many games, I made the point that I had never lost my love of hurling and my campaign with the Glen that year convinced me that I still had something to contribute to Cork's effort to win an All-Ireland. I also went on the record about how important the involvement of Christy Ring as a selector was to me – it was a huge factor. I also mentioned how impressed I was with the calibre of all the other new selectors – all real hurling people.

All of which was true.

THE FACT IS that something exciting was happening in Cork hurling and we had the Blackrock National Hurling Club to thank for it. Having won the county in 1974 they decided to take control of the Cork senior hurling selectorial and coaching process, as was their right. When a team won the county, they had a choice of either taking over the selection process themselves or else letting the county board do it and only once before (in 1961) had a club taken control and that was Glen Rovers. And that didn't happen again until 1975 with Blackrock, who wanted a new approach and it made all the difference.

The first thing they did right was to involve Christy Ring. That was huge, but the other selectors were real hurling people too, and they all ended up playing vital roles. They were: Jimmy Brohan (Blackrock), Denis Murphy (St Finbarr's), Denis Hurley (Sarsfields), Tim Mullane (St Finbarr's) and Frank Murphy (Blackrock, and he was also the secretary of the county board). There were six of them in all but they were rotated over the following five years. They had a very good system and the whole thing gelled.

The first thing that went in 1975 were the cliques. Up to then there were terrible cliques in Cork hurling and the players were as guilty in this as anybody else, with the Glen, the Barrs and the Rockies the main offenders. Players from the same clubs stuck together in the dressing-room and outside it. So, it was very difficult for lads from smaller clubs or from country clubs – younger players especially – to fit into the unit, and to feel part of the whole thing. As a result, many of them underachieved and team performances were affected.

All that literally changed overnight and for the better. I would give great credit to Blackrock for doing that – for bringing in that system and revolutionising and modernising the set-up, getting rid of the old ways which were not best practice nor fit for purpose. It wasn't that we didn't have good hurlers (we did) but you have to have a good set-up to get the best out of them all, individually, and as a unit. And the set-up from 1976 to '80 was excellent.

They appointed Father Bertie Troy as the coach, and Kevin Kehily was in charge of fitness, and both of them also did excellent jobs over the coming years. The atmosphere was very different from the beginning of that year and Cork reaped the dividends.

And that's what the three in-a-row came out of.

My 'comeback' match was against Tipperary. I always loved playing against Tipperary, and I always felt I could play well against Tipp and I think I often did. So, it was on the 5th of October, 1975 in the Mardyke.

Michael Ellard went to town on the superlatives the following day (as only he could) but I knew all during the game I was going well, especially when Tipp moved Francis Loughnane off me. I couldn't do a thing wrong at centre-back the same day, really, and it felt great to be back hurling again for Cork.

It felt right.

Leaving the dressing-rooms, I must admit to a sense of elation but it didn't last long. Christy Ring came over to me and his first words were, 'You know you won't be playing centre-back any more?'

In hindsight, if you didn't know Christy, you'd wonder about this comment, and you could take it the wrong way. But Christy often had a roundabout way of saying things that you might only figure out much later – if you figured it out at all. In fact, this was his way of saying how well I'd just played. It was a compliment. And any praise from Christy Ring was praise indeed – you had to earn it.

But I was shocked.

'You're not serious, Christy?' I said. 'After the way I just played?'

'We've another fella in mind for centre-back,' he said. 'You'll be left half-back.'

'Who?'

'Johnny Crowley,' he said. I knew Johnny, who was from Bishopstown, and even though he was only 19, he came straight in from the 1974 minor team. He was very mature for his age, very strong, and had played brilliantly for Seandún the previous year.

And the rest is history, which was often the case when Christy Ring was involved. I played left half-back for the next three years, winning three All-Ireland medals, three All Star Awards and a Texaco Hurler of The Year Award. Not bad for somebody who was retired, I guess.

I HAVE NO doubt that Christy was behind the whole thing. And he did it brilliantly. If I had been approached and asked would I come back, I'd have said no. But Christy knew me better than I knew myself. He knew that if I was put on the team, I wouldn't withdraw.

Christy also knew that I was ready to play again for Cork. The year away from county hurling and football had done me the world of good. I had loved the training sessions for the Glen and for St Nicks, and I had loved the matches. I had loved the breaks in between them and the extra time with my family. I was relishing everything.

I was enjoying my sport more in 1975 than perhaps I had ever done. And so, when I did come back to join the Cork hurlers in October, 1975, I was completely refreshed, mentally and physically. I felt more like a 20 year-old than a 30 year-old. I was restored.

It was like as if I were starting out all over again, with the same enthusiasm, the same eagerness, the same ambition that I had the first time. With everything to play for, everything to give for the cause.

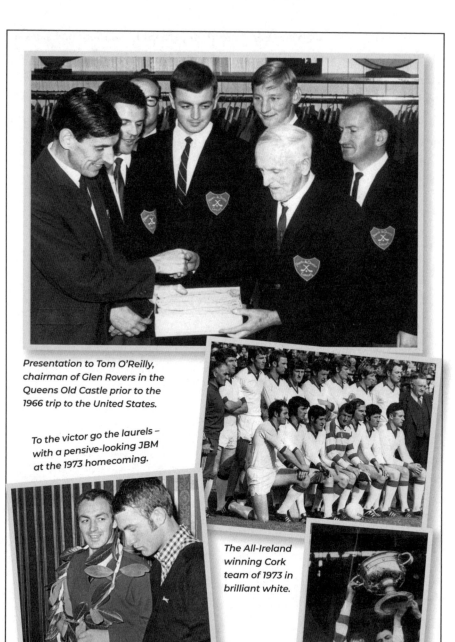

Presentation to Tom O'Reilly, chairman of Glen Rovers in the Queens Old Castle prior to the 1966 trip to the United States.

To the victor go the laurels – with a pensive-looking JBM at the 1973 homecoming.

The All-Ireland winning Cork team of 1973 in brilliant white.

With Billy Morgan and Sam Maguire in 1973.

« CHAPTER 8 »

After My Playing Days

ONE SUNDAY EVENING in 1977 I got a phone call at home from Gene Fitzgerald, who was Minister for Finance at the time. Gene was from Bishopstown in Cork and he was a former treasurer of the Cork County Board.

I was surprised by the call, especially when he asked me could I come into the Metropole Hotel to meet the Minister for Sport, Jim Tunney. When I went into the Metropole, Minister Tunney told me that Jack Lynch had proposed me for a position on the National Sports Council of Ireland – known as *Cospóir* – which was in the process of being set up.

I felt very honoured to have been nominated and so I accepted immediately. I was only 32 and I was very interested in all sports and how to promote sports. I knew as well as anybody how sport can change people's lives, contribute to their well-being and bring with it a host of benefits.

There were some wonderful names among the 25 people on the council. Noel Murphy (the Irish rugby coach), Johnny Giles (the manager of the Irish soccer team), Tony Hanahoe (the manager of the Dublin football team), Eamonn Coghlan, Mick Dowling, Lord Dunraven, Mary McKenna. It was a who's who of sport in Ireland and it was chaired brilliantly by Ronnie Delaney. It was set up under the auspices of the Department of Education and we used to meet in the Department offices in Dublin at least once a month.

Several active sub-committees were also set up and these were doing more hands-on work on the ground. If you were on one of those there might be weekly meetings or events. It was a high-powered council and three civil servants were fully dedicated to it and a secretary, who happened to be a Corkman, Barry Holohan from Dillon's Cross.

I was on the committee for four years from 1977 to '81 and I really enjoyed it. At the beginning, the council didn't have any great teeth or funding – in fact the government funding for sport in 1977 was only £500,000. That would increase to £2 million in a few years, and Jim Tunney was a real believer in the benefits of sport and in supporting it.

Another great aspect of the Sports Council was that it was a North-South initiative and one of the activities I undertook was to go to GAA county conventions in Northern Ireland and to speak at those. Which I was very happy to do, even though this was during the Troubles and it wasn't the safest place for a Corkman or a GAA person to be.

I was also asked to do some coaching in the North and again I was very happy to oblige, even though I was still playing myself at the time. The enthusiasm for hurling and football in the Six Counties was inspiring and I was especially keen to support the small hurling enclaves up there. For about three years I did a lot of coaching in the Ards Peninsula. I used to go up there for weekends – I'd be met around the border and driven from there; it wouldn't do to have a southern registered car around the place – and I must say I loved every minute of it. I was so happy to pass on hurling skills and knowledge – ones that I learned as a child from people like Johnny Clifford and Christy Ring – to the young boys and girls in County Down.

The clubs I worked most closely with were Ballycran, Ballygalget, Portaferry and Bredagh and years later I still check club results to see how they are getting on, especially in the All-Ireland Club championships. I always had a soft spot for them and wanted them to do well.

For many years I have felt that there should be the equivalent of a divisional team from Northern Ireland; that such a "combined counties" team could represent Ulster and compete in the All-Ireland championship. If all the counties in Ulster came together, they could produce a very high-quality team that would be a serious force in the latter stages of the All-Ireland. Look at what Slaughtneil in Derry have achieved on their own. Imagine the best 15 hurlers from all Northern clubs on the one team. They would give it a right lash. Imagine how much it would mean to the development of hurling in Ulster if that team won an All-Ireland, beating Tipperary, Galway or Kilkenny in the final. How much it would enrich hurling, too.

I also travelled to Belfast for the Sports Council and I did a lot of coaching there. Belfast was really struggling at the time – things were very bad and it was very tough on GAA clubs who were often targeted. I used to take the train to Dundalk and then I'd be met by somebody from one of the Belfast or Antrim clubs. I had some hair-raising experiences while I was there; it really opened my eyes to what the people of the North had to put up with, day-in day-out. I also saw the risks that people had to take and the sacrifices they made to ensure that hurling and football survived during the Troubles. I also saw first-hand the harassment and intimidation that Catholics had to endure.

I'd be coaching a group of young boys and girls, and within minutes of the training session a couple of British Army helicopters would arrive and hover over the pitch. They were huge things and the noise and wind they generated at close range was brutal. The helicopters were then lowered down until they were only 10 feet above the ground and we'd all have to return to the dressing-room. After a while they might go away and we'd go back out training but in minutes the helicopters would reappear and the whole process would be repeated. I quickly understood how people could become bitter in the face of such constant intimidation.

The clubs in Belfast had fantastic facilities and clubhouses. The members were at great pains to let me know that every stick of furniture in the club houses was Irish. Nothing British whatsoever was used, and they were very proud that a lot of the facilities and equipment were made by the prisoners in Long Kesh.

My involvement with the Sports Council for those four years was very satisfying. The aim of the council was to create an awareness of sport in Ireland. Coming from a place like Blackpool I would have thought that everybody was aware of sport, but that wasn't the case. The real drive behind the council was the implementation of the government 'Sport for All' policy – that sport would have an inclusive element in society. This is very important. Why should some children, due to socio-economic or geographic coincidences, have access to the best of facilities and opportunities which are not available to others?

Several people on the council were not very involved in sport at all, but they put in Trojan work. Lord Dunraven, for example, who was president of the Irish Wheelchair Association, was very keen that disabled people should have the opportunity to participate in sport and the council did great work in that regard, which I was very proud of. There are many disadvantaged groups in Irish society which, for one reason or another, do not have the opportunities that I and many others had when it came to participating in and benefitting from sport; and they need support and nurturing.

I remember when the Special Olympics World Summer Games came to Dublin in 2003 and what a wonderful inspiring event it was. I thought of Lord Dunraven, how proud he must have been. And how much it must have meant to all the families of young people with special needs.

I was very grateful to have done my own small bit, from 1977 to '81, to promote sport and its benefits in Ireland too. And I owed that privilege to Jack Lynch, for which I will always be grateful.

◄ ◄ ◆ ► ►

I HAD NEVER been heavily involved in GAA administration and I had never represented the Glen or St Nicks on the county board, so when I was approached to mediate on the Cork hurlers' third strike in March, 2009, I had to think twice about it.

Funnily enough, way back in 1968 for some strange reason (when I was only 23) I was proposed at the Glen AGM as the board representative for the club. But somebody else (thankfully) got the job. That year I was also selected to contest the position of membership of the Munster Council as a delegate. I don't know why anybody thought I'd be suitable for that, and when I heard on the radio that I had lost out by six votes, I was very relieved.

Subsequent to that, sometime in the 1980s, I was asked by the Cork County Board to go on a committee to look at club fixture problems in Cork. If you think the current difficulties between clubs and counties in the GAA is something new, you'd be very wrong. There was a committee of six or seven people which was chaired by Derry Gowan.

The purpose of the committee was to analyse the structure of the club fixtures for the year and to recommend possible improvements. We met for six weeks and all the eight divisions in Cork (Avondhu, Beara, Carbery, Carrigdhoun, Duhallow, Imokilly, Muskerry and Seandún) were represented. We met very diligently and we talked it through in depth as to how the club fixtures in Cork could be improved by the county board. The clubs were not happy at the time.

We came up with a series of recommendations and I learned a lot about GAA local politics during the process. What happened was this: somebody got a proposal put through at the county board convention to investigate club fixtures and it was passed. That was why the committee was set up by the executive. And I didn't know anything about that because I didn't go to the convention and I didn't know the background. But it dawned on me afterwards that because it was passed at the convention it had to be acted upon.

But it never saw the light of day. And there was never any hope of it seeing the light of day, even after all the time and effort we put in and the recommendations we made, which were logical and based on factual evidence. And which the clubs badly wanted to happen.

That was an eye-opener for me.

MANY YEARS LATER, maybe around 2010, the Cork County Board asked me would I chair the Cork GAA Urbanisation Committee. This committee was developed to look at the impact of urbanisation and the growth of urban areas on the GAA in Cork. It was over a five-year period and about 10 years ago there was an overhaul of the whole county board and all aspects of its activities were looked at and examined in minute detail. They had set up several high-powered committees to look into the various aspects of the running of the board and the activities of the board. This related to games, coaching, urbanisation and so on.

Because of the way that towns were growing and society generally was becoming more urbanised, it was considered important – and it is important – to plan how the GAA can adapt to that. If society changes, sporting bodies have to change accordingly and to modify themselves; otherwise they become ineffective or even irrelevant over time.

The idea was to look at how the GAA in Cork could adapt to urbanisation and to grow the games and new clubs and facilities, given how the demographics were changing. So, we examined that in depth and went to places like Mallow, Midleton, Fermoy, Macroom Carrigaline, Ballincollig etc. Some of these satellite towns were rapidly expanding and had populations of over 20,000 people but only one club serving them. There was plenty of room for new clubs, facilities and pitches.

But the question is: how do you go about that? How do you develop new clubs – how do they come about, where are they located, and how do they interact with and relate to the clubs that are already in place for many years? These are difficult questions to answer and contentious issues.

One example that we had to go by was in Thurles. Thurles had run into this problem and the Tipperary County Board tackled it to get the most out of Thurles and to serve the people of the town – especially the young people – promoting the games in the best possible way. Ensuring, too, that young people don't migrate to other sports. And this happened in the 1970s in a very progressive manner. They solved the problem by creating a second club in Thurles called Durlas Óg. It is a juvenile club which was set up in 1979. And anybody could play with Durlas Óg – you could come from other clubs to play with them because it was underage only; from under-12 to under-16. And then when you were over 16, you could go back to your old club without any hassle because it was understood that people would drop out in their teenage years anyway – there would be a natural attrition.

It was on this model that we had hoped to modernise the organisation of Gaelic games in Cork. But the moment we launched it, and the further we enquired, and the more people we met in the clubs we engaged with, we realised that not one club – under any circumstances – would be open to it. No club would encourage a second local club – even at underage only – in their locality. In fact, the way things were going – despite the population growth and urbanisation – we would end up with fewer GAA clubs in the future and not more. Which is sad to think about, but there you have it.

Based on the work I did for this Cork committee I was asked by Christy Cooney to become part of the National Urbanisation Committee in Croke Park and I was happy to do so. Christy was the President of the GAA at the time, and he's a Youghal man. So, I volunteered to serve on that national committee for three years and I was also on a similar group set up by the Munster Council which disbanded because it was impacting on the national initiative.

And, of course, this is a national issue. Society is becoming more urbanised all the time. Some small, rural clubs are struggling to get enough girls and boys involved, while clubs in some newly urban areas are struggling with the overwhelming numbers. And the work continues to this day, it's still going on, it's still a difficult issue. Here are some frightening statistics from the GAA website:

Between 1971 to 2016 the population of the eleven Leinster counties outside of Dublin has more than doubled from 619,428 to 1,285,318. Yet, in that time, over 20 clubs have gone out of existence in those counties and an estimated 30 more will either disband or amalgamate in the next 15 years. There were 144 fewer teams registered in Leinster in 2016 than there were in 2010, and up to 40% of teams in secondary competitions either failed to play in them or complete their fixtures programmes in 2016.

Something badly needs to be done to reverse these trends.

And the upshot of this is that young people will either go to other sports or stop playing sport at all, which would be disastrous.

Our games have never been under such threat – especially our club games – and this will only have been exacerbated because of the COVID-19 crisis. We don't know the full impact of the 2020 pandemic and we probably won't for years, but it won't be beneficial to our clubs, that's for sure.

◄◄◆►►

THE FIRST CORK strike happened in 2002. And in my opinion that was probably simmering for a while before it actually blew up into a full strike. When you think of the unresolved and contentious issues since my own time – the way players were treated, the Ban, the politics in picking teams, sponsorships, facilities etc, something had to give. And I don't think that any past players would have disagreed with the actions of the Cork players in 2002, given the situation and the conditions we all had to play under. I certainly didn't disagree nor did any players of my era with whom I discussed it.

Things needed to be improved in terms of facilities, welfare, how players were treated, the systems in place, how the partners of players were treated, and so on. So, when that strike took place and was 'resolved', everybody thought… *Fair dues to the players, they put their money where their mouths were.* We also thought… *That's great now, we can move on and put it behind us.* Because it was very divisive; people were hurt, and the wounds needed time to heal.

Conflict is dangerous, it can easily take on a vicious life of its own and you don't know which way it will turn. Once you let loose the dogs of war you might not be able to control who they attack – which is exactly what happened when the second and especially the third strike unfolded and escalated.

People were badly hurt, their families were badly hurt – people on all sides of the conflict. The bitterness and rancour got out of control. Families were divided and clubs were divided – and still are to this day. Even now, all these years later, it's still talked about and it's still a source of pain, anger and sadness. As late as May, 2020 there was an article by Anthony Daly about the strikes and a podcast in the *Irish Examiner* where my old friend Dr Con Murphy spoke about the stress and hurt he endured during the third strike in particular. In the same month Seán Óg Ó hAilpín also spoke about his regret over the bitterness and acrimony that took place and some of the things he, himself, had said.

But the feeling back in 2002 was that the strike was over and now things would improve and that would be an end to it. And the hurlers did kick on and very nearly won three in-a-row and they were excellent, and it was a thrilling time for Cork hurling.

BUT WHILE THINGS had improved for the county players, what about the clubs and their players? In 2003 I was vice-chairman of Glen Rovers and there were 16 senior clubs in the county at the time, excluding divisional teams. And all the clubs got together after the first strike to discuss their players on the county panels. The number of players on county panels were increasing all the time and had gone from 21 to 25, and then to 30. And this was impinging on the club scene. Mark Landers and I were delegated by the clubs to go on their behalf to speak to the county board. And by extension to the new manager of the Cork hurling team who was Dónal O'Grady.

The specific concern of the clubs was this: all they wanted was for their players to be released from the county panel for one night a week. So that the players could train or interact with the club for that one night – just one night a week. Because that was not happening at the time (and still isn't, I'm sure).

It was on that basis we built our analysis and our set of recommendations, and we went to the county board and we were met by the executive. And I have to say that we put a very good case. Mark was very recently an inter-county player and he was captain of Cork in 1999 – on the team that won an All-Ireland under

Jimmy Barry Murphy. Because of that we agreed going in to the board that I would put forward our findings rather than Mark, that I'd do the talking.

I made the case to the executive and there was a pause after I finished. And then Frank Murphy said, 'Mr Coughlan, as long as I have been secretary of the Cork County Board this is the best case I have heard presented to the executive. It's so good.' he said, (and alarm bells began going off when I heard this), 'I wonder would you make it on our behalf to the management of the Cork senior hurling team?'

I said fine, my heart sinking. Because I knew well that Frank was passing on a poisoned chalice to me. Mark and I felt that the county board should be doing this, not us, and not the clubs, either. But we agreed to do it anyway. I felt I should do right by my club (and the other clubs) even though I had a fair idea what was coming.

We arranged to meet Dónal O'Grady and his selectors. This is before the 2003 championship. We met them and we put our case to them on behalf of the county board. And the thrust of our argument was that the clubs just wanted their players for one night a week. That was all. For example, Glen Rovers had two players on the panel at that time and one of them was our captain. But they were both at the upper end of the panel: at numbers 28 and 29. So the possibility of them getting a game on the Cork senior team was quite slim; they were not getting games for Cork despite being on the panel and training with the panel. But they weren't involved in the clubs, either, where they would have been playing; so nobody was getting the benefit of them, and the players themselves were also losing out. The same was true for several other players on the Cork panel.

I couldn't understand this and I thought it would actually be beneficial for them to go back to the club and to be available for the club one night a week. The players would get more out of this and develop further and be of more benefit to the Cork set-up. And I thought that Dónal would appreciate that as a great Cork player and a great club man himself, for the Barrs.

Now, I can understand where he was coming from too, because I had been there when I was training the Cork footballers in the 1980s. He was saying, 'Look, I'm the manager of the Cork team and in order to compete with Kilkenny or Tipperary or whoever I have to be able to have the players as much as possible, because *they* have the players as much as possible – even more so.' And Mark and I understood that and also that training was becoming very specialised, very detailed at that time. They were getting experts of all kinds to work with the players.

Our main fear was that if we pushed this too far – if the clubs pushed this too far – that Dónal might feel so strongly about it that his hands were being tied and he would have to resign. That was the last thing Mark and I wanted. Because if that happened, there could be another strike in Cork and, whatever else, we couldn't be responsible for that. It would be an utter disaster. So we didn't push it. We made our case and – effectively – the clubs then withdrew in order to prevent another Cork strike.

If anything, the issue of clubs versus county has grown worse over the years – because it was never really tackled in Cork or anywhere else. And when you see great sportsmen like Liam Griffin at the forefront of the resistance now, you know something is really wrong.

This time I don't think the clubs will go away; eventually they will stop backing down to Croke Park – unlike the way that Mark Landers and I backed down to Dónal O'Grady.

Dónal had a good point, too. Why should Cork do anything to damage its inter-county chances when other counties were doing the exact opposite? It has to be done at a national level. And it must be done. Ninety-eight percent of the players are not involved at county level but they are being badly impacted upon by the other two percent. That's not sustainable. I understand the economics of the thing but our games should not be all about money – we're better than that and our games and our people deserve better. At the time of writing, there is a possibility that Croke Park, and the GPA and CPA, are moving closer to resolving the fixtures calendar before the 2021 season begins.

One solution is obviously to reduce the panel of players (at all grades) to 20. Another is to reduce the number of competitions and games – there are simply too many. Then you have the issue that, for clubs, there are often no competitive games between May and August – the very best time for playing sport in Ireland. That can't go on, it simply can't, if the games and the clubs – and most importantly, the young players – are to prosper. But it has to be done at a national level, and the GAA has to lead the change. It has to be the change.

The amount of money now being pumped into the preparation of county teams is unsustainable and impacting on our clubs. Tom Ryan, the Director

General of the GAA reported that, *"The combined cost of preparing and fielding senior inter-county teams for the 32 counties came to €29.74 million in 2019. This was an increase of 11.6 percent over the previous year, a trend that simply cannot continue".* This is for senior teams alone. But while the GAA might deplore such spending, what is being done about the diversion of such huge sums from the clubs to the county teams? I'm not so interested in why this was allowed to happen so much as what will they do now to mend the great disconnect between Croke Park and the clubs across Ireland.

The GAA have now been hoisted by their own petard. They have built up a lucrative market for the games by over-promoting the pay-per-view provincial, All-Ireland and Super 8 series to the neglect of the clubs. This has created a huge new audience of people for whom their county is their club. In the same way that the professional provincial teams in rugby are now the clubs of rugby supporters, who have forsaken the real clubs in their locality. The grass-root, local, community and volunteer-based entities which used to be the very foundation of the GAA have been subverted by the professional glamour county brands.

And I'm afraid it's becoming the same for some players, whose local club-based dreams have transformed into inter-county targets and who have given up all individuality to be part of a cog in very well-oiled machines. Skill is also giving way to size, power and fitness – especially in football. Time in the gym seems to be more important than time with a ball and other players. Individuality in players is losing out to conformity within processes and systems.

History has shown us that segregation tends not to be successful. These days, dual players are frowned upon and are accused of being the cause of failure in clubs and counties; but this is looking at the 'problem' from the wrong direction altogether. Is success the sole aim of our games, or are they meant to foster joy and inclusion and participation in young people? Burnout is correctly identified as the biggest issue facing dual players and this is where the GAA should be focusing its energy. The pressures to perform on development squads, underage teams, school teams, colleges, clubs and county teams are exacerbated by the huge growth in competitions and the number of games in these competitions by the use of 'back doors' and Super 8s and the like – all driven by administrators rather than any bottom-up demand. It is in the nature of players to want to play as many games as possible but it is up to those in charge to ensure player welfare and a more responsible work-load. It is in the nature of county managers to want sole ownership of the players and to push them to the limit to win championships – especially when rivals are doing exactly the same.

But the spiral has to be broken or the results will be disastrous. Balance must be restored – and Croke Park must take responsibility for this. The solutions are clear: fewer competitions and fewer games in competitions (more knock-outs); players to train for the next team in the next competition; panels reduced to 20 players; a more structured and sustainable fixture list facilitating clubs in particular; clubs to take back ownership of players.

These trends were foreseeable 40 or 50 years ago. When I nearly burned out from playing too many games in 1973 and 1974, I said to the *Sunday Press... "A pruning of the inter-county programme would provide time for both club and county teams... The most important factor apart from relieving the prolonged pressure on players is that they spend more time with their clubs"*. That's 46 years ago and, to be honest, things are much worse now.

I remember the late Séamus Coughlan from Nemo Rangers and the Cork football team of 1973 telling me that the next revolution in the GAA will be by the clubs. And that is going to happen with or without Croke Park's say so. I have believed this for some time and I really fear for our clubs – the heart and soul of our association.

So, when I got a phone call from Liam Griffin in April, 2020 (in the middle of working on this book) to invite me on the executive committee of the Club Players Association (CPA) I wasn't surprised. Now, what they want with a 75 year-old man on the committee is another thing but I'm happy to be involved and to contribute in my own small way. Right now, I have only attended two meetings (via Zoom), but I'm very impressed with the group and the chairman, Micheál Briody, I must say.

Everything they are doing is for the betterment of their clubs and their clubs alone. All their work is purely voluntary, nobody is accepting any expenses or anything like that, and Croke Park will have to listen to the clubs sooner or later. When you think of the amazing community-based work and charity fundraising done by clubs all over Ireland during the COVID-19 pandemic, it shows the good authority of the local club. That is the real power behind the GAA and it must be respected. To date, such respect has not been forthcoming by the hierarchy in

Croke Park.

The future of our games is at stake. I'm certain that the fall-out of the COVID-19 crisis of 2020 will impact more on our clubs than it will on the county scene. The county games will bounce back because of the media attention and the money involved. But can we say the same for our club games and our club players? I think that some clubs will seriously struggle and they badly need support from Croke Park and our government.

The question is this: are our games for the betterment of all our people, young and old, or are they a business? Is it about all our young people enjoying one of the greatest gifts that we can give them – the gift of sport, of hurling and football? Or is it about profit? We have to decide, but the longer we ignore this problem the more acrimonious and vindictive the revolution will be when it comes. And come it will.

I just hope the conflict won't be as divisive and bitter as the one I was plunged into in 2009 in Cork.

◄ ◄ ◆ ▷ ►

A SECOND STRIKE did take place in Cork in December, 2007 and it was disastrous. It went on for over three months. Kieran Mulvey, chairman of the Labour Relations Commission, acted as an arbitrator between the players and the county board – it took the best negotiator in Ireland without any axe to grind to sort it out. But did he? It appeared so. One of the key elements of the negotiation was that the players gave a commitment not to engage in future strikes.

But lo and behold a third strike did happen in January, 2009. It dragged on into February and then March, becoming more and more unpleasant, divisive and spiteful. In late March I got a phone call from Christy Cooney, the President of the GAA, to know would I chair a mediation committee comprising myself, Jimmy Barry Murphy and John Fenton to try to resolve the impasse. I agreed and so did Jimmy and John, and our headquarters was the Cork Airport Hotel, where we proceeded to ensconce ourselves.

We were surprised to meet Páraic Duffy there. Páraic was the Director General of the GAA and none of us really knew him. He's a lovely man and an absolute gentleman, I have to say. He introduced himself and we were wondering why he was there. He said, 'Look, the reason I'm here is that there are up to 18 other counties lined up to see how we are going to sort this out.' We looked at him.

As if we didn't have enough responsibility, I thought.

Páraic said he would like us to follow a charter the GAA had developed; it laid out a template of how the dealings between the players and the managers would proceed. We politely told him that we appreciated where he was coming from but that he was in Cork now, and the way we do things in Cork is the way we do things in Cork. Jimmy made a very good point and explained that if he didn't mind, we had to handle this in a specific and very sensitive way because we had special circumstances in Cork that may not apply elsewhere. And in fairness to Páraic he did accept that and he suggested we try it our own way first and if that didn't work, we could take it from there. He asked us if he could stay in the room and observe – without contributing anything or taking part in any way. And we said okay to that.

Effectively, we were mediating between the county board and the players, but our main term of reference was to appoint somebody as a coach to the Cork hurling team; someone who would be acceptable/amenable to both parties. We had to establish first if Gerald McCarthy – the out-going manager – was still interested, so the first thing we did was to speak to Gerald about that.

Then we had to draw up a shortlist of who we thought could be a compatible manager; who would be acceptable to both parties, but also good for Cork hurling. Somebody who could coach and get the best out of the team and get the players to perform to the best of their ability. Then we had to meet the players and the county board separately to try to get agreement on who that person would be.

And I have to say that all of this was stressful – hugely stressful; we felt a massive responsibility to Cork hurling and Cork GAA. Feelings were running very high at the time on both sides and of course we had all played with Gerald, and Jimmy was a friend and a club-mate of his too. But we had to put our personal feelings aside to try to find a resolution.

The other thing was that we weren't Kieran Mulvey with the whole Labour Relations Commission behind us; we weren't experienced in these kind of negotiations, and the dos and don'ts involved. Conflict resolution is a very specific skill and a lot can go wrong, and one thing was for sure: this was certainly a very serious and bitter conflict.

We arranged to meet the players and John Gardiner had been appointed captain, so I rang John and said I'd like for us to meet him to explain the situation and I told him when and where, and that he could bring along as many players as he wanted, it was completely open. And I told him that I would meet him in the foyer of the hotel at 6.55pm on the following Friday (it was the 3rd of April, 2009) because we were meeting the board representatives at 7.55pm and we wanted to give both sides the exact same amount of time to make their cases.

We wanted there to be parity of esteem and we wanted to be completely fair to both sides.

So, I did likewise with Jerry O'Sullivan, who was chairman of the Cork County Board and it was the same thing: he was to bring along whomever he also saw fit, and the players would get an hour and so would the board. And I told him that we were meeting the players between 7pm and 8pm, and then we would meet the board between 8pm and 9pm. I was completely up front about it.

WE HAD BOOKED a special room in the hotel for these meetings and the three of us prepared as best we could and we had it all worked out what was to occur. So, I went down and I was in the foyer at five minutes to seven as arranged to meet the players.

No sign of them.

Seven o'clock, no sign… five past… ten past seven, nobody. Now I had been standing there for 15 minutes, waiting.

And then I twigged it. Somebody had told me before we were appointed that the way the players were dealing with the board or whoever they had to interact with, that they never turned up on time for a meeting. This was the way that they planned it, as a kind of tactic – or so I was told. I went back down to the room and said to the lads, 'No sign of them… what will we do?' And Jimmy looked out of the window.

'I can see them outside in the car park.'

'What are they doing?' I asked. I was standing near the door.

'Nothing,' he said. 'They're just standing there. Now they're coming.'

The last thing I heard going out the door to meet the players was Jimmy. 'COUGHLAN,' he shouted after me. 'Don't lose the head!' Because, of course, my face was as red as a Cork jersey. I was bulling.

So, I met them at 7.15pm, and it was just John Gardiner and Donal Óg Cusack.

'We're running late,' I said. '… we have to meet the county board afterwards.' And I walked ahead of them towards the room and I didn't look back.

I didn't know if they were still behind me.

They followed me into the room and sat down. Myself, John and Jimmy laid out our terms of reference, the background of how we had come together, our duties as we saw them, our remit and what we were proposing to do to end the conflict.

And to be honest, what we heard from the two players for the next 40 minutes, I could have written a whole book on that alone. And I'm not going to elaborate on that. I had my own views on the third strike and the damage it was causing, but I said nothing and we had a civil conversation. They laid out their case very well and we asked them some questions, which they answered very well indeed.

Then the county board members came in and I think it's fair to say that we grilled them in a way that they had never been grilled before. We put all sorts of questions and issues to them, which they answered and addressed; there was no evasion or anything like that. And some of the questions were not the type of questions they were accustomed to having to answer, but we felt we had to do it.

And I have to say that some of the things that were said to us that evening – from both sides – shocked the three of us. These were not public knowledge – at least we had not been aware of them until that moment. We were quite shocked and we realised, there and then, that the depth of the conflict was far worse than we had envisaged. Nonetheless, we had a job to do, so we set about doing it.

The bottom line was that we appointed Denis Walsh as a coach and he was acceptable to both sides. This was on Friday, April 3rd, 2009 and Cork were playing Kilkenny two days later in a National Hurling League match.

I went along to the match in Nowlan Park to ensure that everything went to plan, that Denis had taken over the squad and the players would play. I was afraid of some last minute glitch. And it was a painful experience to be a Cork man on the sideline that day because Kilkenny absolutely destroyed Cork in a way that I have never seen a Cork team being destroyed, before or since. I didn't think I would ever see the like of the beating Cork got, and I hope I never will again. Kilkenny 4-26, Cork 0-11. A 27-point whipping and the Kilkenny fans baying for more in the dying moments of the game.

I met Christy Cooney before the game – a great Corkman who has done the GAA some service – and he thanked me.

'I know it was a dirty job,' he said, sadly. 'I only hope it's all over now and that we can move on.' I could only nod in agreement. The sad fact of the matter was, that there was one more unpleasant task I had to take on the following day to make sure the agreement stood. I can't divulge that, either, but it got done and I was very glad when it was all over.

I SUPPOSE MY emotion about the whole thing now – and even then – was primarily one of sadness. But there was anger too, and upset. Now, I'm sure the board could have handled things better and I know from all I heard that there are two sides to every story – especially that particular story. And, as I said earlier, the first strike in 2002 was long overdue and righted many wrongs done to players over the years – including me. That was an issue relating to player welfare and the county board should have been leading the way on that long before 2002.

But what happened in 2009 was too much, it went too far and it caused too much hurt. I say that with sadness. All of the anger has dissipated, but the sadness still remains.

◄ ◄ ◆ ► ►

THE SHIFT FROM playing to coaching came naturally to me. I think I knew in the latter stages of my playing career that I would end up as a coach. I trained the Glen senior team when I was still playing in 1980 and I also coached the Glen minor team in '83. I was happy to give something back to my club and I was very happy to coach St Nicks later, too.

In 1981 I began coaching the St Catherine's (Conna) junior hurling team. This came about through Johnny Clifford. Johnny had been helping out with St Catherine's but his job was in Dunlop's where he was also a shop steward. At this time Dunlop's was being closed down – a great shock to Cork along with the closure of Ford's. One week, Johnny was too busy with Dunlop's and he asked me would I take a training session or two for him.

I stayed with St Catherine's (or they stayed with me) for three years.

In the first year, we won the East Cork junior hurling championship which was a big thing as the club hadn't done that since 1957 – a gap of 24 years. I remember we beat Dungourney in the final in Castlelyons in front of a huge crowd. There was great joy in Conna that night. We went to the county final that year, too, but were beaten by Milford who had some great hurlers including Seanie O'Gorman. That game was played in Castletownroche and I'd say there were 10,000 people at it – a massive crowd for a junior game. And it was one of the best games of hurling I'd ever been at. It really was, and we were unlucky to lose by two points, 1-10 to 0-11.

But calling it junior hurling does it a disservice. I have to say that from the moment I began training St Catherine's I was amazed at the standard of hurling. The skill and enthusiasm of the players were of the highest quality and I admit to having been surprised at how highly skilled they were. Imokilly's breakthrough as a huge force in Cork hurling afterwards was certainly no shock to me. I should have been expecting it, really, because over the years, Glen Rovers had some Titanic battles with divisional teams like Muskerry, Seandún and Avondhu, who may have been made up largely of 'junior' hurlers. But I saw many players in East Cork that would have easily – easily – held their own at senior club level and some of them at county level. We had some fine hurlers in St Catherine's, too, like Mike Mellerick and John Mangan. There were some excellent underage players like Denis Walsh and Cathal Casey, who were coming into their own.

I really enjoyed my time training St Catherine's and they couldn't have been nicer to me. I was utterly thrilled when we got back to the county final in 1983 and, this time, we did win it in Páirc Uí Chaoimh, beating Aghabullogue. We had a five-point lead at half-time and went on to win by 1-13 to 1-8. The joy of the team and their families and the people of Conna was something to behold that day and I was delighted for them all, and to have been a part of it. It was a proud moment for our captain, Batt O'Connell and his family when he was presented with the cup.

In the three years I was with them, I think I learned more about hurling from St Catherine's than they learned from me. I had never done any courses in coaching or anything like that and I just wanted to pass on some of the things I had picked up as a player for so long, working with great coaches in the Glen and for Cork. And I also wanted to pass on my own philosophy of hurling: to contest for the ball fairly and vigorously and to play to win, but not at all costs.

I coached Ballyclough to win a North Cork junior championship and I was also involved in Father O'Neills in East Cork in the 1990s and it was great to see them get to an All-Ireland final in 2019 so many years later. And I think my time with the smaller clubs was the most satisfying thing I did in coaching – not the county or the senior championships.

The big difference between the philosophy of teams in hurling and football now and in my time as a player was this: in those days you were seen as an individual whereas now you're part of a process – you're basically a cog in a big wheel. It's all about the system now and the structure; and players are selected based on how well they can be part of the process that drives the machine. A player now is a number and not a person. And even the numbers 1-15 don't mean a whole lot anymore.

I GOT A call from Frank Murphy one day in October, 1984 to know would I be a selector for the Cork senior football team. He also wanted me to be the coach. This was an interesting time for Cork football. In 1983 Tadhg Murphy scored a goal in the last minute of the Munster final to stop Kerry from winning nine in-a-row, but that was a false dawn and Kerry went on to beat Cork again in '84 and win the All-Ireland. The domination of Kerry was really incredible and I was always glad that it hadn't happened in my time as a player. This was the context within which the county board asked me to become involved as coach, trainer and selector for two years. A tough task.

The other selectors were Mick Keating, Paddy O'Driscoll (a former chairman of the county board), Eamonn Young, Dave Loughman from Youghal (nominated by Imokilly, who had just won the county) and Frank Murphy.

As selectors, our first act in late 1984 and early '85 was to scour the county for footballers. I remember looking at every sort of a football match from senior to minor and everything in between. I lost count of the number of games I attended.

Obviously, this was a new experience for me and a big step up from coaching a junior hurling team in East Cork. I suppose I was also conscious that I was mainly known as a hurler, having been involved in the three in-a-row, and there were comments about Cork having a hurler coaching their football team. My involvement was also something I had not envisaged and I hadn't looked for it or pushed for it in any way, shape or form. I was also conscious that I hadn't been involved with senior football for St Nicks for about 10 years.

But there were some very good players on the Cork team at the time like Dinny Allen, John Cleary, Dave Barry, Colman Corrigan, Kevin Kehily and

Jimmy Kerrigan, and I was certain we could build on that.

I felt that we gave a very good account of ourselves in the Munster final against Kerry in Páirc Uí Chaoimh in 1985. But Liston, Spillane, Power and Sheehy were almost unstoppable when they were on song. We were only four points down with 10 minutes to go when we hit the crossbar. The ball came out and Kerry got a goal at the other end. That was a killer blow, a six-point turnaround. We could have been just a point down with all the momentum, but instead we were seven down and that was more or less the difference between the teams at the end, Kerry 2-11, Cork 0-11. Kerry went on to win the All-Ireland again.

To be honest, however disappointing that was, we were bringing in new players and developing them and I was genuinely pleased with that. I also think that the county board and the football supporters in Cork had very little confidence in the Cork team at that time. And that can seep down to the players. Just as over-confidence can be a problem, so can lack of confidence, but it was a real challenge to build confidence in Cork football after a decade of domination by probably the best football team of all time.

We were bringing in people like John Kerins, Niall Cahalane, Tony Davis, Colm O'Neill, Barry Coffey, Tony Nation and Teddy McCarthy. We also promoted Conor Counihan to captain. I thought we had a very strong foundation for a team, a very good Cork team, that would challenge Kerry within years. Out of the 20 games we played in 1985, we won 14 and drew two. We lost to Kerry (twice) and Dublin (who would contest the All-Ireland final) and we were unlucky to lose to Donegal by a point.

Again, in 1986, we were building and the average age of our panel was only 22. We desperately wanted to make the breakthrough against Kerry so that those upcoming players wouldn't get disheartened. We very nearly got promotion in the league, but in the end, that Kerry team was too much of a hurdle for our young players. We had injuries coming into the game in July, Tom Mannix and Tony Davis couldn't tog out. Then, after only four minutes our great full-back Colman Corrigan had to go off on a stretcher after a clash with Eoin Liston. So, we had to make all sorts of changes and reshuffle fellows around. Denis Walsh had to be brought on and he was a real newcomer at this level; it was a baptism of fire – he had to mark the 'Bomber' Liston.

In fairness to Denis, he did very well but despite having a lot of possession, we couldn't get the scores we needed and Tom Spillane gave an exhibition at centre-back, breaking our hearts time and again. We only managed two points in the first-half (both from frees) and we were down 0-8 to 0-2 at half-time. We started the second-half brilliantly with great points from Colm O'Neill and Dave Barry – only four down now. But just then we were denied a goal by Ambrose O'Donovan miraculously sweeping the ball off the line. I still don't know how he did it. We could really have done with that lift, it would have put us only one behind, but it wasn't going to be our day. I was proud of our young players, they battled to the very end, but the experience of people like Jack O'Shea and Mikey Sheehy were just too much for us, grinding out the win 0-12 to 0-8.

That was the end of my tenure with the Cork footballers. Billy Morgan returned from New York where he had been for a few years and he took over. Then Larry Tompkins and Shea Fahy joined the panel and suddenly everything clicked. Tompkins, especially, was vital to the team, he had a huge effect on everyone around him. Apart from Mick O'Connell, I don't think I ever saw a better footballer than Larry – he was the missing link and Cork would amazingly go on to win the next four Munster Championships, which I don't think ever happened before or since. Not only that, they contested the next four All-Ireland finals, winning in 1989 and '90 – an unparalleled period of success for Cork football.

And I do like to think that myself and my fellow selectors had a role to play in that success, that we developed a good foundation for Billy to build upon. Even though my involvement as manager from 1984 to '86 is often forgotten, I'm personally proud of it, giving back to Cork football, which I had gained so much from, since my first minor match in 1963 to my final senior game in '74.

I WAS ALSO involved in other teams in the 1980s.

In 1986, working with Kevin Heffernan, I was assistant-manager of the Irish team for the International Rules Series against Australia. This was the second series and the games were played in Perth, Melbourne and Adelaide in October that year. Myself and Kevin had to pick the squad to travel, so we went all around Ireland looking at games; National Football League matches, Sigerson Cup (which was on in Cork), club games. You name it, we watched it.

And it was interesting to work with Kevin. He was before my time as a player and I was just coming to the end of my playing career when he was coming into his heyday as a manager of Dublin. He had masterminded the win in 1974 when Dublin dethroned us as All-Ireland champions, which was also my last year playing county football.

And we finalised the panel to travel – which was the very best panel of footballers in Ireland – to take on the Aussies in the International Rules games. When it came time to go to Australia in October 1986 the GAA decided they only wanted to send the bare minimum of people (just the panel and the manager) and they said they didn't need me to travel with the group, which was fine – I had a lot on, to be honest.

IN 1990 I WAS appointed as manager of the Cork minor hurling team and we won the Munster Championship beating Clare in the final. They were raging favourites, they had hammered Cork the previous year, so that was a great win in a tight and low scoring game. We put up huge scores in the first two rounds, beating Kerry and Waterford with our full-forward line of Mark Landers, Damien Fleming and Kevin Murray scoring for fun. We had Donal O'Mahony in goal and he was only 16 and we had Barry Egan at centrefield, he had a great year for us. Our big player was Brian Corcoran and it was his fourth year on the team. Brian would obviously go on to become a great dual player who later had his own hurling comeback to win All-Ireland championships in 2004 and '05. That Munster final win in 1990 was all the sweeter because the senior hurlers beat favourites Tipperary the same day in the 'donkeys don't win derbies' final.

Our All-Ireland semi-final was against Derry which turned out to be far from the walkover that some people were expecting. Brian Corcoran couldn't play due to injury and we had a man sent off just after half-time, but we dug out the win. In the final against Kilkenny we had a disastrous first-half, we were eight points down at half-time. We brought on Damien Fleming at half-time and in fairness to him, he scored two goals and with a couple of minutes left we were only a point down. Kevin Murray beat his man and passed to Damien who buried the ball in the net. Two points up and the game nearly over. Then the referee, Willie Barrett from Tipperary disallowed the goal because he said he had already blown for a foul on Kevin. The game was afterwards called the 'advantage final'. Willie was quoted years later that he had always regretted his decision, but that wasn't any consolation. We had to go for a point from the ensuing free to draw the match.

To make matters worse, we were well beaten in the replay; Brian Corcoran was injured again and although we brought him on during the game he clearly wasn't fit and we were beaten by 13 points by a very good Kilkenny team.

The strange thing about that 1990 Cork minor hurling team was that there were only two players from the city on the panel and there were no players from the Glen, the Barrs or the Rockies. The two city players were both from Delaney Rovers. It was a foretaste of things to come, really, and a foreshadowing of how the standard of hurling in Cork city would diminish, to the great detriment of our county record over the past 15 years.

In 1991 I was involved with the Cork under-21 hurling team and again we won the Munster Championship, beating Limerick 0-17 to 1-7 in Kilmallock. But Galway caught us in the All-Ireland semi-final in Ennis and went on to win the final, too.

And at that stage, I have to say I felt that I had repaid some of the debt I owed to Cork and Glen Rovers and Saint Nicholas, and the GAA generally. I had gotten so much pleasure as a player being coached and looked after by club and county volunteers. Now I felt that I had done my bit too.

I wasn't keen to take on new teams after 1991 or to get involved as a coach or selector, even though there were many offers. In a way I was not ambitious to further my own 'career' as a coach or to be in the limelight or to be winning championships. I'd done my bit, the best I could, and I was okay with that.

At the 'unveiling' of Denis Walsh (centre) as the new Cork hurling coach in 2009.

« CHAPTER 9 »

Three in-a-Row

1976 WAS A MILESTONE year for me because it marked the last time I played senior football for St Nicholas. We had been beaten in the county semi-final in 1973 by Bantry Blues, but the truth was that the glory days of the 60s were gone.

For me, at the age of 31, it was too much to play both senior football and hurling and I was sad to have to end my footballing days. But not quite. I played a bit of junior football with them over the coming years, whenever I could, and I did other various administrative jobs from time to time.

I'd had some great days with St Nicks and I owed them so much. Winning or losing, I was never as proud to put on any jersey as a Saint Nicholas jersey. Every single time.

It meant the world to me.

◄ ◄ ◆ ► ►

FATHER BERTIE TROY was trainer to the Cork hurling team in 1976. Previously, trainers were usually selectors but Father Troy wasn't and this was something new and innovative. Kevin Kehily was the physical trainer and he was a great footballer in his own right. He was also ahead of his time in the way he prepared players physically for matches. I think he did a course in physical education in Strawberry Hill in London and was one of the first people in Cork to set up a gym. Although 80-minute matches ended in 1975, peak physical fitness was still a prerequisite to win championships. Kevin trained us for the next four years and I actually think he sacrificed some of his own playing career, he was so diligent a trainer.

While we didn't excel in the National League in the spring of 1976, we started out well in the championship – our first match being against our old friends, Tipperary. We trained hard for that match in June. Unlike today your first match could also be your last – your whole season could be over early in June.

In '76 Paddy Barry, my friend and teammate in Glen Rovers, was on the cusp of the team. He was also captain of the Glen that year. Paddy was ordained the day before the Tipperary match in the Society of Missions to Africa (SMA) on the Blackrock Road in Cork. As a result, he could not make himself available for the game. He was also having his ordination reception on the evening of the match, and myself and Martin Doherty (another Glen teammate) rushed back from Limerick to attend.

The match itself was a wonderful game of hurling – one of the best games I think I was ever involved in. And I know I'm biased when it comes to Cork-Tipp games but this was the real deal. Jim O'Sullivan of the *Cork Examiner* the following morning called it *"remarkable"* in the way it ebbed and flowed until Seanie O'Leary's winning point in the dying minutes. Final score: Cork 4-10, Tipperary 2-15.

Cork brought on three subs which made a big difference the same day – Jimmy Barry Murphy, Brendan Cummins and John Allen. Jimmy, especially, who came on in the first-half, made a great impression. For long periods in the game we were second-best to Tipp, especially in the first-half. One thing about the selectors now (Ring included) is they weren't afraid to make changes – that would be a feature of the next three years. If something was wrong, they addressed it, quickly and effectively. And that capacity got us out of many scrapes and pulled us over the line in games where we could easily have been second-best.

But it was such a close-run thing that day. In the very last minute, Seamus Power's shot hit the bottom of the post at the Town End of the ground. I can still see it clearly – a great shot. Having struck the post, the ball ran across the goal line – literally the goal line – with Martin Colman beaten, looking on. And it hit the other post and bounced out. It was cleared and we won by a point.

I don't know how many millimetres of a difference it would've taken for that ball to have crossed the line and for us to have lost and have been out of the championship. Not only would we not have won anything that year, there would have been no three in-a-row. If people ever tell you that luck doesn't have a role to play in sport, they don't know what they are talking about. Millimetres is often the distance between utter glory and total disaster, it's as simple as that. History hinges on the tiniest things.

I played well that day against Tipperary at left half-back and I was nervous because it was my first championship game since my return. I didn't want to make a fool of myself or have people telling me I should have stayed in retirement. The truth is that you might feel great before a game and be flying in training, but you never know how well you will play in any given match.

I always had a theory – I don't know if it's true or not but I certainly believed it at the time – that although the coaching books would tell half-backs to keep the forward on their outside, I always preferred to have him on my inside. I'm not sure why but it always felt more comfortable for me. It used to drive coaches to distraction, but eventually they let me at it because they knew I wouldn't change. Afterwards, when I was coaching, I would always advise the corner-backs and wing-backs to let the forward inside them because – by and large – the ball will arrive outside them both and the player on the outside will get to it first.

I often confused the half-forward because he was used to being on the outside and he tended to prefer it; in fact, he was used to being pushed out sideways. My immediate opponent in that game, Francis Loughnane was a left-handed player and left-handed players especially want to be on the outside. So, we shook hands before the game and he took his place outside me, getting ready for the match to start.

If he did, I moved to his outside.

And he moved to my outside. *Amhrán na bhFiann* started (players used to take their positions before the national anthem those days) and while it was playing I moved outside Francis again. And he moved outside me.

Now we were getting close to the sideline and the national anthem still playing. By the time the song finished, both of us ended up outside the sideline, neither of us wanting to back down. And the whole place looking at us, wondering what the hell we were at – some kind of bizarre version of *Lanigan's Ball*.

The final against Limerick on August 1st was played in the new Páirc Uí Chaoimh and despite Éamonn Cregan scoring four goals and a point, we won 3-15 to 4-5. I was delighted to have played well again. Padraig Puirséal in the *Irish Press* the following day referred to the game as, *"The Denis Coughlan Munster final"*.

Whatever about that, I was thrilled with my form and I was enjoying my hurling more than ever. Of course, when you're winning, it's much easier to enjoy it. But, having 'retired' two years previously I felt I was especially lucky and privileged to be there at all and I was very much in bonus territory. I was 31 in 1976 but I certainly felt more like a 21 year-old.

To make matters even sweeter, Páirc Uí Chaoimh was packed and it was the first Munster final Cork won there, before 47,000 people, many of them ecstatic Corkonians. Sweeter again was the fact that we were now qualified for the All-Ireland final. Those days you went straight into the final some years, which meant that winning a Munster Championship was far more important and prestigious than it is today – another sad feature of hurling and football nowadays.

The Munster final wasn't the only match in the Páirc that year. The All-Ireland semi-final between Wexford and Galway, to decide our opponents in the final, was also played there. It was an awful long distance to drag supporters of both counties, which accounts for the small attendance of 26,000. To make matters worse, the match was a draw and they dragged them back to Cork the following Sunday when only 16,000 attended and Wexford won – very impressively, too. So, it was Wexford in the 1976 All-Ireland final.

I MET A man recently, when I was walking the dog around the Glen, and he was a good age, the same man, even older than me. We got chatting and he laughed.

'Denis, you cost me a lot of money in '76 when ye beat Wexford,' he said.

'Oh?' says I.

'I went to the two semi-finals between Galway and Wexford in the Park, that year,' he said. 'God, they were great matches and I never saw the like of the hurling that Wexford did on both days.' I nodded. I remembered how impressive they had been, too, looking on beside Michael O'Hehir.

'So, you backed them?' I said.

'I went straight out and put every bob I had on them,' he said. 'And I still remember it 45 years later.'

'Good enough for you,' says I, smiling. 'Putting money on a team to beat Cork'.

But the truth is that Wexford were outstanding those days. They had Ned Buggy and Mick Jacob and Tony Doran and a host of top-class players. And, after six minutes of that final in 1976, the man I met in the Glen and everybody who backed Wexford must have been rubbing their hands in glee. They had perhaps the best ever start by a team in an All-Ireland hurling final, with Mick Butler and Ned Buggy scoring two quick points straight after the throw-in. Then Martin Quigley scored a goal in the fifth minute, followed by another a minute later. We were eight points down after six minutes. Six minutes, mind you.

But we never panicked and our experience told on the day. Several of us had been there in 1972 when Kilkenny turned around a similar lead of ours with only 20 minutes left. We had a lot more time in '76 and we just kept at it. It didn't matter so much how you started a game, what mattered was how you finished it. We also had Christy Ring on the sideline and he had been drumming that into us for months.

Pat Moylan, at centrefield, struck a purple patch and he scored 10 points the same day (nine from frees). Himself and Gerald dominated midfield and they both had a huge influence on the game. So, there was no dramatic turnaround, we just kept tipping away, putting over the points and we whittled down their lead until we were level by half-time.

After half-time we got a setback when Tony Doran scored a goal, but almost immediately Charlie McCarthy got a brilliant goal in response. I have to say it was absolutely wonderful. Brendan Cummins was playing on the '40' and he stuck in a ball which Charlie allowed to hop before burying it in the top corner. That gave us a huge boost and we never looked back, winning in the end by 2-21 to 4-11.

I played my part, too. I marked six different Wexford players the same day.

When you're going well in a match it's a great boost if your man is switched – you know then the opposition are in trouble. And I really was having a marvellous year of hurling in 1976, my best ever, probably.

It was a wonderful day for us all and for all Cork supporters. Although I had won an All-Ireland hurling medal in 1970 it never meant much to me because of the circumstances surrounding it. But this did. It also meant that Ray Cummins, Brian Murphy and Jimmy Barry Murphy had now also won hurling and football

All-Irelands. And Ray had the great honour as captain of accepting the Liam MacCarthy Cup on our behalf, the first Rockies man to do so since the great Eudie Coughlan in 1931.

It was very sweet indeed, all the more so for me, because only a year previously, I had thought – with good reason – that my Cork hurling days were over along with my chance of ever winning a hurling All-Ireland medal on the pitch.

HAVING CHRISTY RING on the sideline was critical and he made a great switch with the game in the balance near the end. Wexford's best player on the day – probably the best hurler on the pitch – was Mick Jacob at centre-back. He was truly magnificent and we couldn't cope with him at all; he cleared ball after ball after ball.

Late in the game, from where I was, I could see Christy moving Jimmy Barry Murphy to centre-forward. And Jimmy had the legs on Mick, and he scored four points the same day, which turned out to be our winning margin. Now, I'm sure that moving Jimmy was a collective decision but I'm sure, too, that it was Christy who saw the difference it could make.

Christy had given a great team-talk before the game, emphasising how quickly hurling games can change course and never to panic or give up, no matter what happened. If things turned one way, Christy insisted, they could turn the opposite way, too – advice that greatly stood to us and we eight points down after six minutes.

Christy had also studied the referee for the 1976 final, Paddy Johnston from Kilkenny, a former hurler. Christy went up to Kilkenny to watch him referee a club game a few weeks beforehand and noticed that he didn't blow much for over-carrying. And he said this to Ray Cummins before the game, that he could run more than three steps with the ball and get away with it. And if you look at the video, Ray Cummins got a ball just before half-time and wrong-footed William Murphy and he ran about seven steps before kicking it into the net. It was a vital goal and it's on such small details that championships are won and lost.

Now, I have to put on the record that all the selectors were brilliant that year and in the following years – they all did their bit. While I have singled out Christy Ring, he mostly kept his own council at training and before matches. Frank Murphy did most of the talking and he was very good, in fairness.

And afterwards, I thought too, about Seamus Power's shot at the end of the game against Tipperary. The ball hitting the butt of the goalpost and running along the goal line and hitting the second post and being cleared. It was all just meant to be.

STRAIGHT AFTER THE All-Ireland, it was back to the club because Glen Rovers were in the county final against the holders, Blackrock. Yes, them again. But we had Paddy Barry, Martin Doherty, myself and Pat Horgan, too. Not that I can claim much credit for the win, except to give everybody a desperate fright.

1976 was the first county final in the new Páirc Uí Chaoimh and there were 25,000 people at the match – you get huge crowds at the county final the year Cork wins the All-Ireland. It was an okay day, weather-wise, but the ground was very wet, very muddy, especially under the covered stand, now called the South Stand. There was a lot of controversy about the state of the pitch when the ground was rebuilt in 2018, but in reality, the problem had been going back decades and it very nearly cost me dearly.

I was left half-back on the Glen team and we were playing towards the City End so I was near the covered stand which was very mucky. Just before half-time – I think we were losing at the time – I ran onto a ball and I caught it in my hand but I slipped in the mud.

One of my best friends these days, Donie Collins was playing for the Rockies. Donie is from Castlehaven – there are a lot of Collins's down there. He was coming across to tackle me and when I slid, feet first, he tried to avoid me by jumping over me – something you often see in soccer. But didn't his studs catch me in my right eye as he did so. A total accident, but I went down and stayed down in a welter of blood.

There was a bit of pandemonium when they saw the state of my eye and I was carried off on a stretcher. It must have looked bad; I think there was a photo in the newspaper the following day. I was brought into the new First Aid Room – I was told afterwards that I was one of the first people who made use of it; not the kind of first I was hoping for that day, to be honest. I was also conscious that Margaret was in the stand with Jonathan, who was only five at the time.

Doctor Con came into the room and he said that they had called an ambulance, I had to go to the Regional Hospital immediately. I said okay and I just lay there on the bed. I was bandaged up at this stage. The bandage covered both my eyes, and I couldn't see anything. Next thing, I heard Margaret coming in and Con asking her did she want to see me.

While all of this was going on, I had no idea that a real tragedy had just taken place. A man had gotten very ill in the stand, he had a heart attack.

At half-time, when Dr Jim Young – who was President of the Glen at the time – was coming down to see me, he was called up to the stand to do what he could for the stricken man. Unfortunately, the man had died instantly, there was nothing Jim could do. And when the ambulance did arrive, it took him away instead of me.

So, when Jim went into the Glen dressing-room at half-time, Christy Ring (who was a selector) said to him, 'Well? How is he, how is he?'

And Jim replied: 'How is he? He's dead, the poor man.'

Total shock in the dressing-room, there was a collective gasp.

'Dead?' says Ring. 'Dead! Oh my God, sure we have to call the match off, so. We can't go out for the second-half with Denis dead.'

Jim quickly clarified the confusion and the Glen went out for the second-half and won.

In the meantime, I was brought to hospital by car. Very kindly, Dr McCarthy, a priest who was President of Farranferris offered to bring me. He had to lower the seats in the car for me to lie down – I was badly hurt, in fairness. That evening, Jack Lynch, who was Taoiseach, came to visit me in the hospital with the Lord Mayor, Seán French who use to play with the Glen. It was strange talking to them without being able to see them.

I ended up being in the hospital for a week. I needed surgery to save the sight in my eye and they inserted 24 stitches all around it and down the side of my face to put me back together.

And all this was only a few weeks after we had won the All-Ireland. How quickly things can change, how quickly we can go from the highest high to the lowest low. Having said that, I was lucky again – the eye healed up fine, even if I had to be careful with it in future, especially playing hurling. It probably meant the end of any aspirations of a modelling career, too.

People joked with me later that we would have lost the match against Blackrock if I had stayed on that day, but I do think about the man who died in the stand. While my family and I got lucky that day, his family did not.

Of course, today a player would not have been seriously injured in the first place, with the face masks hurlers use, and that's all to the good. But few of us wore helmets in those days, and a helmet might not have protected me from that particular injury, anyway.

When I did come back to hurling, I tried to wear a helmet, but its wire pressed up against the dressing I had to have over the wound and it was too painful. When we went to play in the Wembley Games in 1977, Dr Con did insist I wear one, but that was a once-off. What I did wear, for a while, was a bandage all around my head, like the one you see on second-row rugby players. I was very self-conscious about it, but needs must.

Anyway, the best thing about that day in October, 1976 is that our players showed what the Glen spirit was all about. My great friend, Finbarr O'Neill was brilliant in goal and our full-back line of Father Paddy Barry, Martin Doherty and Teddy O'Brien were inspiring, keeping the famed Rockies to only 10 points. Our half-backs, Donal Clifford, Jerry O'Sullivan and Frank O'Sullivan (who went left half-back when I was injured) were outstanding, too. Joe Joe O'Neill and Liam McAuliffe (who came on for me) worked their socks off and our forwards were tireless, causing real problems. I'm going to name them all for the record: Patsy Harte (who scored 2-2), Pat Doherty, Pat Horgan, Vince Marshall, Frank Cunningham who came on as a sub, Tom Collins and Red Crowley. All proud Glen men and the great heroes of 1976.

But we weren't finished yet.

A FEW WEEKS after the county final we played Newmarket-on-Fergus in the Munster Club Championship. This was my first game back after the eye injury and I must admit I was nervous playing with my big bandage strapped around me. It was a very sticky game and we were lucky enough to scramble the win. Clare teams always put up a ferocious challenge to you and the same club had beaten us by a point in the same championship eight years previously. This time, we were able to get revenge, winning – just about, 2-9 to 1-13. Finbarr was brilliant in goal again and I was very relieved, my eye having stood up to its first stiff challenge.

The Munster club final was played on the 19th of December. This was against South Liberties who had Éamonn Grimes, Joe McKenna and Pat Hartigan among other Limerick senior hurlers. The match was played in Limerick in bad conditions and it was a tough game with three players sent off, two from South Liberties – both for late and dangerous tackles on our goalkeeper, Finbarr O'Neill. Despite this, we were losing by two points at half-time. At the start of the second-half, Joe McKenna scored a point to put them three up, but from then on the extra man told for us and we kept them scoreless for 20 minutes, eventually winning 2-8 to 2-4, a true December scoreline.

I was delighted, because for a while after the county final I wasn't sure if I would ever play again, so severe was my eye injury. And I ended up at centre-back against South Liberties, marking Joe McKenna, which was no easy task. I think I did okay on him.

It was a great joy to win my third Munster hurling club championship, my first one having happened 12 years before, in 1964. I was always so proud of my club, but in a way, in those Munster and All-Ireland championships, the Glen were representing Cork too, and that was a great honour and something we took very seriously.

This was a time of great dominance for Cork clubs. Between 1964 and '80, Blackrock won five Munster titles, St Finbarr's won four and Glen Rovers won three. Cork clubs winning 12 Munster Championships in 17 years. Between 1971 and '80 a Cork club won every single Munster Championship – 10 in-a-row!

Don't tell me that the dominance of these three great Cork city hurling clubs was not a significant factor in the dominance of Cork hurling, too, especially in the 1970s, when Cork won five Munster Championships in-a-row. And club hurling mattered a lot in Cork those days. There were an estimated 38,000 people at the county final in 1977 between St Finbarr's and Glen Rovers. Think about that number for a minute. These are two inner city club teams but 38,000 people wanted to see them playing. In 2019 there were just over 5,000 people at the county senior final between Glen Rovers and Imokilly in Páirc Uí Rinn, even though there was a second county final played just before it. What does that tell you?

The Glen went on to play St Gabriel's of London in February, 1977. That took place in Páirc Uí Chaoimh. In March, we beat Tremane of Roscommon in the All-Ireland semi-final – again in Cork (the Mardyke this time) – in what was a terribly one-sided game, not doing us much good at all – even though Tom Collins must have created some kind of record, scoring five goals. Tremane had shocked Kiltormer in the Connacht final and there was another shock in Leinster where Camross of Laois beat James Stephens of Kilkenny.

We knew Camross would be good in the All-Ireland final, you didn't beat James Stephens with a bad hurling team. The Camross backbone comprised four Cuddy brothers, PJ, Martin Tim and Sean. PJ was quite young but a serious hurler, nonetheless, and tough. The match was played in Semple Stadium on the 27th of March, 1977 and it was tight enough until the very end when we pulled away a bit, winning 2-12 to 0-8. Again, Tom Collins was the hero, scoring another two goals and it was a great day for my friend Finbarr O'Neill who was captain.

But most importantly, Glen Rovers were champions of Ireland, and we all – and everybody in Blackpool – took great pride in that.

◄◄◆►►

WITH ABOUT 13 MINUTES to go in the first round of the Munster Championship game against Waterford in June, 1977 Cork were seven points down. We had lost Tim Crowley in the first-half to injury. Waterford were fired up like a hive of angry bees. We were in trouble all over the pitch and I had a bad feeling. I was thinking of our defeats to Waterford in 1967 and '74 – Déise teams really were a problem for us and this was a right dog fight in Semple Stadium.

To make matters worse, we were All-Ireland champions and ripe for the taking. To make matters worse again, I was captain, the Glen having won the county the year before. Pat Horgan and Martin Doherty were on the panel but I was the only Glen player on the team.

Luckily, we turned it around. Our forwards came good and our backs conceded only two points in the last 25 minutes of the game. But up to Ray Cummins's goal with three minutes left, the match could have gone either way.

All this forced me to think about my captaincy. My track record as captain of teams was dire. The Cork under-21 footballers in 1966 – we lost to Kerry. The senior footballers in 1967 – we lost to Meath. In 1970 I should have been Cork hurling captain but was dropped. In 1973, the Glen – beaten by Blackrock. In 1973 the Cork hurlers – beaten by Tipp. I was captain of Munster in hurling and football – both lost. Any year I was captain of St Nicks – lost.

This crept into my mind and I couldn't get rid of it. My concern wasn't so much of the effect on my own game as the effect on the team. I knew I'd be okay personally, it was the team I was worried about. We had such a good team that we should be winning and I didn't want to jeopardise that, so I approached Martin Doherty.

'Martin,' I said. 'I'm going to step back as captain and let you take over. My record as captain isn't great.' And I had no qualms about saying that to Martin, who was a fellow club man and a great Glen Rovers hurler.

Martin said fine and to this day I have never – not once – regretted that decision. Not in over 40 years. When we did win in 1977 and Martin lifted the Liam MacCarthy Cup I felt completely vindicated. I was utterly thrilled.

There was a problem and I had dealt with it. The fact that the problem was in my head was immaterial – it was still a major issue for me and once it went away the team flourished again and I flourished, too. Winning the All-Ireland was the only thing I wanted, any personal glory beyond that was of no interest to me whatsoever.

I'm not saying my decision was an easy one. It wasn't. I knew well what I was giving up (after 1970 I knew it better than anybody), but it was the right thing to do and the selectors didn't mind and we moved on. That was that. Martin would be captain for the Munster final against Clare.

There was an exceptional spirit and purpose about the camp that summer. And that sense of togetherness had been mainly created by the selectors (which in my experience was very unusual). All the players from the different clubs slotted in well with each other. The starting fifteen and the subs – it didn't matter. Which club – it didn't matter. Older or younger – didn't matter. We were all in it together.

For example, Brian Murphy and Johnny Crowley came from clubs that weren't as strong as the Glen, Barrs or Rockies but they fitted in so well, as did our goalkeeper, Martin Coleman. That year, two young players had come on to the team: Tom Cashman and Dermot McCurtain from Blackrock and they gelled right in immediately.

Clare had gotten the better of Tipperary in the first round after a replay and then they beat Limerick. So we knew they would be battle hardened and a serious threat on the 10th of July in Thurles.

Now, Clare had just won the National Hurling League, defeating Kilkenny in the final. And they would retain it the following year. They had an outstanding half-back line: Ger Loughnane, Gus Lohan (a veteran and father of Frank and Brian) and Seán Stack. But they had great hurlers all through the team and they believed it was their time.

It was a very high scoring game that swung our way when Ray Cummins got into some kind of a tussle with the Clare full-back, Jim Power. It was innocent enough, really, but Ray lost his footing and fell, and the full-back was sent off. Very harshly in my opinion. But we kicked on to win 4-15 to 4-10.

Clare felt that they had been robbed with the sending off, but an actual armed robbery took place in Semple Stadium during the game. Shortly after half-time three armed men burst into the counting room under the stand terrifying Tadhg Crowley, the Munster Council treasurer and his nine year-old son along with council official, Seamus Power and stileman, Timmy Grace who was making his returns.

The robbers packed £24,594 into a briefcase (all they could fit of the £48,000 takings of the day) and escaped. The Taoiseach, Jack Lynch and the President, Paddy Hillery were sitting in the stand above their heads along with half the Cabinet, watching the match during the whole thing. I think there were around 45,000 people at the game, a big hopeful crowd had come from Clare.

WE WERE DRAWN against Galway in the All-Ireland semi-final in Croke Park. Galway were like Waterford in the sense you didn't know which Galway were ever going to turn up. On their day they could be unbeatable but maybe they didn't produce it as often as they should and that could lull you into a dangerously false sense of security.

They had been in the final two years previously, having beaten Cork, and were desperate to make their big breakthrough. Like Clare, they had a great half-back line of Joe McDonagh, Sean Silke and Iggy Clarke and other outstanding hurlers such as John Connolly, Michael Connolly and PJ Molloy.

In the first-half, PJ gave a display, scoring four points, and we were two points down at half-time. We rearranged our half-back line putting Dermot McCurtain on the left, me in the centre and Johnny Crowley on the right to mark PJ. That didn't work at all and now John Connolly was doing damage on me in the middle. But when I went out to the right on PJ and Johnny went centre-back we got on top. We pulled away in the last 20 minutes, outscoring them by 1-7 to 0-2. Tim Crowley had a mighty game the same day and we needed him badly. He was a powerhouse of a man, he really was.

THERE HAD BEEN a bit of tension around Cork the week before that match because of the so-called 'Three Stripes Affair'. The Cork footballers, including Jimmy Barry Murphy and Brian Murphy (who were also on the hurling team) had defied the county board and worn Adidas gear with three stripes (not manufactured in Ireland) in a Munster final replay against Kerry. The board suspended the players but only from playing football for Cork – which meant they could still line out for their clubs and they could also play hurling. So, Jimmy and Brian got to play against Galway and in the final against Wexford. Eventually the players relented in the dispute, which led Billy Morgan to remark in his book *Rebel, Rebel*, "I suppose it was in the back of our minds that we had relatively short playing careers. If we had a Dónal Óg Cusack, we might have kept it going. Maybe if we kept at that battle back in 1977, the troubles of the last few years would have been avoided".

◄ ◄ ◆ ▷ ►

YOU THINK MATCHES and All-Irelands are important until your newly-born daughter is put into your arms. Then you know what's important in life. Our lovely daughter, Ciara arrived in August 1977, to keep her brother and sister company, and to keep her mother and father busy.

That was a happy and wonderful day, the best day of 1977 by far for me. Another gift and another blessing for Margaret and I, and I'll say more about such blessings later in this book.

◄ ◄ ◆ ▷ ►

IT WAS WEXFORD again in the final and we were very determined not to let them build up a big lead like they had done in the opening minutes the year before. It wasn't as good a game, or as high scoring as in 1976 but we weren't complaining. Cork tend not to win the 'classics' as Christy used to say. Seanie O'Leary got a broken nose in the warm-up, but he's made of tough stuff and scored 1-2 after.

Although we won by only three points (1-17 to 3-8) in reality we were by far the better team and our 16 wides (10 in the second-half) flattered Wexford. They were very dependent on Tony Doran in 1977 whereas they had far more potent threats all over the pitch the year before.

I have to pay special tribute to Gerald McCarthy for 1977. Our big fear against Wexford was that Mick Jacob would repeat his heroics of the year before – he really was unplayable that day. So, Gerald was given a very specific job at centre-forward. At all costs he wasn't to let Mick get the ball into his hand. Now, Gerald was a much better centre-fielder in my view and he was also an artist with the hurley and sliotar. But he completely sacrificed his own skills that day to keep the ball moving and away from Mick Jacob and he did a great job, feeding untold amounts of possession to the wing-forwards and the full-forward line.

And so, Martin Doherty was the first Glen Rovers man since Christy Ring to lift the Liam McCarthy Cup. There's a great photo of Martin raising the cup and me looking on. I'm smiling, but I may have had a little tinge of nostalgia at that moment – of what might have been. But it was only for a moment. It was a very joyful day for me, and I was so grateful to have been a part of it.

It was a great year for me, personally. I won another All Star award and was selected as Texaco Hurler of the Year. That's the highest accolade you can get in hurling and I was in august company the night of the presentation in Dublin. Eamonn Coghlan (Athletics), Phil Sutcliffe (Boxing), Eddie Macken (Equestrian), Jimmy Keaveney (Gaelic football), Christy O'Connor Snr (Golf), Terry Gregg (Hockey), Vincent O'Brien (Horseracing), Derek Daly (Motor sport) and Willie Duggan (Rugby). It was a proud night for myself and Margaret, and for Glen Rovers and Cork too, I suppose. But the All-Ireland win was all that mattered. It was the first time since the 1950s that Cork had won back-to-back all Ireland championships.

And, most importantly, it gave us a chance to try for three in-a-row.

Jack Lynch, who was Taoiseach at the time, presented the Texaco award to me that night. One Glen Rovers player to another.

GLEN ROVERS GOT to the county final again in 1977 and there was a huge crowd in Páirc Uí Chaoimh to watch us play our old rivals, St Finbarr's. Officially there were 34,000 at the game but it was probably closer to 42,000. Basically, the Páirc was full for a club match.

Because the Cork hurlers were going so well, in part, the county final was a celebration of that – the 'little All-Ireland' as we humble Corkonians like to call it. But it was a remarkable occasion, even if the Barrs were too good for us on the day. As club All-Ireland champions, we felt we had a point to prove, but not much went right for us. It was very disappointing.

It's fair to say that there was a great rivalry between Glen Rovers and St Finbarr's, going back to 1934 when the two teams first met in a county final. The Glen won that day and the dominance of the Barrs and Blackrock in Cork would never quite be the same. They would now have to contend with their noisy northside neighbours. Blackrock had won 20 county championships and St Finbarr's had won 10 before the Glen won their first, but we weren't long making up for lost time. Including 1934, Glen Rovers won eight in-a-row, and we dominated the 40s and 50s, too. And those were the great teams that I was hearing about, growing up in Madden's Buildings.

◄◄◆►►

THE NATIONAL HURLING League was a big competition in my time. It had a much higher status than it does now. It was a very good national competition and counties – even like Cork who were winning All-Irelands – didn't hold back the way they do today. That time it would be very rare if you didn't put out your best team, but the other factor was that people valued winning a National League. Also, the selectors of All Star teams took the league seriously and factored in league performances all through the year into picking their teams. That doesn't happen anymore.

I never won a National Football League medal. It's one of the very few medals I don't have, but we never even managed to get to the final for some reason. In 1969 we reached the play-offs, but were beaten by Kerry – ruining my chances of being the first ever player to win both hurling and football league medals in the same year.

In truth, football medals of any description are a rarity in Cork, so for me to win one senior All-Ireland, one junior All-Ireland, five senior Munster medals, one under-21 and one junior Munster medal is really remarkable. Especially because you had to best Kerry to win any of those, let alone all of them. But no National Football League medal.

In hurling it was a different story. Cork won the National Hurling League in 1969, '70 (in which I didn't feature, as I've said) '72, '74 and '80.

WE GOT A bye into the semi-final of the Munster Championship in 1978. We played Waterford in Thurles on the 25th of June and, unusually, we beat them well.

There was a bit of controversy in Cork in 1978 due to the restructuring of the county senior championships and the creation of a 'back-door' system. Some of the smaller clubs were happy with this, but the players on the Cork panel were far from happy. We also felt that the county championship would be robbed of its glamour and I was one of those who spoke out against it. Dermot McCurtain said in one newspaper article that the same interest in the championship would not be there anymore. Gerald McCarthy went further, saying that the county board didn't *give a damn about the players*" and that money meant more to the board than players did. Everybody (me, especially) knew that the players were already being overplayed and now the board were bringing in extra games, with the championship being contested on a league basis. But Gerald predicted that the public would not generate extra income for the board and that supporters would stop going to club games in Cork.

How prescient: that's exactly what happened and now we have a paltry 5,000 at county finals when once we had over 30,000.

Gerald made an even better point, however – and this is in February, 1978, remember. He said that he could foresee a time when this format would lead to the decline of the big clubs in Cork and that such a decline would also damage the quality of Cork hurling teams. He pointed out that the lack of a prominent club in Tipperary had been a strong factor in the deterioration of the Tipp senior hurling team. Tipperary really were in the doldrums at this time – they went an amazing 16 years without winning a Munster hurling championship, between 1972 and '87. Gerald's words are chilling when you think of the situation now in Cork, without an All-Ireland title in 15 years. He said, *"I fear the same might happen in Cork and what a tragedy that would be."*

The issue raised its head again before the Munster final in July when extra club championship games were scheduled as we got ready to play Clare. We were going for three in-a-row and Ray Cummins couldn't train with us because he had to prepare for a football match with St Michael's against Milstreet. To add to our problems, Dermot McCurtain, Johnny Crowley and Seanie O'Leary all picked up injuries. There were rumours in the newspapers that morale was low. That wasn't true, however annoyed the players were, but it wasn't the ideal preparation for a do-or-die Munster final against Clare on the 30th of July, that was for sure.

That day got off to a terrible start. At that time players went by car to games and there were different cars for different groups of players. I was in the East Cork car, since I was living in Carrigtwohill. Paddy Roche from Roche's Garage used to pick up myself and some of the others and drive to Thurles or wherever. And we headed off in plenty of time that morning – or so we thought.

At the Kilcoran Lodge between Mitchelstown and Cahir the traffic was gridlocked. I can recall three lines of cars lawlessly driving up the (pre-motorway) road, even though we were more than 30 miles away from Thurles. We were going nowhere fast, and four Cork players in the car.

Paddy turned the car around and headed back for Mitchelstown to try to find another route – this was in the days before Sat Navs or Google Maps. We were getting a bit panicky, I have to say. The other team cars were in the same boat but we didn't know that. The heart-rates were fairly high when we made it to Semple Stadium but those were the days before Fitbits too. In fairness, there were 54,180 people in the grounds and another 4,000 had to be locked out because it was full. Most of those at the game seemed to be from Clare, they had all but evacuated the county. They were convinced this was their year – with good reason, too.

Clare were very fired up. The sending off of Jim Power the previous year was used as a motivational tool and it raised its head a lot in the pre-match analysis. Winning leagues was fine, but it wasn't enough for Clare – they were after Munster and All-Ireland championships and they felt they were good enough to achieve them. This was their time to break through, today was the day. They were managed by the great Father Harry Bohan and coached by none other than Justin McCarthy, my old centrefield partner.

It was a dry day but very windy – there was a fierce wind blowing down the pitch and we had it behind us in the first-half. Not only did we not make use of it, we hit 13 wides. The half-time score: Cork 0-5, Clare 0-3. Eight scores in the first-half of a Munster final – surely a record low. A measly two-point lead for Cork with a gale of wind behind us.

It was an especially embarrassing first-half from our forwards – ALL of whom failed to score in that first 35 minutes. I'm going to name them all to rub it in: Gerald McCarthy, Jimmy Barry-Murphy, Pat Moylan, Charlie McCarthy, Ray Cummins and Seanie O'Leary. As good a forward line as ever represented Cork but the scorers in that first-half? John Horgan at corner-back scored four points from placed balls and Tom Cashman at centrefield scored our only point from play. The chant of ... 'CLARE... CLARE... CLARE' rang in our ears as we left the pitch at half-time and greeted us back onto it for the second-half.

We knew at half-time that the name of the game in the second-half would be to defend with our lives. We knew that Clare were going to throw absolutely everything at us to win their first Munster championship since 1932.

WHO DID WE turn to in the dressing-room to regather and stir ourselves? We turned to Christy Ring and he gave one of the finest speeches I have ever heard, and I have heard many of them. I've never forgotten it and by the time we returned to the pitch we were as ready as we would ever be.

But where were Clare?

We waited, and we waited and we waited, but no sign of them. I'm not sure how long they kept us waiting – it felt like a lifetime. But if they were trying to psyche us out of it, that was not going to happen. If they thought it would rattle us, they were wrong. If they thought this was the day they would brush Cork aside, they were also mistaken. We had no intention of going anywhere and we weren't going to give up our Munster and All-Ireland Championships without a hell of a battle. They didn't hear Christy Ring giving the speech of his life in the dressing-room that day – we did. And if they kept us waiting minutes, hours or days to play the second-half it didn't matter.

The second-half was one of the finest defensive performances Cork has ever produced. Against a gale force wind we held them to eight points, winning out by 0-13 to 0-11. It was the lowest scoring Munster final since 1963 and only the second ever since 1888 without a goal. None of that mattered to us. You have to win the dirty games as much as the classics.

We were especially determined not to concede a goal and we didn't. A goal would have lifted Clare and the roar would probably have blown Thurles off the map. Not only did they not get a goal, they didn't get a sniff of one; I don't think

Martin Coleman had to make a serious save. As a back, that made me very proud. Our three in-a-row was still on and we were still Munster champions at the final whistle.

This was Tom Cashman's finest hour; it was his Munster final. He gave an exhibition of hurling, left and right – there should be a poem or song written about the Blackrock man's heroism that day. He broke Clare. I've seen him play many brilliant matches but this was the greatest I ever saw.

It was a wonderful win in adversity and it meant the world to us. You don't have to wait over 40 years for hunger, we were as hungry as we ever had been. And, as a defender, it's lovely to win games where one team scores 30 points and the other scores 29. Or when there are nine or 10 goals flying in from all angles. But with our backs to the wall and into a gale of wind that day in 1978 we showed our mettle. We showed what Cork steel really was. Christy put it up to us at half-time and we answered him in the second-half. I was very proud of my fellow defenders. Denis Burns came in for Brian Murphy and he did a great job, as did Martin Coleman in goal, along with Martin Doherty, John Horgan, Dermot McCurtain and Johnny Crowley. Ray and Charlie got some great scores in the second-half when we needed them, too. All around the pitch there were Cork heroes that day.

We didn't need to believe in Biddy Early to win that Munster Championship in 1978 – our fourth in-a-row, the first time Cork had done that since the 1920s – we needed to believe in ourselves. And to back up that belief. Which we did.

And so, we won through to an All-Ireland final on the 3rd of September, a five-week wait. It would be Kilkenny in the final.

Good. We had unfinished business with them.

Three in-a-row was all the talk in Cork that August. But within the squad we were very disciplined and focused. We never mentioned the three in-a-row, not once. Not in training, not in the dressing-room, it never raised its head in any way, shape or form.

And this was a deliberate act by the selectors. We were playing a hurling match and we had to prepare for that like any other hurling match. The selectors were very focused on the small things that each of us had to work on; how we could improve our own games individually, while at the same time preparing as a team for the old enemy. And that was all we were focusing on. While the county was in a lather of speculation and a frenzy for tickets, we went quietly about our preparation.

As players we had to get ready to beat Kilkenny and we were to do this by playing a certain way. Very simply, we were not going to allow Kilkenny to get the ball into their hands. This was the instruction and we prepared accordingly. In the training sessions the ball was moving quickly, always moving, always with purpose. Get the ball to the wings, get it into the full-forward line, keep it moving – doubling, flicking, tapping, whatever it took. It was drilled into us and we worked at it very hard.

Funnily enough, I loved this and I was well used to it. In the Glen we often used to prepare the same way to play the Barrs, focusing on keeping the ball away from Gerald and Charlie and Jimmy.

There is no point in trying to be physical against Kilkenny or trying to psyche them out of it. That's a waste of time, as Davy Fitz found out when Waterford tried it in 2008. It just won't work. Kilkenny can match you in physicality all day long. You have to play to your own strengths against Kilkenny and stop them playing to theirs.

You can't hurl if you don't have the ball. And, of course, one of the things we wanted to ensure was that the final would not be a classic like it was in 1972. Classics are no good if you don't win them. We were quite happy for it to be a low scoring game as long as we kept their danger men quiet. They had run up 4-20 in the semi-final against Galway with Matt Ruth scoring two goals and Brian Cody and Liam O'Brien getting two more. We certainly didn't want a repeat of that. Billy Fitzpatrick, Mick Brennan and Kevin Fennelly were all capable of scoring at will, if they were allowed.

So, we had prepared very well, physically and mentally for the final. Christy Ring played a big role in that. A few nights before the Sunday, things were tense and he made another amazing speech, very far ahead of its time. Christy told us a story, and the way he told it made the image very vivid.

It was about the All-Ireland final against Kilkenny in 1946, which they say was his greatest ever game – and that's saying something. How he picked up a ball in midfield and before anybody knew anything he had gone through the defence and then – it had been a wet day – the only thing the people could see was the rain falling off the net. But he had imagined that scene himself in advance, and seen that rain and that net before the game ever happened. He was talking about visualisation, essentially, although this was long before the word existed or was ever used in sport. Dr Con described it very well in an *Irish Examiner* article in 2019 on the 40th anniversary of Christy's passing.

"That [visualisation] was a very new idea at the time, but he broke it down for the players. He spoke about his playing days, and how he'd envision everything the week of a big match — togging out in the dressing-room, the parade around the field, all of that, so he'd be calm when it came time to play the actual match itself. Then he described the goal he got against Kilkenny in the 1946 All-Ireland final. In detail, the raindrops falling off the net when the ball hit it. All of that gave the team a huge boost."

I'm sure when Christy saw the headline in the *Irish Press* the day after the final, he smiled. *"No Classic but Cork had Champion Touch"* it said. Exactly what we had planned. We were more experienced than Kilkenny – they had some young players – and our experience told. We were able to take the setbacks when they came. We didn't panic, we kept to the plan, we played our own game all through. We had visualised what we wanted and then we were able to execute it. When we conceded a soft goal after five minutes, we responded with a point. When we had to make changes, we did. Switching Ray to corner-forward was a great move and got him out of the clutches of Fan Larkin. Moving Timmy Crowley to centrefield worked, as did switching myself and Johnny Crowley in the second-half.

Our scores came at vital times, especially Jimmy's goal in the second-half which gave us some breathing space, but again I felt our back-line was the foundation for the win. Holding Kilkenny to 2-8 was a great day's work in any language and they could never build the kind of momentum that swept us away in 1972. We never gave them space or time on the ball and we limited their possession – which we had worked on all during August.

The usual heady mix of joy and relief flowed through me at the final whistle. We had really done it; we had really won the three in-a-row. For the first time in over 25 years.

Winning an All-Ireland with Cork was beyond my childhood dreams, but winning three in-a-row? Being part of that? That was far more than anything I could ever have imagined. And the feeling when we had achieved it? It was everything I could have hoped for – absolutely everything.

Although I was now 33, I felt as fresh that year as I ever had. I had trained as hard that summer as I ever did and I enjoyed the training, too.

I was the oldest man on the team (Gerald was a few months younger) but I didn't feel it.

I felt so healthy that I could go on forever. Sure, what could go wrong?

What, indeed? I was about to find out.

◄◄◆►►

NOW, THERE IS something about the three in-a-row that I hesitate to mention but I will anyway – I suppose I should. In the 1978 final I was marking Kevin Fennelly – his family would become quite the dynasty later, fair play to them, comprising many stunning hurlers. Kevin scored a goal off me early in the game. In my defence, in the three All-Ireland campaigns of those years, that was the first score I gave away.

There was no other score against me in 1976, '77, or '78. Nor was there a score against me in 1979. I went four years, playing 15 matches at wing-back for Cork, without conceding a score, marking maybe 25 different players – apart from Kevin's goal.

And how the goal came about was this – I can still see it vividly. Matt Ruth got the ball – he was left corner-forward for Kilkenny and he was under the Hogan Stand and Kilkenny were playing into the Railway (Hill 16) End. He hit in a high looping ball towards the square and myself and Martin Doherty both went for it. I read it first and I got there ahead of Martin and Brian Cody (who Martin was marking) and I caught it.

The next thing was, both Martin and Brian hit into me. Their momentum carried them into me and we were all still reaching up for the ball which I had just caught – I was wide open. They knocked me over and the ball fell out of my hand in front of the goal.

Kevin was there and he just tapped it in.

And it was very frustrating because I had made up my mind even before I caught the ball what I was going to do. This sounds strange but I can remember it clearly. My plan was to head off on a solo run with the ball and get it away from the goal as quickly as possible out towards the wing. I thought... *This this is going to be great... I'm in my glory here with the ball and away I go.*

But you can't go on a solo run without the ball and before I knew it, I'm on the ground and the ball is in the net and my record is gone. Now, we still had a match to win, and luckily we did and I played okay after.

And I'm only saying this in the following context: I was considered a stylish player but my first instinct *always* was to defend. I was a back first and foremost, before anything else and – as a back – my job is to stop the man I'm marking from scoring. If every defender does that your team will win, it's as simple as that.

While some people might think that it was more important for me to be stylish or to catch the ball or strike the ball well – that wasn't my first priority at all. Anytime I stopped my man from scoring was a good day, even if I hardly touched the ball myself.

My other priority was this: I felt very strongly that there was no point whatsoever in dragging your man down. When you do that, you're losing, and 99 times out of a 100 you're handing the opposition an easy and a guaranteed score. Free-takers very rarely miss at the higher levels. And if you foul somebody that score is against you.

I don't ever recall in my whole career deliberately fouling anybody knowingly when contesting the ball. I may have given away frees but it was never deliberate, because when you do that, you're giving up. Whether that is innocence or naiveté or whatever on my part, that's the way I approached both football and hurling. Doing otherwise simply never occurred to me.

When I was sent off in 1972 the last thing in my mind was to hit my opponent, let alone foul him. It never occurred to me to strike that man on the head – I would never do anything like that and I don't mean that in a boastful, or holier-than-thou way. It's just the way that I was hardwired – for whatever reason I don't know – and I'm only thinking about it now in the context of this book, trying to say something about my philosophy of play. I never even considered doing otherwise or consciously decided I wouldn't foul people. It simply never occurred to me.

It was the ball, the ball, the ball… all the time and all the way. Rightly or wrongly, I don't know. Maybe I should've been more cynical; maybe I should've been thinking about fouling at times but I just didn't want to do it.

I had to smile when I read an article by a Dublin journalist one day – while I was still playing – describing me as a dual playing dilettante. I had to look the word up, I must confess. It means *"somebody who dabbles in an activity, an amateur who seems to know something about it, but doesn't"*. I'm not sure what the writer was getting at. Maybe he was implying I wasn't playing hard enough or tough enough. Maybe he thought I should have been flaking fellows or that I wasn't trying my best. I can tell you I was trying very hard in every single game I played. But I don't equate fouling or hitting fellows with trying hard.

One of my teammates in the Glen told me once that he used to hit me during a game, to get me going. He used to do it when there were opponents around so that I would think it was one of them and he thought it would drive me on. Maybe it did, but I always felt I was giving it everything and that you didn't have to be dragging players down or hitting them or shouting and roaring to do your level best.

In a way, I did feel I had an ability to read the game. That I could see where the ball might come and as a result I didn't have to foul as much as other players – backs, especially. I think I am justified in saying this because I do remember one particular foul and I was mortified I did it. It's my only memory of deliberately dragging somebody down and I was disgusted with myself.

IN THE ALL-IRELAND football final against Galway in 1973 I was marking Jimmy Duggan. Now, Jimmy was, in my opinion, their best player – he really was the most beautiful footballer you could imagine. He is a lovely man too, and he'd wish you well before the game.

And he got to a ball ahead of me and was heading off towards goal, towards the Railway End and I was chasing him. And I don't know whether I tripped over myself or if I panicked, but what did I do except drag him down. It was almost like a rugby tackle, I just dragged him down unceremoniously.

Nowadays you'd get a black card for it and rightly so, but those days it was just a free in. But I was so horrified at this and I was so ashamed – and this is an All-Ireland final now, the stakes are high – I said to him, 'God, Jimmy… I'm so sorry for doing that'.

I was so embarrassed that I apologised to him there and then in the middle of the game in Croke Park with 73,308 people looking on and hundreds of thousands watching on television.

But my philosophy was that I didn't care how many scores my opponent got off me. You don't foul him. And it was the same when I was coaching afterwards – particularly coaching defenders.

If you foul, you lose.

It's an automatic and stress-free point. If you tackle carefully, on the other hand, if you hassle the forward and put him under pressure (legally), it is much harder for him to score.

The Cork team against Tipperary in 1976, the first step on a great journey.

On our way back to Cork in 1976 – myself and Jonathan in the middle, holding the Liam MacCarthy Cup.

Watching Martin Doherty lift the Liam MacCarthy Cup in 1977.

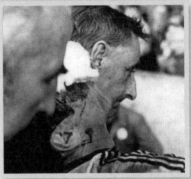

Being carried from the pitch in the county final of 1976. John 'Kid' Cronin in the foreground, Mick 'Langton' McCarthy on my other side.

With two hurling and sporting legends, Jimmy Doyle and Ray Cummins in San Francisco, 1972.

My memento of the county final in 1976 and strapped up like a rugby second-row forward before the 1976 All-Ireland Club final against Camross.

« CHAPTER 10 »

Jack

JACK LYNCH WAS from a different era to Christy Ring – another generation back again – and a much different era to me. He played with St Nicholas and Glen Rovers until 1951 but he was long gone as a player before I had any contact with the clubs. But he was often spoken about and he might appear at Glen Rovers or St Nicks matches or events and that always generated great excitement, especially among the older people who held him in awe.

I think he was still playing when he was a TD, and I remember older men in the club saying that they dragged him back playing long after he should have finished. Apparently, he once said to them, 'When I'm dead, you'll want my bones'.

But the reason they brought him back was because he had such an aura about him. Even when he wasn't playing, you just wanted him around. And, of course, as a player, he was peerless. Imagine somebody winning six All-Ireland medals in-a-row, in hurling and football. Only one man did that or will ever do that: Jack Lynch from 1941-1946.

He was a very gentle person with tremendous charisma. Mícheál Ó Muircheartaigh tells a lovely story about Jack. When Mícheál was at Christy Ring's funeral in 1979 he was sitting beside a Cork man in the church, and the same man had been captain of the Glen a year or two after Jack had retired from playing. When they got to the county semi-final, he wrote to Jack appealing for him to come back and he took out Jack's letter of reply and showed it to Mícheál at the funeral.

It said, *"Thank you for thinking of me, but I have to reject your kind offer because it would mean dropping a promising young fellow for the sake of an old fellow"*. That was the calibre of man Jack Lynch was, and I would get to see that quality up close.

Jack (whom I always referred to as Mr Lynch) had presented medals to me for the Glen and St Nicks but I was very young then and never really met him properly on those occasions.

When my father died in 1968, he was very good to send a Mass card to my mother, which meant a great deal to her.

ONE OF MY first in-depth conversations with Jack Lynch was a strange one because I couldn't see him. It was after that county final in October 1976 and both my eyes were completely covered with bandages when I had been injured and admitted to the Cork Regional Hospital. On the night of the game, as I was awaiting my fate in my hospital bed, I was told that Jack Lynch and Seán French (the Lord Mayor of Cork) were out in the corridor and would like to say hello; they had come to visit. I was very touched that two busy and eminent men had made the effort, and so it was very nice to chat to them, although I couldn't even see them.

IN THE MID-1970s I had heard rumours from people in Fianna Fáil that I was being talked about in a political sense. Now, I had little or no connection to politics – no real political involvement at all – so this was news to me. But, of course, everybody was conscious that Jack Lynch was Taoiseach and leader of Fianna Fáil, and that he was a proud Blackpool, St Nicholas and Glen Rovers man like myself.

And politics was mentioned to me from time to time by various people but they were probably just feeling me out to know if I would be interested in becoming involved. There wasn't any serious approach. I had no political experience; neither my mother nor father were political in any way. Having said that, we all voted for Jack Lynch, but that was true of almost everybody in Blackpool.

THE INSURANCE DINNER, hosted by the Insurance Institute, was a black-tie affair held annually in the Metropole Hotel and in 1977 Jack Lynch was the guest of honour. Before the meeting I was in the gents toilet and I got a tap on the shoulder. And who was it only Jack Lynch and he asked if he could have a word with me. We went upstairs to his bedroom – he and his wife, Máirín were staying in the hotel that night. Máirín wasn't attending the event – no partners were – but she was staying in the hotel with Jack. I was concerned about the time, I didn't want him to be late for the dinner and it was getting quite close, but he said not to worry, he just wanted to have a quick chat.

Up in the room he told me that Fianna Fáil were very interested that I would be a candidate for them in the upcoming general election. He didn't apply too much pressure and we didn't have much time, but he told me to think about it and to let him know if I would be interested or what it would take for me to become interested.

So, this was very different from any previous meeting I'd had with him. I wouldn't say we were talking as equals or anything like that, and the conversation took only 10 minutes, but we weren't chatting about sport or anything casual – this was serious business. And this was Jack Lynch the serious politician, not just a fellow Cork, St Nicks or Glen man.

I didn't follow up on it, and the 1977 general election came and went and I didn't think much more about it. In any case, it looked like Fianna Fáil didn't really need me, they won the election in a landslide, ousting the Fine Gael/Labour government with over 50% of first preference votes and a majority of 20 seats in the 21st Dáil. In the Cork City constituency, Fianna Fáil won no less than three of the five seats, with Pearse Wyse and Seán French also being elected along with Jack Lynch.

THE NEXT TIME I met Jack he showed his kindness and quality again. It was the evening of Christy Ring's funeral in March, 1979, a desperately upsetting day at which Jack Lynch gave the graveside oration. I, myself was ill at the time and as I was at home packing a bag to go back into hospital, I saw a car entering the driveway of our house in Carrigtwohill. It was a big car and I didn't recognise the driver, but who was with him only Jack Lynch. He was calling in to see me, to find out how I was and if there was anything he could do for me. I greatly appreciated the visit.

NOW, I'M NOT sure how serious Jack was in his 1977 approach – later I felt that he was really only planting a seed to consider it as a future career or life-choice. I guess that if I'd been gung-ho and really committed, they might have put me forward. But when the second approach came in September, 1979, it was very different. The Cork hurlers had been knocked out of the All-Ireland championship by Galway in August and this was the Friday before the football final between Kerry and Dublin, so it was on September 14th.

At 2pm I got a phone call in my offices on the South Mall that Jack Lynch wanted to meet me in the Imperial Hotel which was just down the street. And immediately alarm bells began to ring in my head. All that summer, there had been speculation in the newspapers that I would be running in the Cork City constituency by-election, which was due because the Labour TD, Patrick Kerrigan had died on July 4th. It was all news to me but something must have been afoot in political circles.

One headline from *Hibernia* in July said... *"Coughlan Seeks Cork FF Nomination"* which was completely untrue, but in August, the *Cork Examiner* – on its front page – had the headline *"Hurling ace Coughlan to lead FF election attack?"* And in that I am quoted as thinking about running for office, even though it was months to any by-election and nominations were nowhere near being finalised.

So, when Jack asked me to meet him in September, I knew what it was about. I'd probably been expecting it. And, of course, I agreed to meet him – he was the Taoiseach of the country and a great hero of mine. But there was something else, too.

Older men in Glen Rovers had often told me I was like him. That I played hurling and football like him, and carried myself like him. People have even shown me old photos in the club or elsewhere and said, *'Don't you think you look like him, there?'* I honestly couldn't see the resemblance, but they weren't making it up, in fairness.

I'd never seen him play. I was too young, but it was obviously flattering. And everybody also said what a nice man he was, what a gentleman, but he wasn't soft either. As well as his six All-Ireland medals with Cork, he won 12 county senior medals with St Nicks and the Glen and six Railway Cup medals with Munster at a time when you wouldn't even take to a playing field if you were soft, let alone win anything.

They say he was the most popular Irish politician since Daniel O'Connell and, of course, he was like a god on the northside. He was revered, and I don't think there has ever been so popular a person in Cork since Jack Lynch – in sport or the arts or in any field. The only person who was ever as popular was probably Michael Collins, even if he came from a different political party and lived in a very divisive time. If somebody ever spoke about 'Jack' in Cork they could only be speaking about one person.

So, I went along to the Imperial Hotel at the appointed time and I sat down with him in a meeting room that had been set aside. And, of course, he was concerned about my health – he asked me all about that and I told him that it was much improved since I had last met him after Christy's funeral, and I thanked him again for visiting me that evening. He asked all about Margaret and the children – we had been to his home in Skibbereen on a couple of occasions, with mutual friends from San Francisco, Frank and Kathleen O'Keeffe – about my family life, what age were the children, how were they and so on. And he wanted to know about my work, how that was going. He was well aware that I had a new job in an insurance brokerage firm on the South Mall because I had asked him to open the company offices a few months previously but he hadn't been available.

I suppose he was getting to know me better as a person, how I spoke and how I came across. We were there for two hours in all, which is a long time to speak to somebody on a one-to-one basis. And he had these deep, piercing blue eyes. When you were speaking, he really looked at you, you knew he was looking at you. Needless to say, he was a very intelligent and perceptive man.

So, I had a very wide-ranging chat with him before he got down to the business of what he really had wanted to talk to me about. He told me in confidence that he would be retiring in December as leader of Fianna Fáil and as Taoiseach. He also told me in confidence the reasons for his retirement, the changes that were coming down the line in Irish politics, and I won't breach that confidence. But it wasn't so much what he was asking me, but the way he asked me, that hit me to the core.

Effectively, he wanted me to be the Fianna Fáil candidate in the Cork City constituency in the next by-election which would take place in a few months. But he didn't phrase it like that. The way he phrased it really blew me away. There are some expressions in your life that you never forget, in moments of special intimacy or importance; things said by people of great value to you.

And I will never forget the exact words Jack Lynch said to me that day. He looked at me with those eyes and in a soft clear voice he spoke up.

'Denis... Máirín and I have decided that you are to be my successor in Cork. We want you to continue on my legacy.'

Now, because I had partly been expecting Jack's approach I was humming and hawing and I wasn't particularly positive towards the idea. And, being the astute man that he was, he could tell this from my reaction immediately. It's very difficult to say no to somebody like Jack Lynch, a man – a hero – you have idolised since you were a child. But the way he asked me...

I immediately felt a huge burden of responsibility to him, to Cork and to the country. I also felt it was a huge honour, that he would pick me, the boy from Madden's Buildings. I have to say that in my whole life this was one of the most extraordinary moments that I have ever experienced.

How could I say no to that? To him? Of all people.

God, it was tough. It really was, even all these years later, I can tell you it was tough. But I knew too, that I would say no.

Then he raised the stakes. He outlined my future within the party and in government over the next 10 years. He was in no doubt that I would be successful in the by-election and he had a pathway arranged for me within Fianna Fáil that had been agreed between himself and some very senior party members. He laid it all out: how I would move up through the system over the following decade. That was all said in confidence, so I don't want to divulge the details. And, of course, I would have had to prove that I was capable of fulfilling those roles and so on but again he didn't seem to be in any doubt that I could.

I began to put forward reasons why I couldn't enter politics. My ill-health; the upheaval to Margaret and my family; leaving our lovely home in Carrigtwohill, upping sticks completely; my business commitments – I had just started a new job I was very happy with. I think I used hurling as an excuse, playing for the Glen and Cork. I was listing out all these things – probably not very coherently.

He listened to all of this and he nodded away and then he said that I couldn't make any commitment there and then, anyway, that I needed to talk to Margaret about it first. And he asked me what did I think Margaret would say and I told him that I knew what Margaret would say: that she would leave it up to myself completely; that whatever I decided she would back me one hundred percent. Whatever I decided would make no difference to the way we felt about each other.

In fairness to me, although I was flustered and emotional and making excuses left right and centre, I wasn't going to blame Margaret for my decision and, of course, she and I had talked about it in advance, I knew what was coming.

He told me that he had been in the same position himself once. He had to make the decision that I was now facing and that it was a crucial moment for me, that it had been thrust upon me, as it were, but sometimes that's how the best things in life can occur. And he was up front, too, about the fact that having a political career meant that one had to make many sacrifices – he wasn't sugar coating it.

He didn't want a decision there and then, he was very fair about that. He asked me to give it some thought and I said I would. If it were anybody else in the world I would have said no there and then. My mind was made up, and I would have left it at that. But because it was Jack Lynch I promised I would give it some more thought. And if it were anybody else in the world offering what Jack Lynch had just offered me, it would have made my decision easier.

BUT IT WASN'T anybody else.

He asked me if I was going up to the All-Ireland on Sunday and I said I was. He said, 'Look, don't go to Dublin, will you stay at home and think about your decision and talk to Margaret, so you can make a fully formed decision? I'll phone you Monday and you can let me know.'

I said I'd prefer to talk to him in person on Monday, that this was one of the biggest decisions of my life, but he said, 'No, I'll ring you Monday'.

We shook hands and I walked out of the hotel, my head reeling. I went back to the office and sat at my desk and looked blankly at the wall.

Máirín and I have decided that you are to be my successor in Cork.

To be honest I didn't need any more time. I had made my decision, really, and it was an agonising one. I spent the weekend looking things over every which way. Trying to convince myself that I was right, wondering if I was wrong.

Trying to weigh up all the pros and cons.

Talking to Margaret. I didn't go to Dublin to the match but I wasn't looking forward to Monday's phone call. If only he hadn't made it so personal. If only he hadn't involved Máirín and worded it the way he did.

We want you to continue my legacy.

I need to give some background, here too. At that time, Jack Lynch was fighting for his political life. The party had run away with the 1977 election as I said but since then, things had not been good, externally, or internally within the party. Within the party, Charlie Haughey was vying for power, he wanted the top job.

Haughey had been fired as a minister for his role in the Arms Crisis back in 1970 but in opposition Jack had put him back on the front bench in 1975 as spokesperson on health and he became Minister for Health in 1977 when Fianna Fáil retook power. The so-called 'Gang of Five' – Jackie Fahey, Tom McEllistrim, Seán Doherty, Mark Killilea and Albert Reynolds – were actively lobbying for Haughey within the party and trying to get rid of Lynch. Party discipline had eroded with the backbencher revolt against George Colley's proposed two percent levy on farmers. Colley's humiliating climbdown showed how frail the hold that Lynch had on his own party, which Haughey was actively exploiting for his own ends. There were other problems around the *Family Planning Bill of 1978*.

The Irish economy was not going well at that time, either. The national deficit in 1978 was 17.8 percent and the national debt had increased by £2 billion. In the European elections of June, 1979 Fianna Fáil were badly defeated all over the country. The Troubles had come to a head in August when Lord Mountbatten was killed in Sligo. Increased security measures were opposed by Síle De Valera, further embarrassing Lynch. There were two by-elections due to be held in November, in Cork North-East and the one Jack wanted me to run for, in Cork City. And he needed to win those elections to have any hope of resigning on his own terms, in his own time. And, so, by refusing to run I risked damaging Jack's ability to bow out gracefully as befitted the great man. What a responsibility.

While I agonised all that weekend, I often wondered... *Why me, why did he have to pick me? And why did he bring up his legacy?*

I wondered, too, if people had said to him about the resemblance between us, as a person or as a player. Jack and Máirín never had children. I wondered if he saw a resemblance – he would have often seen me play – and if that influenced his decision. I wondered about a lot of things that weekend.

Clearly this was important to him. This was his legacy, he was talking about his successor, for God's sake. He was fighting for his political life. He wanted somebody whom he could trust and somebody who would follow on where he left off.

And I was saying no.

I remember vividly on that Monday afternoon sitting in my office, unable to eat lunch, and looking at the phone, waiting for it to ring. When it did ring, it gave me a start.

I picked it up and it was Jack, and he asked me if I had made a decision?

And I said yes, and I told him what it was.

WE HAD THREE children under the age of eight – all of them in vital, formative years. Now I was at home with them early most evenings (even when I was training which wouldn't be for much longer) and if I were a TD or Minister or whatever, how much time would I really spend with them? I'd be in Dublin or campaigning or doing God only knows what.

And even Jack Lynch and his legacy couldn't compete with that. I had a good life, the life I'd always wanted, and I wasn't giving it up for anything or anyone. Still, it was hard, it really was.

There was something else, too. I was not ambitious for power or fame. Whatever fame I got from sport was given to me, I wasn't out there looking for it or dreaming of it. Secondly, I think that I didn't have the confidence in myself to do it. I just didn't see myself succeeding as a politician, I was certainly no Jack Lynch.

If I went for it, I would definitely have given it my all, but deep down I didn't really believe I could do it.

In my defence there were still serious concerns about my health. Elections are stressful and demanding undertakings and, while I felt I could still hurl – hurling never having taken much out of me – I didn't know how well my immune system would react to a whirlwind political campaign. And I would be entering the bearpit of politics in Dublin.

The government was in turmoil, Fianna Fáil were in turmoil, the country was in turmoil. Did I really want to put myself through that? Especially after what I'd been through in February and March?

But that wasn't much of an excuse, either. After I said no to Jack that day I was distressed. I really was miserable and at first, I wondered if I had made a terrible mistake.

The two by-elections were called for November 7th and I played a small part in supporting the Fianna Fáil candidate in Cork, John Dennehy. I spoke at a few meetings and did a little bit of campaigning – out of guilt, as much as anything else, I think.

When the election results were released, I felt sick. Fianna Fáil were beaten and Liam Burke of Fine Gael won the Cork City seat. Myra Barry of Fine Gael won the Cork North-East seat. To make matters worse, not long afterwards Jack Lynch announced his resignation as Taoiseach and leader of Fianna Fail.

As if that wasn't bad enough, his chosen successor George Colley was defeated and Charles Haughey became party leader and Taoiseach.

I felt awful. I'm not arrogant or stupid enough to think that anything I could have done would have changed things for Jack, but I could have tried. When he asked me to do something for him and for Cork and for Ireland I could have said yes. But I didn't.

That regret faded and I have firmly believed for a long time that I made the right decision. I did what I did for myself and for Margaret and our children, and I have never regretted that. I was true to myself and I think that's what we all have to do in the end. The years since then have been good to us, thank God. And I'm more convinced now than ever that the path I chose was the right one.

◄ ◄ ◆ ▷ ►

JACK LYNCH RETIRED from politics on June 11th, 1981 at the next General Election. The newspapers early that year were also predicting that I would run in the election to replace him, but that was without any foundation and no approach was made by Jack or Fianna Fáil.

One morning in late May that year – almost two years after I had turned Jack Lynch down – I came out of my office in the South Mall and who did I meet only the man himself. He must have been campaigning in Cork, even though he wasn't running.

He saw me on the footpath, came over and shook my hand. He nodded, smiled and winked at me. He said, 'You made the right decision, Denis.'

He had been in a bad place in his career when he asked me for help, and I had refused it. But no, his real greatness shone out that day in his gesture of magnanimity, kindness and generosity to me. And I'll never forget it.

AS A SMALL postscript, my name cropped up again in newspapers from time to time afterwards in relation to running for Fianna Fáil. But there was no further approach from the party.

Until 1988.

I got a phone call from an acquaintance asking would I meet Albert Reynolds in University College Cork. I was taken aback but I partly guessed what it would be about. I went along, anyway. Albert Reynolds was Minister for Finance at the time, Fianna Fáil were back in power.

The meeting was held in the UCC Council Room which is an imposing room with panelled walls and a large boardroom table. But when I was ushered in, I got quite a shock at the number of people sitting there. I think there were 10 people, many of whom would be very well known in various elements of Cork society – business, the arts, sport and so on. They were all Fianna Fáil people, needless to say. I won't name them.

Albert came to the point quickly. Cork didn't have a Minister at the time and Fianna Fáil wanted to rectify that situation. He wanted me to run in the next general election and if I did, and I was successful, I would be that Minister.

It immediately brought me back to my meeting with Jack Lynch almost 10 years previously when I was also being offered a high office in the Irish government. And I knew my answer would be the same. But I listened to the various people who spoke and said their pieces. And my reply came into my head just before I responded.

I thanked Minister Reynolds very much for the offer, but I told him that Jack Lynch himself had made a similar offer in 1979 and if I said no to Jack, I would find it very hard to say yes to anybody else.

To be honest, I didn't have to think much about the offer this time. I was older and there wasn't the emotional link to Jack Lynch for starters. I felt I had made the right decision in 1979 and I had never looked back.

Politics was not for me. It wasn't for me in the 70s or the 80s and it would never be. That was that.

BUT WHAT A man Jack Lynch was.

He embodied everything that was best about Cork people and Irish people.

Being presented with my St Nicks 1965 county medal by Jack Lynch.

The night of the 1973 All-Ireland final. From left, Máirín Lynch, myself, Jack Lynch, Donal Aherne (captain of the Cork minor team) and Éamon de Barra (chairman of the Cork Reception Committee).

« CHAPTER 11 »

Something Always Happens

ON THE 13th OF February, 1979 I attended a Sports Council meeting in Dublin. At dinner that evening, I felt very uncomfortable when I was sitting down. There was something wrong but I didn't know what it was.

I was sitting next to a doctor, Kevin O'Flanagan, who was also a member of the Sports Council. He had represented Ireland in both soccer and rugby and he had played for Arsenal in the 40s. He looked at me and said, 'Are you okay Denis? You look like you're in pain there'.

'I don't know,' I said. 'I can't sit down properly… there's something wrong.' I pointed at my groin area.

He stood up immediately and told me to follow him. I did. He marched me down to the nearest gents in the hotel and he told me he needed to examine me, which he proceeded to do.

He looked at me with concern and said, 'Denis, you have to go to hospital immediately'.

'What?' I said. 'What is it?'

'I don't know,' he said. 'But you have a lump in your groin and that is not a good place to have a swelling. You need to go straight to St Vincent's. If I were you, I'd go down there straight away.'

I hummed and hawed, and said I had to be back in Cork the following day for a meeting. But I did get a shock. Up to a few moments before I had felt in the very best of health with no symptoms whatsoever. It wasn't as if I had been neglecting my health or ignoring anything. I was 33 years-old and I had just been part of a Cork three in-a-row, what could be so wrong?

He shook his head.

'Denis, if you don't go tonight, please promise me you will check yourself in tomorrow morning. It really is very serious… time is of the essence.' He wouldn't be drawn on what it might be but he repeated the need for urgent medical attention.

This was 10 o'clock at night and I had no intention of going to hospital. I told him that I'd get it looked after in the morning.

I drove back to Cork the following morning – St Valentine's Day – full of worry. I went straight home and told Margaret what Dr O'Flanagan had said. I told her I had a board meeting of my company that evening in the Metropole Hotel but I'd go to Dr Con Murphy to get checked out first. I told her not to worry, in an attempt to reassure myself as much as her, maybe. I'm not sure if I wished her a happy Valentine's Day. I rang Con and made an appointment. I went over to his surgery in Mardyke Street in the afternoon.

CON EXAMINED ME and told me that I had to go straight to hospital.

'You won't be going to any meeting tonight,' he said. 'You're going to the Regional Hospital this minute.'

He made a phone call to facilitate my admission and I didn't come out of hospital for four weeks.

They did some tests that night and the following morning. The day after that I met the consultant. His name was Professor Denis J. O'Sullivan, an eminent physician. I went into his offices and he introduced himself. He was a distinguished looking man, but he was kindly, too, not at all aloof. I will always remember the words he said to me.

'I've often admired you playing hurling and football, Denis,' he said. 'But I'm sorry to say we won't see you playing anymore.' If that wasn't shocking enough, what he said next floored me.

'What do I have?' I asked him. 'What's wrong with me?'

'We have narrowed it down to one of two conditions,' he said. 'According to the tests, we think you have either leukaemia… or Hodgkin's disease, also known as Hodgkin's Lymphoma. I'm very sorry.'

My world turned upside down in an instant. I immediately thought of Margaret and the lads. Jonathan was eight, Mags was six and Ciara was only two and a half. In moments like that, things like hurling and football and All-Ireland Championships and jobs and everything else fade quickly away into the far distance. All you think about are your family and what this would mean for them.

I left his office in a daze. I can't remember now how I broke the news to Margaret. She must have visited me in the hospital, I'm sure I didn't tell her over the phone. For several weeks I was a patient at the hospital getting tests done every weekday. I was living in a new world and it wasn't a good one. In my worst nightmares I could not have imagined anything like this.

They couldn't do any tests at weekends and most of the time I wasn't particularly ill – at least I wasn't feeling very unwell apart from the lumps – so they let me go home some weekends, and I used to admit myself in to the hospital again on Sunday nights.

It was mostly blood tests but they had to a lot of biopsies too. Those are unpleasant. They took several biopsies from under my arms and around my groin. In those days a lot of the tests had to go abroad – they couldn't be analysed in Ireland – which meant delays, and this was the reason why I had to spend so much time in hospital. I was also put on various medications, which were very strong and flattened me from time to time.

I was in a kind of limbo, but not a good one. There's a feeling of dread hanging over you at every waking moment and all I could think about was what would happen to Margaret, Jonathan, Mags and Ciara. It's frightening, I'm not afraid to admit it. It's your last thought at night and your first thought in the morning.

I can't even imagine what Margaret was going through, it must have been pure hell for her. It must have been a very lonely time for her when I was heading off to hospital on Sunday nights and during the week. Margaret is from Dublin and her family were all in Dublin. My mother was living at home in Blackpool on her own. My two sisters were away and my father had died over 10 years before.

One of those weekends at home I got what was called the rigors. I didn't know what was happening to me, I just couldn't stop shaking. I felt hot and cold at the same time but I was shaking uncontrollably and it was very frightening.

Margaret rang Dr Con and he drove straight down to Carrigtwohill to attend to me. It was a bit of a journey on the weekend but he came straight down. He knew what it was, which was a relief for me, but I had to go immediately to the hospital and be readmitted. The doctors could not confirm one way or the other what I had; the tests were inconclusive. Leukaemia or Hodgkin's Lymphoma were the two possibilities but we didn't know where we stood.

ONE EVENING, BEFORE I was going for another biopsy Dr Con visited me in the hospital – he really is a great friend. We were just sitting there in my hospital room, chatting, and who walked in, only Christy Ring.

Christy sat down and the three of us started chatting. He sat on the side of my bed and I was glad to see him; just to have him there was a great boost. He had such a presence that you always felt better in his company. Two of my greatest friends there with me in the hospital. Moments like that give you heart.

Christy was asking how I was and so on and I was telling him about the tests and how things were, how we still didn't know the final prognosis. He was telling us about a trip to Lourdes he had just been on. Then there was a lull in the conversation.

Now, we never talked about the four in-a-row.

Even in the celebrations in September, we didn't talk about it, we kind of knew better. We didn't want to jinx it, either. Of course, the newspapers mentioned it and some people you would meet on the street or at work might ask about it but we never really did. It was on but it was a long way away too, and now I didn't know if I'd even be alive for it, being honest. Things weren't looking good for me. Anyway, what was there to talk about?

But Con took some kind of a figary the same day and maybe he did it out of devilment or to lighten the tone or to be optimistic, given the situation. Whatever possessed him, didn't he say, 'Christy, what do you think our chances are of winning the four in-a-row?'

I said nothing, waiting for Christy's reaction. I didn't think he'd want to talk about it. But he gave it some thought, and he kind of winced and shook his head.

'I don't know,' he said. He had an intense way of speaking, he thought very deeply about things. He was often quiet in company but when he did say something, he really meant it. 'Four in-a-row?' he said and he shook his head again.

'It's a very hard thing to do.'

'Why is that?' Con said. I was wondering the same, myself.

Christy shook his head again. He was looking inward, or into the past. He had a profound knowledge of hurling.

'Something always happens,' he said. And he said it in a way that indicated he didn't want to be drawn. End of conversation. Very often when Christy said something, you'd have to tease it out with him, but there was a kind of finality about this. Con and I didn't speak. Perhaps I was thinking about my own situation, and so were my two friends. So, I said nothing.

Christy rose to leave. He produced a bottle of holy water he had brought all the way from Lourdes where he had gone as a volunteer to help bring disabled people there.

He gave me the bottle. I said thanks.

He looked at me, then, and he said, 'Ring will pray for you tonight.'

And he put his hand on my head and I was so moved. I looked at Con and saw that he was crying and, of course, I started crying too. Well, if I did, Christy started crying as well. There we were, three grown men, crying in my room in the Cork Regional Hospital.

That was on the Tuesday and they let me home to Carrigtwohill as usual at lunchtime on the Friday for the weekend. The phone rang about four o'clock. Margaret answered it and she came in to me and told me that it was Dr Con on the phone. She looked worried and I immediately realised why. The results of my biopsies. Of course, they would send them to my GP first.

Oh, Jesus, I thought. *Here it is.*

Time seemed to slow down.

I went to the phone – a little shakily, I admit.

'Hello Con, how are you?' I said.

'I have bad news, Denis,' Con said.

'Oh, God,' I said. 'What it is?'

Con realised what I meant. That I was talking about myself, about my tests.

'Oh, no,' he said. 'No, Denis, it's not you. It's Christy.'

'What's wrong,' I said. 'What happened?'

'Christy was found dead this morning, on the street by the School of Commerce.'

Christy Ring was gone.

Something always happens.

CHRISTY DIED ON a Friday and his removal was on the following night from Forde's Funeral Home, but I was too sick to attend. He was buried on the Sunday and, again, I was too unwell to go to the funeral Mass in the Church of Our Lady of Lourdes in Ballinlough. And the irony of the name of that church wasn't lost on me, either. Only a week earlier Christy had been praying to Our Lady in the town of Lourdes itself, between tending to the disabled people he was looking after out there.

The scenes at his funeral were extraordinary. My old friend, Michael Ellard pointed out that such a vast outpouring of shock and grief hadn't been seen in Cork since the burials of Terence MacSwiney and Tomás Mac Curtain, our Lord Mayors in 1920 – the very year Christy was born in Cloyne. Up to 60,000 people lined the streets of Cork to pay tribute and say goodbye to the man who had done so much for them. Many of them were weeping openly, knowing that part of them had gone forever with Christy – the better part, perhaps.

It took the cortege three hours to make its way back to Cloyne, such were the crowds of mourners lining the road, anxious to honour their great fallen hero. I drove to Cloyne from my home in Carrigtwohill and parked my car on the outskirts of the village. Myself and some other men had been told that the cortege would stop at a certain place and we were to be ready there.

When the hearse arrived and I saw the jerseys of St Nicholas and Glen Rovers on the coffin, I had to fight back tears. I felt the weight of the coffin on my shoulder and I thought of Christy's last words to me – that he would pray for me. It was very moving because – as somebody said – this was the first time that any of us who had played with Christy Ring ever carried him. But I did feel honoured to carry my great friend and mentor on that day.

Jack Lynch gave the oration at the graveside and it is worth quoting.

'As long as young men will match their hurling skills against each other on Ireland's green fields, as long as young boys swing their camáns for the sheer thrill of the feel and the tingle in their fingers of the impact of ash on leather, as long as hurling is played the story of Christy Ring will be told. And that will be forever.'

◄◄◆►►

WHEN I WAS very sick in February and March of 1979, it was the last thing on my mind that I would ever play hurling again. When Christy died, hurling itself seemed lessened, somehow. But those emotions passed as the days lengthened and as clubs and counties began to prepare for another summer of championship hurling.

But will I be part of it?

Here I am, at 33 years of age. I have a wife and a young family, and all the responsibilities that go with that. I have a job and a career and I need to look after my financial obligations to my family, too. I have just been part of the three in-a-row, winning three All Star Awards and a Texaco Hurler of the Year. Christy is gone and I'm very sick, just coming out of several surgeries. I'm still weak after dozens of blood tests and I don't know how many biopsies.

Why on earth would I want to play again? I have no need to play whatsoever. None. And yet ...

And yet, by April, I knew things were changing and that the longing to be back was growing inside me. But playing again would be madness, surely. I still hadn't received the all-clear. What the hell was wrong with me, thinking about going back to hurling? Where were my priorities?

One factor definitely was the fact that we were drawn against Tipperary in the first round. From the very first hurling moment I can remember – my father bringing me to Cork and Tipperary matches in the 50s – and when I knew I wanted to hurl, I wanted more than anything to hurl against Tipp.

The match was set for the 3rd of June in Páirc Uí Chaoimh and at some point – I can't remember exactly when – I knew I wanted to play in it.

In retrospect I think it was probably irresponsible of me even to be thinking about playing again when I had been so ill; and even at that time nobody could say to me that I was over it or that it wouldn't recur.

I wondered afterwards if it was a need to hold onto something; to have something to aim for that summer, something reassuring or affirming to which I could aspire. I don't know. Maybe if I could play again, it would undo some of my illness or the illness would go away. Maybe it was something to do with Christy. I don't know what was going through my head, really, what I was thinking at all.

I didn't know if I would be able to manage it – if I would be physically strong enough, for starters. But eventually I knew that I did want to play again. And I wanted to hurl that summer and to make history – to win a four in-a-row.

So, I came back.

The medical people could still not prove one way or the other if it was Hodgkin's Lymphoma or leukaemia. Then, although they had not ruled out either of those, they began to wonder if it was some kind of tropical disease. So, they put me through a whole raft of tests for all sorts of tropical diseases that I might have picked up.

In April I talked to Margaret and we decided I'd give hurling a go and if it didn't work out, I'd drop it. By then I certainly wasn't ready to train, so time was running out. In May I began to train. I had missed out all the spring league campaign and all the other usual obligations with Munster, Cork and the Glen. It was now or never.

In training I could see the selectors looking at me, assessing what kind of a state I was in. But the man I'd have needed most to tell me what to do – and to tell me straight where I stood – wasn't there anymore. Christy was gone and there was a vacuum that nobody else – with the best will in the world – could fill. We all missed him, our selectors most, probably, but we all had to get on with it and to fulfil our obligations. We felt now that we *had* to do the four in-a-row for Christy; for his memory if for no other reason. And I probably owed him more than anybody else in the set-up. I wouldn't even have been back playing hurling for Cork without him, for starters. In hindsight, that was probably a big factor in my returning to the team.

By May 14th it was three months since the first symptoms and training seemed to be going okay. I wasn't as fit as I would normally have been but I wasn't as bad as I thought I'd be, either.

A MATCH WAS arranged between Cork and a Rest of Ireland team – an All Star team, effectively; they had the top players from Kilkenny, Limerick, Galway, Clare and Wexford. It was a charity event and it was played in Páirc Uí Chaoimh on the 27th of May, the Sunday before the Tipperary championship game. It was my first match since February or possibly January. I don't remember much about it but I must have done okay – and in fairness, I must have been physically okay for them to put me on the team in the first place. You can't play wing-back if you're not up to it but there is a difference between being 'okay' and being championship ready.

One thing I do remember about that game is getting hit on the back of my right hand. My hand swelled up, alarmingly. In other circumstances, I would have come off, but I felt I needed the game badly, so I said nothing. At a reception afterwards Dr Con saw my hand. I didn't want him to look at it, but he insisted – it was all swollen.

'Don't tell anyone,' I said to him.

But, of course, Con examined it and got me an ice pack and Michael Ellard saw that, and it was in the newspaper the following morning. So much for not telling anyone! The X-ray didn't show up any bone damage so I had injections every day that week and I was picked for the game. I got another two injections before the match. I was happy enough the way I could hold the hurley, otherwise I would have cried off, in fairness.

We beat Tipp by a point and we were lucky to come through.

They had been in the doldrums for a while but were building a good team and they gave it everything. We had John Fenton at centrefield; he was maybe 23 or 24 at the time and he played instead of Tom Cashman. It was the start of a glittering career for the Midleton man. I was marking another youngster, Eamonn O'Shea who was a real speed merchant and I must admit to having been nervous about whether or not I could manage him. I was 34 now and Eamonn had at least 10 years on me. In a way this was my second comeback; the first being in 1976 after my 'retirement' and now after being so ill.

Could it be one comeback too many? It did occur to me. I didn't want to make a fool of myself after all these years. But I did okay and lasted the whole game, which was a bonus. I was told that Michael O'Hehir was very kind to me in his commentary of the game and singled me out for praise when I caught a good ball near the end, saying that he had wondered if he'd ever see me play again. It was a nice gesture from the great man but we went back a long way.

Medically, I still wasn't out of the woods. I continued to be monitored by the specialists for the next two years. But I was back and we were in another Munster final. We had made it over the first hurdle without Christy. So far so good.

THE FINAL WAS against Limerick and I felt I was getting much fitter and stronger in the build up to that game.

Pat Hartigan was full-back with Limerick at that time and he was a truly great player. I think he was on the first five All Star teams and I had the honour of playing with him for Munster in the Railway Cup. But didn't the ball hit him in the eye in training coming up to the final and he couldn't play. I was very sad to learn afterwards that he actually lost the sight in his eye from the incident. His absence was a huge psychological blow to Limerick and they never really got going. They also had 11 wides in the first-half and when Charlie and Ray scored goals after half-time we pulled away. Our back line was very settled and composed.

I was marking a young player, Paddy Kelly from Kilmallock and he was very fast, a flier. I wondered at the time if it was a coincidence that opposition teams seemed to be putting the fastest players they had on me. Somehow, I don't think it was. Also, I noticed around this time that newspapers were referring to me as a *"veteran"*.

Still, it was lovely to win another Munster Championship, Cork's fifth in-a-row.

While Christy had often been quiet before games, his presence spoke volumes in the dressing-room. It was only after he had gone that we realised what a great influence he had been; what a huge impact he had on us all, individually as players and collectively as a team. A feature of the team was how adaptable our panel had been and the many on-field switches that had improved our play, especially at critical times.

In any championship there will be key moments where changes have to be made. But they have to be the right changes.

We would face such a moment very soon.

NEEDLESS TO SAY, we were raging favourites coming into the All-Ireland semi-final against Galway. In hindsight, I can't say for certain that we were complacent or were thinking about the final, and I don't think we were.

Having said that, I think there was a certain level of complacency in Cork among our supporters – that we were invincible or something. We hadn't been beaten in 12 consecutive games and I wonder if people were expecting that run to continue at least to the final, because if memory serves me right, only 12,000 people turned up to Croke Park for the match against Galway. That's a very small crowd for Cork. I wondered after if people were waiting for the final against

Kilkenny and the four in-a-row. But that game would never come for us. If people had better memories, they might have reflected on the last team to have beaten us, four years earlier, in 1975 – it was Galway.

And however hard you try, sometimes a sense of expectation can permeate into a team – when people expect something to happen, rather than taking on the responsibility for making it happen. As a coach, later, I would find this a major challenge – however hard you try, if something takes root in players' minds that they are bound to win, it's a disaster.

All credit to Galway, they took the game to us from the beginning. They weren't worried about reputations or four in-a-row. They had a match to win and they went about it. Our forwards never got going. In the first-half we only scored six points and were losing 0-9 to 0-6 at half-time. In reality we were lucky to be only three points down because the Galway forwards gave our half-back line a torrid time in the first-half – including me.

After half-time, when we drew level at 10 points each and Seanie O'Leary put us ahead, we were in the ideal position. In previous years we would have built on this and killed out the game, but not this time. In truth, at stages we were outplayed all over the pitch. John Connolly and Steve Mahon won the centrefield battle. Our half-forwards struggled, only scoring two points. Our full-forward line was stymied, Ray Cummins getting our only goal from a rebounded penalty.

Galway were brilliant – they played just as Galway should be playing all the time – aggressively, at a high tempo and with real direct purpose. They were fantastic and Babs Keating, their coach, had them hurling with verve.

LOSING WAS A bitter disappointment. We were gutted, we were actually distressed after the game. We had not lost a championship match in Munster in five years or any game in four years. We weren't used to losing; it was hard to come to terms with the idea that there was a final coming up and we wouldn't be part of it. The newspapers made much of the fact that some of us had been playing for Cork since the mid-60s and now this was nearly the 80s. Headlines like, "*Age Finally Catches up with the Champions*" made us feel old, whether we were or not.

The three in-a-row was a great achievement. It hadn't been done by Cork since the 50s (1952 to '54) and it hasn't been managed by Cork since. Effectively, since 1954 (almost 70 years ago) Cork have only won one three in-a-row and for me to have been part of that great team was a wonderful thrill, especially since I thought my county hurling days had ended in 1974.

But we had lost Christy and our All-Ireland crown and our dreams of four in-a-row.

That was a sad dressing-room after the Galway match.

There were a lot of tears that day.

I think we felt that we had let Christy down and it was another good-bye to the great man – a painful one, a final one. We also knew it was the ending, not only of a dream, but of an era, too. And an end of this great team.

Something always happens.

◂◃◆▷▸

WE HAD A good run in the National Hurling League of 1979-1980. We beat Galway in the semi-final in April. It was scant revenge for them getting the better of us the year before but at least we beat them. We played Limerick in the final on May 4th 1980. It was on in Páirc Uí Chaoimh on a lovely sunny day and there were 33,000 in attendance.

The Cork footballers had beaten Kerry in the National Football League final the previous Sunday, which was lovely to see, and we really wanted to emulate them. But Limerick were never going to make it easy for us and it was a real dog fight. Their forwards, including Joe McKenna, Ollie O'Connor, Éamonn Grimes, Éamonn Cregan and Brian Carroll were a real handful. Around midway in the first-half McKenna struck a goal which gave Limerick a bit of a lead and a huge lift. Soon they were six points up and cruising, and we had to dig deep. Éamonn O'Donoghue got a goal for us which we badly needed but we were still six points down at half-time.

We rallied well and controlled the second-half and were winning by three points with time up. Limerick got a dubious sideline and as the ball came across, Ollie O'Connor got a stick to it: goal. A draw. I felt I was playing well in 1980 and contributing to the team – even though I would be 35 that June.

We were expecting to go to Limerick for the replay but it was played in the Park again. In any case we won by nine points, 4-15 to 4-6 which was a bit flattering but we did put up a good score. Our goalkeeper, Tim Murphy's amazing save from Joe McKenna was a great boost but Limerick were the better team for a long time, and were winning 0-7 to 0-0 after 13 minutes. Then Ray Cummins and Éamonn O'Donoghue got two quick goals from rebounds and we were right back in it. Pat Moylan and John Fenton were on top at centrefield and the team overall played very well. We grew in momentum as the game went on and, although Limerick's four goals kept them in touch, Jimmy Barry Murphy's inclusion in the 44th minute gave us a fierce boost and caused a bit of panic. We pulled away in the last 10 minutes to complete the league hurling and football double for Cork.

Just a few weeks later we beat Tipp in the Munster Championship semi-final to set up yet another Munster final against Limerick.

Now we were going for six in-a-row in Munster and this would have been a record, but it wasn't to be. On a sunny day we played into a strong wind in the first-half and were only four points down at half-time. Our forwards – which was unlike them – weren't going well and we ended up with 17 wides. I remember John Fenton taking a 21-yard free in the first-half and he went for a goal and it was saved. It wasn't one big thing, it was a lot of small things that went against us.

Limerick led for most of the game, even if we were only a couple of points down for periods of the second-half. I was marking Willie Fitzmaurice, one of two brothers from Killeedy – he went on to become a Canon. Dermot McCurtain's loss to injury was a real blow and our selectors did try everything they could to get us going, with a lot of positional changes. But no joy; Limerick held on to win 2-14 to 2-10.

The game was played on the 20th of July, 1980 and it was a big day for Limerick. It was their first Munster Championship win against Cork since 1971 and their first final win against Cork since 1940.

It was a big game for me, too. I didn't know it at the time, but it was the last championship match I would ever play for Cork.

I TOOK A break for the winter games in the National Hurling League but I went back training after Christmas. Then in early February I got a phone call from one of the Cork selectors, Johnny Clifford, who was a fellow Glen Rovers man.

It was on the Wednesday before a match.

And it was at 8:30 in the morning. I remember the call well; the phone was in the hall of the house. I was just about to bring the lads to school.

'Hello?' I said.

'Hello, Denis… this is Johnny Clifford here.'

'Hello, Johnny… how are you?'

'I'm fine, Denis. I'm just ringing you about the team for Sunday.' There was a pause. 'I'm just ringing to say you're not on the team, Denis. Sorry about that.'

'No bother, Johnny… the rest will do me good, anyway.'

'That's just it, Denis. I'm afraid you won't be on the team this year at all. The selectors think it's the end of the road for you.'

Another pause.

'That's okay, Johnny… thanks for ringing me and letting me know,' I said.

And I hung up. *Well, that's that*, I thought.

The end of my Cork hurling days.

My son, Jonathan must have heard some of the call because he said, 'Are you playing on Sunday, Dad?'

'No, Jonathan,' I said. 'I think I'll take a bit of a rest.'

'But aren't you going to play anymore?' he said.

'You know, I don't think I will play anymore, Jonathan. I think that's it now.' I didn't want to come out and tell him I was dropped.

'Fan Larkin played until he was 38,' Jonathan said.

'Did he?' I said. 'Well, I won't be playing until I'm 38, I'm afraid.' I tousled his hair and said, 'Come on, you. Time for school.'

I don't know where Jonathan heard about Fan Larkin playing until he was 38. I guess it's funnier now maybe than it was at the time.

SO, IT WAS February, 1981 and my county career was finally over. This time for good. I would be 36 that summer. I'd had a great innings, I knew, but still I was disappointed. I felt I was fit enough and playing well enough to make a contribution, but the selectors obviously felt differently and they wanted to build a new team. Which was fine.

And when I began to think about it over the next few days, I realised that I would miss it all, the training especially. I think I got more enjoyment out of training than playing, which seems strange but I loved the sense of purpose in training sessions, the sense of incentive, of getting things right. I loved the learning and the physical and mental preparation. Even years later, when I was long retired, the training was the thing I missed most and not the matches I was training for.

And I wasn't upset or anything like that when I was told it was the end of the road. There was never any fuss those days when players came to the end of their careers. There might have been something in the papers when they realised that I wouldn't be playing any more – I can't remember. But I was lucky to have gotten the phone call and I was genuinely grateful to Johnny for letting me know.

A lot of fellows wouldn't have gotten such a call, that was the way things were done those days. And it didn't matter who you were, you might learn that your playing days were over when you saw the panel listed in the newspaper.

Had I not come back to Cork in 1976 I think I would have regretted it. I was only 29 then and even if Cork had not won the three in-a-row, I think it would have been a pity for me to lose out on those extra years. I had played my first football match for Cork in 1963 and my first hurling match in 1965. I played football for Cork for 12 years and hurling for 16 years.

I had been donning the iconic blood and bandage jersey for 18 years and how fulfilling it was to do so; what an honour it all had been.

Everybody loves their county and I certainly love mine. I'm proud of many things in my life but my pride to be a Corkman probably surpasses anything.

But I had no regrets about finishing for Cork in 1981, I didn't take a backward glance. I'd given Cork everything and gotten everything in return.

Absolutely everything.

I continued to play with the Glen and again we made it to the county final in 1981, but again, we lost to the Barrs. In our defence they really were an outstanding team. And I also played for the Glen in 1982, but I was 37 by then and that was my last year wearing the beloved green, black and gold.

I CONTINUED TO play some junior football for St Nicks and I enjoyed that. And we made it to the county junior final in 1983 which was very exciting. And after that was done and dusted, I realised that I had played for St Nicks in the county junior final in 1963 as an 18 year-old. And I played in a county junior final in 1983 as a 38 year-old and also the following year when I was 39.

I must remind Jonathan of that, the next time I see him. Fan Larkin indeed.

Seriously, I was absolutely fine about bowing out from club hurling and football, just as I was for Cork. It was time. I felt I'd done my bit – I had certainly done the best I could. I had played so many games and I had been so lucky with injuries and my health. Even to come back from my illness in 1979 had been such a great bonus.

I had been playing for the Glen and St Nicks since I was a child in the 50s, waiting on the Watercourse Road to see if the lads from Gurranabrahar and Cuchulainns would pass by and there would be a game up in the old Glen Field. I might have been nine or so when I began doing that, and 30 years of playing sport is as much as anybody could reasonably ask for. When I think back on all the friends I made and all the memories we created together, I feel nothing less than blessed.

It was a great privilege and a great pleasure to play for so long with two wonderful clubs, Saint Nicholas and Glen Rovers, and I treasure every single moment. The two great clubs I loved so well as a boy and as a man, and still love to this very day.

And I know I'm biased but I couldn't have wished for two greater clubs to have been part of. If I could have picked anywhere in the world to have grown up and in any time, I wouldn't change a thing.

I owe my clubs so much; they gave me so much.

They gave me everything.

The cortege at Christy Ring's funeral crossing Patrick's Bridge.

« CHAPTER 12 »

Everything

ALL OUR CHILDREN grew up in Carrigtwohill and I hope they all had joyful childhoods, as did their mother and myself. I think they did, in fairness – we always did our very best for them.

Jonathan went to the boy's primary school in the village, Scoil Mhuire Naofa and it was a very good school. He was keen on sport at a young age and he played under-12 for Carrigtwohill with all his friends. One evening, when he was maybe 13 or 14 there was a knock at the door. It was Jack Walsh (the father of Denis Walsh, the sportswriter) and two other men. There was a rule in Cork at the time (this would have been around 1984) that if you played under-16 for a club you had to stick with that club from then on; it would be very hard to transfer.

And the reason the three men called was because they were thinking of putting Jonathan on the under-16 team, but they wanted to let us know because they knew I was a Glen Rovers man. They didn't want to tie Jonathan into the club without letting us know first. It was very decent of them, I must say, and Margaret and I really appreciated it.

So, I just put it to Jonathan and I talked him through it – that if he wanted to continue to play for Carrigtwohill he would probably have to stay with them afterwards, but it was fine with his mother and myself whatever club he chose. Many of his friends were playing with the local club, which is a great club I must say, and it was his decision completely. I didn't influence him in any way nor would I ever do that.

He said he wanted to play with the Glen, which was fine by me, too. He was already going to secondary school in Farranferris in Blackpool as a day-boy and some of his schoolmates there were probably Glen Rovers hurlers too. And my mother was still living in Madden's Buildings so that was somewhere very close to Farna he could call into before meeting me after work to go home, or getting a lift out to Carrigtwohill from myself or Margaret.

But I laid it out for him that if he wanted to play for the Glen, he would have to train with them and a lot of that training might be on days where his mother or I might not be able to drop him. So, he would have to get the train to Glounthane or the bus to Carrigtwohill. And he understood all that, and in fairness he stuck with it and he was very dedicated in his training and his preparation for teams and matches. He might have to walk from the train station in Cork up to the Glen for training and all the way down afterwards, and that's a long walk, but he never complained and just got on with things. He was a great player for the Glen, at underage and also for the senior team in due course and Margaret and I were very proud of that.

Jonathan played under-21 championship hurling for Cork but (unlike me) he was very unlucky with injuries. In his twenties he tore ligaments in both knees, each of which took him out of the game for a full year and there were very tough rehabilitation and recovery programmes both times. It really did curtail his hurling career in a big way; he was never the same athlete going back after those.

Jonathan keeps his cool which is a great trait – I think he might be a bit calmer than me and he's very solid. He married a lovely girl, Deborah Deane from Derry in 1998; they met at a wedding. She teaches in the community school in Glanmire. Her father is from Dunmanway, originally.

Deborah and Jonathan have four children: Niamh, who is 20 and studying at UCC; Leah, who is 18 and has completed her Leaving Cert year in St Angela's College in Cork; Donagh, who is 16 and a student in the North Monastery, and Beth, who is 12 and at primary school in Carrignavar.

Donagh and Beth have the sports gene and play football in St Nicks and hurling and camogie in the Glen. Niamh used to play sports, too but she had juvenile arthritis in her teens and doesn't play anymore. She's flying now and won the title of Miss Cork City in 2019 and used the platform to raise awareness of that condition in young people. Leah is a great girl, too; she's quiet and does her own thing and her Leaving Cert was disrupted by the COVID-19 outbreak like so many others. She is hoping to study criminology in UCC next year and I really hope that works out for her.

◄◄◆►►

MAGS WAS BORN in December, 1973 (just after an Oireachtas final as I mentioned earlier) and she went to a great primary school in Carrigtwohill called Scoil Chlochair Mhuire which was run by an order of nuns called the Poor Servants of the Mother of God. That school was so good that girls used to get the bus from the northside of the city to attend it.

She also went to the secondary school in Carrigtwohill – a very good school called Saint Aloysius' College. Unlike Jonathan, when she was growing up, Mags had no interest in sport. Absolutely no interest, I don't think she ever even saw me play. And that was the way all through her teens. She was a great girl growing up and was good at school and did a very good Leaving Cert.

We were very proud when she went to UCC to study commerce; she was the first person on my side of the family to go to college, so that was exciting and she did really well there. And, lo and behold, in UCC didn't she take up rowing. Not only that, she became captain of the UCC Rowing Club. Now, this was before the current popularity of rowing, since the great success of the O'Donovans and Sanita Puspure and others. Nor would there have been a tradition of rowing in the family or the school or the town. But she really got into it, she took to it (no pun intended) like a duck to water.

Mags was very serious about rowing (she never does things by half) and it's a sport at which you have to be very dedicated. She insisted on cycling from Carrigtwohill up to the marina in Cork and all the way home. She wouldn't take a lift from myself or Margaret – she insisted on cycling herself. That's a serious cycle both ways, maybe 40km in all. With a serious training session in between, no doubt.

And she loved that for the four years she was in UCC. When she graduated with a B Comm, it was a proud day for myself and Margaret. After qualifying she went off to Australia for a few years and she was living in Sydney. Margaret and I went out to see her in 1995; it was a lovely five-week trip. She was 23 at that stage.

When she finished in Australia she moved to London and she had a good job with the Irish Tourist Board there for two years. Mags always loved travelling, she has a really adventurous spirit which I've always envied. Then she came back to Dublin and she worked as an Operations Manager for several years. She had bought herself an apartment in Kildare and was commuting up and down to Dublin like so many others.

One Friday evening in 2010, she came home for the weekend with news. Now the funny thing about Mags is that she would always have her mind made up before she would tell us anything. She wouldn't ever put any worry on us (although like all parents we worried from time to time about all our children); she would have it all figured out. I think she got that from me – I used to internalise and analyse things and work it all out in my head before I told my parents anything (about a change of job or something big) and Mags is the same. On that Friday she arrived in and looked at us and she told us she had something to tell us.

'I'm giving up my job in Dublin,' she said.

And we said that was fine, she could do whatever she wanted to do as far as we were concerned as long as she was happy. And we asked her if she knew what she did want to do. She had looked into this of course and she was going to sign up for a Job Bridge Course and she would find something she liked through that. And she had arranged a position in Ballymaloe Gardens as a trainee gardener.

And we said fine, we'd support her one hundred percent in any decision – which we would and did – but I suppose we did worry a bit too. It was a total change going from Operations Manager in a multi-national business to a gardener. While she always did have green fingers, there's the financial aspect of any job, too. But we also knew that whatever Mags did, she would make a great success of it, and of course that's the way things turned out.

She is still working in the very famous and prestigious gardens in Ballymaloe. Now she is head gardener there and she lives down in East Cork and is very much embedded in the local community in Ballycotton.

She is an avid swimmer and she swims down there practically each day of the year.

◄◄◆►►

CIARA, OUR YOUNGEST, was born in August, 1977, just in time for the three in-a-row. She went to the same primary and secondary school as Mags, but unlike Mags, she was always keen on sport. We always remind her that she began the camogie club in Carrigtwohill. When she was eight or nine, Ciara wasn't happy that the local boys were getting coaching and training but the girls weren't, so she organised the girls to group together and she asked me would I go down some night and coach them, which I was happy to do.

I was already coaching some of the younger boys, so fair is fair, why wouldn't I help out the girls? And the camogie club grew out of that and is thriving now.

But that would be Ciara's form. If something had to be done it should be done and she'd take it on herself without a second thought. When she was coming up to the Leaving Cert, all she wanted was a career in physiotherapy, so she decided to do a degree course in Bristol University. No bother to her, and she only 17. Margaret and I were worried, we felt she was very young to be going abroad alone. Of course, she flourished there and achieved her degree and is now a physiotherapist.

It was a huge achievement for somebody so young to head off like that and make such a success of it. In many ways, Ciara is the opposite to myself and Mags, she worries about things and externalises them. She discussed everything with Margaret and myself before making a decision like that, for example.

Ciara played basketball and other sports. She used to go to matches with me. When I was coaching other clubs she would come along and hang around on the sideline, not a bother on her. Most kids would be bored doing that, but she wanted to be there and to be involved. Now, when she went to matches with me, I might have to promise her a bar of chocolate but that's fair enough.

One of her first jobs after she came back from Bristol was in Limerick. She used to visit patients with respiratory disease in their homes. She became really interested in that approach. When she came back to Cork, through the Mercy University Hospital, she started that system there, too – the physiotherapist and nurse would treat people in their own homes.

The doctors were very happy with that because it allowed them to discharge people back to their own homes which is healthier. Now she is working for the School of Physiotherapy in University College Cork, where she lectures on their Masters programme.

Ciara married Joe in 2012 and he's a lovely man, I must say. He's from West Clare, near Mullagh – good football country (Kilmurry-Ibrickane) and he works in horticulture. Ciara and Joe have two children, Rory, who is seven and Jane, who is five. It's lovely when they visit, to have small children around the place, and we love Jane and Rory and Ciara and Joe to bits, needless to say. They, and all our grandchildren, mean everything to us.

Reunited with the Cork three in-a-row champion team.

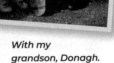

With my grandson, Donagh.

Myself and Margaret, with Jonathan, Mags and Ciara at the end of the summer of 2020.

« EPILOGUE »

THOUGH NOW 75 YEARS-OLD, I still retain a great interest in all sports, particularly hurling. Football, which I played and enjoyed very much for over 20 years, has to a large degree lost its identity. It has become an amalgam of other sports where a football is used.

Though the players' skill, fitness, physique and dedication are to be admired, and is not in question, the game I am watching is no longer enjoyable for me.

Croke Park might say that attendances at big inter-county games would suggest otherwise. But when only 4,000 people turn up for a county final (2019), in hurling or football, in a sports-mad county like Cork, then clearly people are voting with their feet at club games.

There is no doubt, inter-county hurling and football are the showcase brands of the GAA, but in becoming the games they are, a disconnect has been created between Croke Park and clubs.

Much has been written on the subject of club vs county. Inter-county players seldom train with their clubs now because of the 'programme' laid out for them by the county team manager and his backroom team, which can be up to 25 or 30 people. Also, it's not unusual to see inter-county panels of up to 40 players now.

However, a few of things concern me about these large panels:

1, Players are becoming 'strangers' in their own clubs

2, At the wrong time of the year, there are too many competitions in which, by and large, it's the same cohort of players who are training and playing in these competitions

3, The regular club players get no meaningful games until April (when they may get two) and then there is no more activity for them until September

4, This has a significant effect on clubs, which results in little or no activity on the playing fields during the summer-time.

Effectively, county team managers are deciding when players can play or train with their clubs. Croke Park and county boards, by extension, are abdicating their responsibilities to the clubs.

As a result of this the number of injuries and the increase in burn-out is increasing, and it is alarming to see the number of inter-county players who are just walking away from the game, disillusioned.

I truly believe a small panel (21) of players is the best option.

The manager or coach can work much more efficiently with 21 players as opposed to 35 or 40. The players get to play more games, and at the same time you don't have to worry so much about competition, because ALL of the players are involved. You have NOBODY switched off.

I DON'T THINK I would wish to be part of a 35 or 40-man panel of players, not knowing when I will get a meaningful game. I think it would effect me, both physically and psychologically. Nobody can keep that many players happy.

But, if I was part of a 20-man panel, I would have a different attitude, assured that I was one of the 20 best players in the county (or my club) and not just along to make up the numbers.

This would also release a huge number of players back to their clubs, where they would get regular games. Plus, it would also improve the fixtures programme greatly, and it would allow all of our players to play the games they love at the best time of the year.

From a county board perspective, there would be a huge reduction in expenditure. I know a number of county boards and clubs that are in financial difficulties and, only for the assistance of Croke Park, they would be in even greater trouble.

I also believe that the present large panels are devaluing the status of All-Ireland medals, and also club county championship medals.

HURLING, WHICH IS recognised worldwide as unique, has changed very much in the last 10 years. I know the game is still seen as very exciting, with scores every minute, and that the skill and speed of players is magnificent. I understand and admire all of that.

But I still find it difficult to watch the short puck-out from the goalkeeper and the playing 'through the lines', the hand-passing and the increasing reliance on retaining possession. Most games are now being decided on the form of the free-taker on a given day.

The art of defending is slowly being eroded. Coaches now want defenders to take the ball out from the back, adapt and become a midfield player (or even a forward), while at the same time being a defender.

It is not easy to do all of these things. Personally, I liked to defend. I did not want my opponent to get any ball; I didn't want him to get a single score.

That's why we have defenders, midfielders and forwards on the field. They all have different roles.

This is not entirely the players' fault, but in the modern game, in every game, we are reminded of what we have lost from our great game – over-head striking, ground hurling, goalmouth thrills.

Croke Park needs to act.

And it needs to act soon.

◄◄◆►►

I WOULD LIKE to conclude, at this time of division and conflict within the GAA, with the following sentence taken from a speech by Jack Lynch in March, 1983, at the Church of the Sacred Heart in Donnybrook, Dublin, in a thanksgiving service for the gift of sport.

'A friendship with sports and sportspeople is a friendship for life… a friendship that transcends political boundaries and religious divides.'

« ACKNOWLEDGEMENTS »

UNTIL RECENTLY, I never seriously considered the notion of writing my life story, and resisted the suggestion whenever it was put to me. Eventually, the gentle persistence, encouragement and support of Liam Hayes, publisher at Hero Books, broke down my defences. In hindsight, I am delighted that his Meath football persistence had the staying power to keep faith with his idea.

Putting all my thoughts and memories into print was no mean feat, and for that I would really like to thank Tadhg Coakley, who somehow managed to co-ordinate and make sense of all the games and events of my life over the past 75 years.

In order for me to have lived the life I did, many people have helped me along the way. Heartfelt thanks to my parents, the late John and Margaret Coughlan, who gave me great encouragement in my early years; to my sisters, Anne and Catherine, who didn't see me play very often but always had a great interest in my career.

Thanks to the many people of Glen Rovers and St Nicholas, who nurtured my hurling and football career for nearly 30 years (and still play a big role in my life); to the players of St Nicks and the Glen I had the pleasure and honour of playing with and also to my colleagues on Cork hurling and football teams. Thanks also to all my friends in Cork Golf Club and those I have met through school, work, badminton, squash, poetry, music and elsewhere.

To Dr Con Murphy, who has been a wonderful friend and confidant since

1973, who managed on many occasions to get me through injury and illness so I could line out in important club and county games.

To my children, Jonathan, Mags and Ciara, who have been a great joy to Margaret and I over the years, never more so than during the recent lockdown due to COVID-19.

And finally, but most importantly, to Margaret, my wife of 50 years. She has been at my side for all the great (and not so great) days I have had. She has helped me to recover from injuries and illness; listened to me complain for years; and put up with my mood swings (particularly before games).

I would like to thank her so much for a wonderful life and a great friendship. She is my greatest hero.

Denis Coughlan
August, 2020

‹‹◆▷▶

I WANT TO thank Denis for trusting me with his life story, it was a great honour and a great pleasure to work on the book with him. I want to thank Liam Hayes and Hero Books for bringing me on board; it was a brilliant experience to work with Liam, I learned so much.

Thanks to Denis and Margaret for their hospitality and kindness.

Thanks to the authors of the great books *The Nicks of Time* and *The Spirit of The Glen*, which were invaluable to me. Thanks to Mary White and Denis Hurley for the advice, I really appreciate it. Thanks to my writers' group who critiqued some of the book; they are, Rachel Andrews, Madeleine D'Arcy and Arnold Fanning.

Thanks to Tony Leen of the *Irish Examiner* for all his support along with Deirdre Roberts of Mercier Press and all the other publishers who have put my writing in print. Big thank you to my own GAA club, Mallow, and all the volunteers who helped me as a player back along the years.

Thanks, always, to Ciara.

Tadhg Coakley
August, 2020

Author Biography

TADHG COAKLEY IS from Mallow, for whom he played hurling, football and soccer in his younger days. He also hurled with St Colman's College Fermoy, UCC, as well as on Cork minor and under-21 teams.

His first novel, *The First Sunday in September* was published in 2018 by The Mercier Press to great acclaim. It tells the story of a fictional All-Ireland hurling Sunday when Cork play Clare. Donal Ryan described it as *"vibrant and authentic, brimming with intensity and desire"*. His second book, *Whatever It Takes* (2020) is a crime novel set in Cork about a garda detective, Collins, who goes to war against the leading criminal in the city. Collins is a former inter-county hurler who hates to lose. *Whatever it Takes* won the 2020 Cork One City, One Book Award and will be followed by a sequel called *Everything He's Got* in 2021. Tadhg is currently also working on a book of essays about sport which he is hoping to publish in 2021.

His short stories, articles, sportswriting and essays have been published in the *Irish Examiner*, *The Irish Times*, *The Holly Bough*, The42.ie, *The Stinging Fly*, *Quarryman*, *Honest Ulsterman*, *Silver Apples* and elsewhere. He is a graduate of the MA in Creative Writing course in UCC.

He lives in Cork city with his wife, Ciara.

www.tadhgcoakley.com

MORE
GREAT
SPORTS BOOKS
FROM
HEROBOOKS

www.**HERO**BOOKS.digital

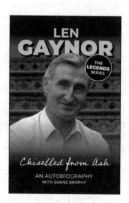

Chiselled from Ash
Len Gaynor: An Autobiography

CHISELLED FROM ASH is a story of love and honour.

It's the story of Len Gaynor's great love for the game of hurling, and how he has honoured the great game his whole life.

Len Gaynor won it all with Tipperary, finishing his career with three All-Ireland hurling titles, four Munster titles and two National League titles in the 1960s and 70s. But the flamboyant wing back also wanted to give back at the end of his career.

The Kilruane MacDonaghs clubman - and winner of three county titles - quickly proved himself to be one of the smartest and most ambitious coaches in the game.

At club level he strived to teach and help the next generation, and led his own Kilruane and neighbouring clubs to success – and at county level through the 1990s Len Gaynor managed Tipperary and Clare on the biggest stages in the game.

Chiselled from Ash is the story of one man's great love for a great game that has remained undimmed over seven decades.

Authors: Len Gaynor with Shane Brophy
Print Price: €20.00
Ebook: €10.00
ISBN: 9781910827208

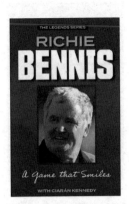

'A Game that Smiles'
The Richie Bennis Autobiography

RICHIE BENNIS IS one of the true legends remaining in the game of hurling. A towering figure in Limerick GAA, he played a central role as the county won the All-Ireland title in 1973 and then he strived as hard as anyone to see the Liam MacCarthy Cup return to the Treaty County.

It was a wait of 45 years – during which time Bennis worked at grassroots hurling in the famed Patrickswell club, where he hurled into his 40s and won 10 county titles. He also led Limerick as team manager to the 2007 All-Ireland final where they lost to Kilkenny.

In 2018, Limerick were crowned All-Ireland champions.

For Richie Bennis, a long agonising wait ended. His story is one of triumph, and heartache and personal tragedy, and a courage that was never dimmed.

Authors: Richie Bennis with Ciarán Kennedy
Print Price: €20.00
ISBN: 9781910827093

Available on
Amazon
Apple Books
Kobo
And all good book shops

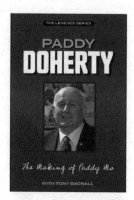

The Making of Paddy Mo
Paddy Doherty: An Autobiography

TO THIS DAY, Down's Paddy Doherty is still remembered as one of the most lethal finishers in the history of Gaelic football. The Ballykinlar clubman was fast, and breathtaking on the ball.

He led his county to a long awaited All-Ireland victory in 1960, and the following summer he captained the Mournemen and brought the Sam Maguire Cup back across the border a second time.

Doherty continued to rip apart defences throughout the decade and won a third All-Ireland crown with Down in 1968, when the Mournemen defeated Kerry in September for the second time, to add to seven Ulster titles and three National league titles.

The 1960s was a decade which is best remembered for the legend of Paddy Doherty.

And... The Making of Paddy Mo.

Authors: Paddy Doherty with Tony Bagnall
Print Price: €20.00
Ebook: €10.00
ISBN: 9781910827178

Available on
Amazon
Apple Books
Kobo
And all good online stores

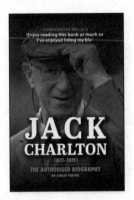

Jack Charlton
The Authorised Biography

AS ONE OF the true legends of Irish and English football, Jack Charlton was a man both loved and feared, but now the people who have lived with him all of his life introduce the real 'Big Jack' in this brilliant authorised biography which is presented in a foreword by Jack himself.

For the first time Jack's wife and family, his teammates as a World Cup winner with England in 1966, and his players during his management years with Middlesbrough, Sheffield Wednesday, Newcastle, and Ireland tell their stories of the man who dominated their lives.

Graeme Souness, Chris Waddle, and Peter Beardsley amongst others, are joined by Mick McCarthy, Niall Quinn and the greatest footballers who played under Big Jack for 10 years as Ireland team boss.

This is the most personable, inviting and intimate account of Jack Charlton's life, and the book contains photographs published for the first time from Jack and Pat Charlton's personal collection.

Jack Charlton: The Authorised Biography is written by former Daily Mail Northern Football Correspondent, Colin Young.

Author: Colin Young
Print Price: €20.00
Ebook: €10.00
ISBN: 9781910827017

Available on
Amazon

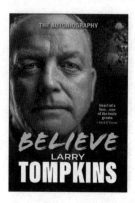

BELIEVE

Larry Tompkins: An Autobiography

HIS SELF-BELIEF WAS unbreakable.

His iron will inspirational.

Nothing could stop Larry Tompkins. No man, no team, as he made his football life the greatest story ever told in the long and brilliant history of the GAA.

Six years with his native Kildare left him empty-handed and heartbroken. He emigrated to New York to find a job and find a team he could lead to championship glory. In the United States, Tompkins' belief in himself never dimmed. He led Donegal to four New York championships in the Big Apple. He also found a new home for himself in Ireland and led Castlehaven to two Cork and Munster titles. In between, he also became the most valuable and feared footballer in Ireland.

BELIEVE is the story of a man who defied all the odds. In Cork's magnificent red shirt, he led his adopted county to two All-Ireland titles in 1989 and 90, one National League and six Munster titles, and he also was honoured with three Allstar awards.

Upon his retirement, Larry Tompkins continued to lead and inspire, and make others believe too. He managed Cork for seven years, winning Munster glory again, and drove Cork to the 1999 All-Ireland final where they agonisingly came up short.

BELIEVE is a story which proves to everyone, in every sport, that anything is possible and everything is there to be won!

Authors: Larry Tompkins with Denis Hurley
Print Price: €20.00
Ebook: €10.00
ISBN: 9781910827123

Available on
Amazon
Apple Books
Kobo
And all good online stores

TIPPERARY
GAME OF MY LIFE

THE GREATEST TIPPERARY hurlers over the last 50 years remember the one game in blue and gold that defined their lives...

Jimmy Finn, Theo English, Tony Wall, Tadhg O'Connor, Dinny Ryan, Babs Keating, John Sheedy, Ken Hogan, Colm Bonnar, Cormac Bonnar, Declan Carr, Michael Cleary, Pat Fox, Conal Bonnar, Declan Ryan, Michael Ryan, Joe Hayes, Eamonn Corcoran, Tommy Dunne, Shane McGrath, James Woodlock, Brendan Cummins, Eoin Kelly, Michael Cahill, Brendan Maher, James Barry, Seamus Callinan and more...

A game that will live with each man forever.

Author: Stephen Gleeson
Print Price: €20.00
Ebook: €10.00
ISBN: 9781910827185

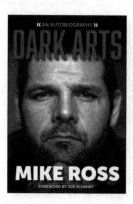

Dark Arts
Mike Ross: An Autobiography

FOR THE FIRST time, Mike Ross brings sports fans into the dark heart of the professional game of rugby union. Ross is recognised as the greatest scrummager in Irish rugby history – and the man who was the foundation stone for the beginning of the Joe Schmidt era, which saw Leinster win back-to-back Heineken Cups and Ireland become the greatest team in Europe.

But Mike Ross might never have been a professional rugby player. He did not turn pro until he was 26 years of age. And he spent three years learning his trade at the toughest end of the game with Harlequins in England before coming home at 30, and chasing the dream of an Irish jersey.

Ross would play 61 times for Ireland, and over 150 times for Leinster. His story is one of big dreams and amazing courage, on and off the field.

He writes about the good times and the hardest times, facing the true beasts of the professional game every weekend. And he writes about his own life, and the suicide of his younger brother, Andrew at 16 years of age with an honesty and compassion that is rewarding for everyone who has experienced the sudden death of a loved one and has to rebuild their lives.

Authors: Mike Ross with Liam Hayes
Print Price: €20.00
Ebook: €10.00
ISBN: 9781910827048

Available on
Amazon
Apple Books
Kobo
And all good online stores

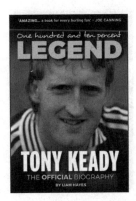

One Hundred and Ten Percent Legend
Tony Keady: The Official Biography

WHEN TONY KEADY died suddenly in August of 2017, at just 53 years of age, a whole county mourned and the rest of the country stopped in its tracks to say goodbye to a legend of the game of hurling.

Except Tony Keady was more than a legend.

In 1988, after leading Galway to a second All-Ireland title in succession, he was crowned the greatest hurler in Ireland. He was 25 years of age and there was nobody like him, nobody to touch him in the maroon No.6 shirt.

But, four years later, and still not 30, after being wrongly banned for 12 months by the GAA, he was also discarded by his own county and refused a maroon jersey the very last time he walked out onto Croke Park behind the Galway team.

A few months before his death, Tony Keady visited Liam Hayes and told him he wished to tell his own story. He felt it was time, but tragically time was not on Tony's side. One month after he died Galway won the All-Ireland title for the first time since 1988, and 80,000 people rose from their seats in the sixth minute of the game to applaud and remember a man who was more than a legend

Tony's wife, Margaret and his daughter, Shannon and his three boys, Anthony, Harry and Jake, decided to finish telling the story of a father and a hurler who always asked those around him for '110%.

Author: Liam Hayes
Price: €20.00
ISBN: 9781910827048

Available on
Amazon
Apple Books
Kobo
And all good online stores

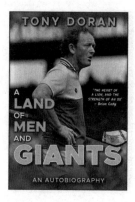

A Land of Men and Giants
The Tony Doran Autobiography

WEXFORD'S ALL-IRELAND winning hero Tony Doran was a giant in the game of hurling through the 1960s, 70s and 80s, at a time when full-forwards were ordered to plunder goals.

In his 19 years and 187 appearances as a Wexford hurler, Tony Doran successfully went for goal 131 times.

But Doran also played against giants from Kilkenny, Tipperary and Cork, and so many other counties, at a time when the game of hurling tested the wits and the courage of every man on the field.

Some of these men became giants.

A Land of Men and Giants is the story told by Tony Doran of a life spent living and competing against legendary men and true giants of the game.

A Land of Men and Giants: The Autobiography of Tony Doran is edited by award-winning writer and author Liam Hayes.

Authors: Tony Doran with Liam Hayes
Print Price: €20.00
ISBN: 9781910827031

Available on
Amazon